The Contemporary British Mosque

Islam of the Global West

Series editors: Kambiz GhaneaBassiri and Frank Peter

Islam of the Global West is a pioneering series that examines Islamic beliefs, practices, discourses, communities, and institutions that have emerged from 'the Global West.' The geographical and intellectual framing of the Global West reflects both the role played by the interactions between people from diverse religions and cultures in the development of Western ideals and institutions in the modern era, and the globalization of these very ideals and institutions.

In creating an intellectual space where works of scholarship on European and North American Muslims enter into conversation with one another, the series promotes the publication of theoretically informed and empirically grounded research in these areas. By bringing the rapidly growing research on Muslims in European and North American societies, ranging from the United States and France to Portugal and Albania, into conversation with the conceptual framing of the Global West, this ambitious series aims to reimagine the modern world and develop new analytical categories and historical narratives that highlight the complex relationships and rivalries that have shaped the multicultural, poly-religious character of Europe and North America, as evidenced, by way of example, in such economically and culturally dynamic urban centres as Los Angeles, New York, Paris, Madrid, Toronto, Sarajevo, London, Berlin, and Amsterdam where there is a significant Muslim presence.

American and Muslim Worlds Before 1900
Edited by John Ghazvinian and Arthur Mitchell Fraas

Anarchist, Artist, Sufi
Mark Sedgwick

Amplifying Islam in the European Soundscape: Religious Pluralism and Secularism in the Netherlands
Pooyan Tamimi Arab

The British Muslim Convert Lord Headley, 1855-1935
Jamie Gilham

Interrogating Muslims
Schirin Amir-Moazami

Islam and Nationhood in Bosnia-Herzegovina: Surviving Empires
Xavier Bougarel

Islam and Muslims in Victorian Britain
Edited by Jamie Gilham

Islam and the Governing of Muslims in France
Frank Peter

Islam as Critique: Sayyid Ahmad Khan and the Challenge of Modernity
Khurram Hussain

Muslims Making British Media
Carl Morris

Sacred Spaces and Transnational Networks in American Sufism
Merin Shobhana Xavier

The Ministry of Louis Farrakhan in the Nation of Islam
Dawn-Marie Gibson

The Contemporary British Mosque

The Establishment of Muslim Congregations and Institutions

Abdul-Azim Ahmed

BLOOMSBURY ACADEMIC
LONDON • NEW YORK • OXFORD • NEW DELHI • SYDNEY

BLOOMSBURY ACADEMIC

Bloomsbury Publishing Plc, 50 Bedford Square, London, WC1B 3DP, UK
Bloomsbury Publishing Inc, 1359 Broadway, New York, NY 10018, USA
Bloomsbury Publishing Ireland, 29 Earlsfort Terrace, Dublin 2, D02 AY28, Ireland

BLOOMSBURY, BLOOMSBURY ACADEMIC and the Diana logo are trademarks of Bloomsbury Publishing Plc

First published in Great Britain 2024
This paperback edition published 2025

Copyright © Abdul-Azim Ahmed, 2024

Abdul-Azim Ahmed has asserted his right under the Copyright, Designs and Patents Act, 1988, to be identified as Author of this work.

Series design by Dani Leigh
Cover image © Brian Stablyk

All rights reserved. No part of this publication may be: i) reproduced or transmitted in any form, electronic or mechanical, including photocopying, recording or by means of any information storage or retrieval system without prior permission in writing from the publishers; or ii) used or reproduced in any way for the training, development or operation of artificial intelligence (AI) technologies, including generative AI technologies. The rights holders expressly reserve this publication from the text and data mining exception as per Article 4(3) of the Digital Single Market Directive (EU) 2019/790.

Bloomsbury Publishing Plc does not have any control over, or responsibility for, any third-party websites referred to or in this book. All internet addresses given in this book were correct at the time of going to press. The author and publisher regret any inconvenience caused if addresses have changed or sites have ceased to exist, but can accept no responsibility for any such changes.

A catalogue record for this book is available from the British Library.

A catalog record for this book is available from the Library of Congress.

ISBN: HB: 978-1-3502-5897-6
PB: 978-1-3502-5901-0
ePDF: 978-1-3502-5898-3
eBook: 978-1-3502-5899-0

Series: Islam of the Global West

Typeset by Deanta Global Publishing Services, Chennai, India

For product safety related questions contact productsafety@bloomsbury.com.

To find out more about our authors and books visit www.bloomsbury.com and sign up for our newsletters

Contents

Note on text		viii
Note on transliteration		ix
1	The British mosque	1
2	The interspatial mosque	21
3	The congregational mosque	43
4	The sacred mosque	71
5	The diverse mosque	93
6	The civil society mosque	109
7	The unwelcome mosque	133
8	The women's mosque	153
9	Conclusion	175
Notes		179
References		183
Glossary		216
Index		221

Note on text

1. Unless otherwise stated, all translations of the Quran are taken from Abdel Haleem (2005). Chapter and verse numbers are provided in text, and a full reference for Abdel Haleem's translation can be found in the bibliography.
2. *Hadith* citations refer to the collection and chapter title. Translation used are indicated through endnotes.
3. The original date of publications is included in the text. If the date of the reprint is misleading, it is only included the first time.
4. Author-date referencing has been used, along with references. Endnotes are used for webpages when evidencing a point that is not a written source (i.e. a news article, report, blog post or similar).

Transliteration

English spellings have been used for romanizing non-English names, if accepted spellings exist and these persons or institutions are best identified with them. Whenever necessary, Arabic and Urdu names and terms have been transliterated according to a simplified and adapted version of the IJMES system.

1

The British mosque

If you were to sit in the corner of a British mosque, notebook (or smartphone) in hand, with the express intention of observing and understanding what goes on inside the walls of that institution, what would you see? Undoubtedly, you would witness worshippers gathering five times a day for prayer. It may be a handful of people or it may be hundreds. You would witness other gatherings of religious devotion as well as sermons, classes and education. You might see moments of social interaction, the exchange of *salam*[1] between two strangers or the warm embrace and casual conversation between lifelong friends. You might see other organizations and institutions using the space of the mosque for meetings or fundraisers. Perhaps even elected politicians, speaking to the gathered congregants about parking, Palestine and everything in between. If you sat long enough, you would see wedding ceremonies, funerals and the celebration of new births. What you saw would depend on which mosque you went, when you went how long you stayed, and it would soon be very clear that mosques, what they do and the purpose they serve differ significantly. This book is an attempt at making sense of that and to approach the mosque as an institution in Britain, shaped by the immediate context, and to try and speak of the sprawling diversity and differences in a way which recognizes that which is shared and salient.

Why the British mosque?

Since 2010, I have been researching mosques in Britain. During this time, I have amassed many books on mosques. They take up two shelves in my study, each shelf over 2 metres in length across. These include dated academic works, such as Stephen Barton's *The Bengali Muslims of Bradford* (1986) – a small book with a soft-spine and typewriter print. These are accompanied by many architectural studies. They are almost always large, hardback and heavily illustrated. Fatima

Gailani's *The Mosques of London* (2000) and Shahed Saleem's *The British Mosque* (2018) are two representative examples of such works. There are newer books too, written by non-academics with a polemic angle such as Ed Husain's *Among The Mosques* (2021) and Innes Bowen's *Medina in Birmingham, Najaf in Brent* (2014). There are other academic publications with understated covers and niche foci – Zacharias Pieri's *Tablighi Jamaat and the Quest for the London Mega Mosque* (2015) or Humayun Ansari's *The Making of the East London Mosque, 1910–1951* (2011). Accompanying these monographs and edited collections are several reports produced by charities, think-tanks and Muslim organizations (see, e.g. the Muslim Council of Britain's (MCB) *Voices from the Minaret* (2006) or *Mosques Made in Britain* published by the Quilliam Foundation (Dyke 2009)). It is surprising to me that in this considerably broad, inter-disciplinary and growing genre of literature on mosques in Britain there is not yet a book that provides a sociological overview of British mosques. One that seeks to answer fundamental questions about what mosques in Britain do and how they do it, how they differ, their role in broader society and the debates within and about them. This book will begin to fill that gap.

Goals

If there is a single comprehensive objective of this book, it is to advance our understanding of the British mosque. Some of this will be done by adding detail to existing understandings. For example, as Chapter 3 shows, it is not uncommon to hear the British mosque described as a community centre. This book does not seek to challenge that description but rather provide more meaningful depth – how are British mosques 'community centres'? In other cases, *The Contemporary British Mosque* will trouble inherited commonplace understandings of the mosque, such as the notion that mosques are equivalent to churches (Chapter 4) or are places of isolation and segregation (Chapter 7). The operation and significance of theological diversity within mosques (Chapter 6) will be explored. The book will engage with the phenomenon of mosque conflicts and what these conflicts tell us about Britain today (Chapter 8), and while the issue of gender (in the broadest sense) is considered throughout, particular attention to debate about the inclusion of women in the mosque will be given in the penultimate chapter (Chapter 9).

The book is not comprehensive. There are many dimensions and aspects of mosques I leave unexplored. For example, I pay very little attention to the role of the imam, to debates about radicalization or mosque architecture and design. These omissions are intentional. I seek to draw attention to the dimensions of mosque understudied or overlooked, for example, the centrality of the congregation, the diverse activities of mosques and the tension between the everyday and the more overtly sacred[2] functions of the mosque.

It is worth stressing why this book has been written now. First is the growth in the number of mosques as a whole. The exact number of mosques is unknown and so estimates are based on official records (such as the 1398 in the database of Places of Worship Registered for Marriages[3]) or privately maintained databases (such as Mehmood Naqshbandi's 'MuslimsinBritain.org', which records 2,200 mosques). Mehboob Naqshabandi's database has been used in academic and journalistic work since its inception (being used widely by Innes Bowen in her work *Madina in Birmingham, Najaf in Brent* (2014)). Cataloguing and documenting British mosques is an ambitious project, not least because of how active Muslim congregations are. New mosques are built, old mosques are re-purposed, existing mosques are expanded – data becomes out of date very quickly. Naqshabandi's methodology is to be commended; he lists the accuracy of his information and provides references for his sources, allowing the user to ascertain how up-to-date the information is, and how reliable it might be. There are other databases too, such as the mosquedirectory.co.uk, a more temperamental site and with less reliable information, and the private databases maintained by a large array Muslim charities (for whom mosques are a central resource for their fundraising), local councils of mosques, and organizations like the MCB – these tend not to be as comprehensive as the online databases, but have the benefit of often being more in-depth, detailed and reliable in their data. All databases point to a single fact however, there are thousands of mosques in Britain and they are continuing to be built. So why write this book? Mosques are now a sizable, commonplace, part of Britain and the British Muslim experience, present in numbers that allow for a study of typology, function and purposes.

If this growth is combined with the demographic shift underway amongst British Muslims, another important facet of the contemporary period is highlighted. In the 2011 census, just under half of British Muslims were born in the United Kingdom. One can expect this to have grown by the 2021 census to indicate the majority of British Muslims are now British-born. This shift impacts mosques as they undergo a "changing of the guard" as younger, British-born Muslims assume leadership over an older generation who often founded them. On the one hand, this signifies a period of change and adaptation. New mosque leaders are more reflective over their purpose and organization, and there is a growth in networks, associations, conferences and similar aimed at developing mosque activity. This book responds and engages with this period of change, presenting an account of contemporary British mosques that tie together their history and future.

Approaches

In my attempt to understand contemporary British mosques, I have drawn on the ethnographic tradition within sociology and anthropology. The broad conceptualization of the field, the emphasis on human presence, and as I discuss later, the incorporation of rhythm provided the methodological and theoretical tools necessary to explore what is important and significant in and about the British mosque. The Manchester School provided inspiration, as they eschewed an emphasis on a single location for fieldwork and decided instead to 'follow the conflict' (Marcus 1995: 10). In 'Ethnography in/of the World System: The Emergence of Multi-Sited Ethnography' (1995) Marcus outlines multi-sited ethnography with trepidation, proposing its utility while simultaneously outlining the anxieties multi-sited ethnographies hold for him; namely, 'testing the limits of ethnography', 'attenuating the power of fieldwork' and 'the loss of the subaltern' (1995: 99–101). In the years since however, multi-sited ethnography has shifted from being an innovative method at the periphery, to a familiar part of the landscape of qualitative research. Indeed, there are now several textbooks on conducting multi-sited fieldwork (Falzon 2009; Coleman and Von Hellermann 2011). Candea however provides an articulate defence of the bounded-field site. Candea's main critique of multi-sited approaches is 'its lack of attention to the processes of bounding, selection and choice' in fieldwork (2007: 169). He argues that the value of a bounded-field site is to take agency and control for the decisions the researcher must inevitably make in the field about what to investigate, where to look and what to ignore (Candea 2007: 180). My own strategy for bounding the field site was to place emphasis on the places referred to as 'mosques'. It is both multi-sited, with fieldwork taking place across the United Kingdom, but also bounded, with an intentional focus on those places named or referred to as a 'mosque'. I chose not to define what a mosque was, and instead allow the language of participants to guide me, not only in where I looked but also in how I conceptualized the mosque, its activities and its congregation.

The congregation also provided an analytical frame important to my approach. I locate my scholarship in the social scientific study of religion, which shares ground with the sociology of religion but holds an interest in a broader range of questions than the latter. While the sociology of religion has concerned itself primarily with the question of modernity and its impact on religion vis-à-vis society, the social scientific study of religion has pursued broader questions around what is religion, religious practice and belief, its manifestation in everyday life, identity and history. I draw on contentions made by Spickard in *Alternative Sociologies of Religion: Through Non-Western Eyes* (2017) to reimagine the foundational conceptions of sociology by engaging with the ideas, conceptualizations and theories outside of Western Christianity and Europe. Thus I consciously adopted the concepts and frameworks utilized by research participants, putting them in conversation with existing literature. Throughout this work, I attempt to engage with the everyday realities of British Muslims involved in mosques and to view these realities on their own terms, but with theoretical insight provided by literature and research undertaken. Like many scholars of religious studies, I am sceptical of careless comparative religion, but equally I do not consider it unreasonable nor always incorrect to put different religious traditions (and the scholarship around them) in relation to each other. This too informs the analysis I provide on the contemporary British mosque.

As such, I sought to synthesize and bring together two approaches in the sociology of religion. The first is the study of institutional religion, specifically congregational studies (see Ammerman et al. 1998 and Guest, Tusting and Woodhead 2004). I discuss this further in Chapter 3, but it became evident to me that the 'congregational studies' common in the sociology of religion had value to the study of British Muslims. However, a turn away from institutional and congregational studies in the sociology of religion in recent decades has depopularized this approach. Instead, a second approach became prominent. That of 'everyday religion' (Ammerman 2007) or 'lived religion' (McGuire 2008), which emerged as a reaction to congregational studies, focused instead on the individual, non-institutional and sometimes heterodox expressions of religion found outside of places of worship. Ammerman (2016) and others however have argued that this has created an artificial and misleading binary in the literature. This book and its research findings could be both described as 'lived religion' and 'congregational studies', and throughout I have sought to adopt the strengths of each tradition. Drawing on congregational studies, I have given attention to the ways in which Muslims do religion together, negotiating questions of orthopraxis and identity (a topic explored in Chapter 5). I have also created typologies of the mosque (Chapter 2), an endeavour directly inspired by similar attempts in Christian congregational studies. Mosques are also located in a wider civil society sphere (Chapter 6), shifting attention from the individualized/personalized and towards the communal/social dimensions of religion (Chapter 6). The foregrounding of the everyday manifestations and contestations of religion however are present within this book too, for example, in Chapter 4, where the sacred character of the mosque is explored, or Chapter 7, which considers conflict and contestations in, around and about mosques. Everyday religion is noted for also turning away from real/perceived hierarchies of religious authority. In my own study, interrogating questions of hierarchy and authority where necessary throughout. Chapter 3 presents an example where I explicitly sought to connect the phenomenological approach of everyday religion with the structuralist emphasis within congregational studies.

The book

Chapter 2 is titled 'The interspatial mosque' and introduces a typology to understand mosque function. Mosques provide a range of services to Muslims and wider society, however the term 'mosque' implies a singular model of institution with a singular model of operation. This disguises the variety of mosques by ambiguating internal diversity and heterogeneity. This chapter is aimed at disturbing that picture by presenting a model which distinguishes different types of mosque activity. It does this by identifying three levels of mosque activity. The first level (*fard*) focuses on the individual obligation of daily prayer, the second level (*fard kifaya*) introduces communal elements, such as the funeral prayer and religious instruction. The final and third level (*sunna*) concludes by tying the typology with an emerging vocabulary for mosques in Anglophone Islam, one that provides a greater sense of the diversity of mosques.

Attention then shifts in Chapter 3 to 'The congregational mosque'. This chapter argues that the congregation has become the primary form of communal religious organizing amongst Muslims in Britain. This congregational turn amongst Muslims is significant in the operation of mosques, which are financed, run and managed primarily through the congregation (rather than by external networks, states or a religious hierarchy). By focusing on the congregation, a deeper understanding of mosques can also be obtained by foregrounding the activity of those involved, which is necessary to establish and maintain a mosque. The chapter argues existing studies of mosques have collectively and inadvertently overemphasized the leadership role of mosque committees and imams. The majority of British mosques, with a few notable examples discussed, locate their authority in the congregation, sustain themselves financially and practically through the congregation and are products of the congregation's ambitions.

Having thus far provided an overview of mosque diversity, functions (what mosques do) and functioning (how mosques do what they do), Chapter 4, 'The sacred mosque', examines a core element of the mosque and its worship. This account is important since its omission would fail to adequately convey the significance and meaning of a mosque to its participants. The chapter not only demonstrates how a process of sacralization operates within mosques that construct its importance in place and time but also how this sacralization is managed and contends with other demands on the mosque (notably the more 'everyday' concerns). The chapter uncovers a tension in many mosques, between the practical social ('worldly') benefits of a mosque outlined in Chapter 2, with the 'otherworldly' and transcendental meaning invested into it, and how this tension is navigated by congregants.

'The diverse mosque', Chapter 5, places mosques in a landscape of intra-religious diversity. Mosques do not hold a straightforward denominational identity that is uniform amongst both mosque leadership and worshippers. The congregation can, and often are, diverse in terms of their denominational background which in turn can influence leadership and can just as often be divorced from it. I speak of denominations to emphasize a focus on the names that groups give themselves rather than looking for underlying divisions or categorizations. This chapter provides an overview of denominational diversity, while also arguing that mosques are moving in two directions. They are either becoming more ecumenical (i.e. constructing an inclusive identity that transcends denominational, sectarian and ethnic boundaries to an extent) seeking to service a broad spectrum of Muslims. Alternatively, they are becoming stronger in their specific religious, linguistic or ethnic identity. The two directions are mutually reinforcing. The ecumenism of most mosques allows some to adopt a more niche-denominational role.

Chapter 6 frames mosques as sites of civil society. I begin with the contention that mosques are valid sites of civil society. This should not be a controversial statement, but nonetheless, I demonstrate in Chapter 6 that the mosque is often overlooked when considering British civil society as a whole. This chapter presents the way in which mosques function to provide an important site of social capital for Muslims, with implications for issues ranging from social mobility to democratic ac1tivism. The contemporary British mosque is an exception to the decline of civil society organizations witnessed in other parts of British society, and as such, understanding the British mosque sociologically promises to contribute to academic inquiry into civil society as a whole.

Chapter 7 considers the reception of mosques in wider British society and focuses on the conflicts, controversies and contestations that regularly surround mosques, especially in relation to construction or expansion. Such conflicts are well documented in both the press and academic publications. This chapter explores the driving factors behind the conflicts and argues that they stem from a powershift in which a once small minority religious community is maturing into to a more confident and expressive one, who are increasingly making claims to the British landscape.

Women's (lack of) access to mosques has been an area of debate within the British Muslim community for several decades. Younger Muslims have increasingly made calls for more equal access to mosques – not only to access the religious knowledge available but the wider community of believers. Chapter 8 explores the different ways in which Muslims in Britain have debated, campaigned for or resisted women's access to mosques.

The conclusion draws the key findings together, the future path in front of mosques, and the questions that remain unanswered and deserve academic attention. Collectively, the chapters provide an overview of the British mosque, an insight into its everyday realities and the landscape of mosques more widely, and it highlights the salient developments internal to Muslim communities and the mechanics and diversity of the mosque itself, as well as covering the ways in which British Muslims themselves perceive the mosque and how it is perceived by those outside the religious community. The mosque is a new institution in Britain, connected to a very old tradition globally. It contains both continuities and innovations, contradictions and symmetries. This book aims to show how it is central to the ambitions of the British Muslim community and a key institution in British society. In the remainder of this chapter, a brief account of mosque establishment in Britain is provided, beginning with the pioneer mosques.

The pioneer mosques

The story of the contemporary British mosque can be traced over several periods. The first period is one of pioneers who were the founders of the earliest mosques in Britain. These founders were few and far between, predating the wider migration of Muslims in Britain that followed the Second World War. They remain important in establishing templates for mosque activity that would be followed by others. The story of British mosques largely follows the story of British Muslim settlement. Wherever Muslims gathered, for work and to live, they would invariably establish mosques. The reasons why are explored elsewhere in this work, but here the story of the establishment of these first mosques will be told. There is an academic interest in early mosques which can be observed by the dedicated accounts of their origins that have been published in such works as Humayun Ansari's *The Making of the East London Mosque* (2011), Muslim Purwez Salamat's *A Miracle at Woking* (2008) and Ron Geaves's *Islam in Victorian Britain* (2010) which looks at the Liverpool Institute (see also Ansari 2002; Gilliat-Ray and Mellor 2010; Gilliat-Ray 2010a; Petersen 2008 for other historically focused accounts). More general publications tracing the settlement of Muslims in Britain also reflect this growing historical interest amongst scholars of British Islam (Halliday 2010; Seddon 2014), an interest succinctly summarized by Sophie Gilliat-Ray:

> The active documentation of past historical events and achievements seems to be part of a concerted effort to enable British Muslims to feel embedded in and connected to UK society, while also constructively challenging assumptions about the supposed segregation and disconnection of British Muslims from wider society. (2010a: 189)

The study of early mosques of Britain are important thus not only for their role in the story of Muslim settlement but also in helping resituate Muslims as part of the fabric of modern Britain. Three of the earliest mosques in Britain do well to illustrate this point, the Liverpool Muslim Institute (founded in 1887 – the earliest mosque opened in the UK), the Shah Jahan Mosque (established in 1889 and the first purpose-built mosque in Britain), and Noor al-Islam Mosque in Cardiff (established sometime between 1936 and 1939, though with some uncertainty about exactly when). The establishment of these three mosques are valuable to understanding the contemporary landscape. As discussed subsequently the mosques, their structures, the figures behind them and the role they occupied in society reflect and raise many of the key issues raised throughout this work.

Liverpool: 'The birthplace of Islam in Britain'

The first mosque, established in 1887, was the Liverpool Muslim Institute founded by the British convert Abdullah Quilliam. Quilliam was an English Victorian gentleman and a lawyer by profession. Liverpool, during the nineteenth century, was a busy port and connected to international destinations of note. Its commercial importance during this period place as a contender for the unofficial and highly contested title of 'the second city of the British Empire' (London being the first). The Muslims in Liverpool during this *fin de siècle* were lascars, itinerant seamen taking up employment in the ships to-ing and fro-ing from ports in the British Empire. It was in this context that Abdullah Quilliam opened the first mosque in Britain.[4] The Liverpool Muslim Institute is a large converted terraced house. Quilliam ran the mosque with missionary zeal. Alongside an orphanage, he ran regular classes and lectures, ministering to the local Muslims, as well as acting as a representative to the British government of its countless Muslim subjects (he was keen to remind the government that its Muslim subjects outnumbered its Christian subjects). He was aided in this role through the singular title of 'Shaykh al-Islam of the British Isles', echoing a title normally issued by the Ottoman caliph Abdülmecid II, though in this case he most likely adopted it of his volition. Through a regular publication, *The Crescent*, Quilliam noted the new converts to Islam in Liverpool and surrounding areas (including many notable members of high society, such as Henry Stanley, third Baron Stanley of Alderley, the first Muslim member of the House of Lords, and Robert 'Reschid' Stanley, who would have been the first Muslim mayor in Britain during his tenure as Mayor of Stalybridge). His writings, which include prose and poetry, present a vociferous thinker, at times deeply patriotic to Britain, at other times seemingly agitating for the Ottoman Empire. His mosque was a base for his varied activities, and as a converted house, it also sets the model for many more converted domestic homes that would become mosques in the future. The mosque fell into disrepair after Quilliam departed Liverpool. It was eventually sold, and its historic importance largely overlooked until scholars (such as Ron Geaves) and activists (such as members of the Abdullah Quilliam Society) worked to revive public interest, and renovated the building, reopening in 2015. It now once again serves the Muslim community in Liverpool from 8–10 Brougham Terrace. Today, Brougham Terrace has been swallowed by the A5049, a dual-carriageway running through the east of Liverpool. I visited it once in 2010, at which point plans for renovation were still embryonic. The building maintained its historic character, though its appearance from the outside was of a forgotten and unmaintained terraced home, completely unremarkable for anyone passing. I passed through Liverpool again in 2015, at which point the mosque was once open to the public (for the first time in over a century) and functioning as a mosque. The renovation was not yet complete however, though the builders present took me through the building, including the parts unfinished, proudly indicating the quality of material and efforts to preserve the original features of the mosque installed by Quilliam himself. Today, it stands painted in brilliant white and ornately refurbished and decorated; it no longer looks forgotten. During my most recent visit in 2021, my informal tour-guide for the mosque turned to me and said 'welcome to the birthplace of Islam in Britain', a poetic but not inaccurate title that captures the historical and symbolic importance of the mosque.

Woking: 'The Mecca of the West'

The second mosque in Britain, though the first purpose-built mosque, is the Shah Jahan Mosque in Woking. It opened officially in 1889 and stands in stark contrast to Quilliam's mosque in many ways. The Shah Jahan Mosque was commissioned and built by Gottlieb Wilhelm Leitner, an orientalist and scholar of languages fluent in Arabic and Turkish. It was a part of a larger Oriental Institute that sought to cement and further the study of the 'east' in Britain, attracting numerous students from abroad and publishing journals in Arabic, Sanskrit and Urdu, as well as in English. The mosque on the site of the institute was funded by Sultan Shah Jahan Begum, the ruler of the princely state of Bhopal in India. It was built with the familiar onion domes of India and though grand in its architectural design it is a diminutive building, only able to accommodate between fifty and eighty worshippers (less than the Liverpool Muslim Institute). While it served as a mosque to students studying at the Oriental Institute, its significance beyond that was initially limited. It may not have survived the closure of the Oriental Institute after Leitner's death in 1899, but a trust was established to take over the mosque and it reopened in 1913. The mosque attracted the attention of Khwaja Kamal-ud-Din (d. 1932), an Indian-born lawyer and theologian who was an early advocate for the Ahmadiyya movement. During his first visit to the Shah Jahan Mosque, enamoured by the sight of an architecturally Islamic building in the heart of England, he is reported to have prayed that God make the mosque 'the Mecca of the West' (Salamat 2008: 26). For a time at least, it seemed his prayer was answered. The mosque became a landmark mosque in Britain during the interwar period. It hosted Muslim dignitaries, including politicians and even visiting heads of state, being utilised as a symbol of Britain's religious liberty and tolerance by the government. The Shah Jahan Mosque also became, during the early part of the twentieth century, a site of activism for several important Muslim intellectuals, authors and scholars. Marmaduke Pickthall and Yusuf Ali, well known for their translations of the Quran into English, worshipped at Shah Jahan Mosque. Their graves can now be found at the burial site associated with the mosque. Quilliam too, in his later years, would assume a pseudonym and began frequenting the Shah Jahan Mosque. The mosque's central role in British Muslim public life slowly diminished, as catalogued by Salamat (2008), to be replaced by a more ordinary role as one of the many mosques in operation Post Second World War, though its important historic role remains intact. A visitor to Shah Jahan Mosque today might be disappointed by its surroundings. It lies within a thoroughly ordinary suburb of London. On my first time to Woking to see the mosque, I got lost several times driving down quiet roads with semi-detached and townhouse homes, many of them new build, struggling to locate the mosque (doing several drives up and down the appropriately named 'Oriental Road'. The mosque itself however doesn't disappoint. The complex is tucked away behind a shopping centre, giving it perhaps intentionally the feeling of an oasis. The mosque itself is a small but stunning building that evokes the Anglo-Indian culture emerging during the British Raj. While it may no longer hold such a prominent role in civic life, it is still celebrated for being a site of Muslim activism during the earliest period of British Muslim history, and through historians and activists, its history is increasingly well documented and accessible to a wider public (for example, Muslim heritage group Everyday Muslim developed a walking trail that covers its history).[5]

Cardiff: The mosques of Tiger Bay

> A venerable patriarchal gentleman wearing a green turban and white and green robe is a familiar figure as he walks about followed by a tall slim man clad in a white burnoose and white turban – the Sheikh and his secretary. (Drake 1954: 328)

This was the description offered by Chicago School ethnographer St Clair Drake describing the founder of Wales' first mosque, Shaykh Abdullah Ali al-Hakimi (d. 1954) and his deputy, Hasan Ismail.[6] Drake, already well established as an academic following the publication of *Black Metropolis* (Cayton and Drake 1946), undertook his doctoral thesis in Cardiff's Tiger Bay. A bustling multicultural, multireligious port city. It was here that al-Hakimi established Noor al-Islam (spellings for the mosque vary, even in official records; Nur ul-Islam, Noor-el-Islam and Noor al-Islam are all used in various places). Al-Hakimi was a Yemeni student of the North African Shaykh, Ahmad al-'Alawi (1869–1934). The latter was the leader of the 'Alawi *tariqa*, a mystic with a pronounced importance amongst European Islam, especially converts (Lings

1993). In 1936, al-Hakimi obtained *ijaza* or permission to begin working in Britain from Shaykh al-'Alawi (Seddon 2014: 74). Al-Hakimi was particularly active in Cardiff and South Shields, but it was Cardiff and the historic 'Tiger Bay' that became the site of much of his work, moving from South Shields to Cardiff permanently in 1938. Halliday (2010) suspects that al-Hakimi's insistence on educating Muslim women (the wives of the sailors, often converts) was the reason he departed from South Shields, though I suspect the untimely death of his wife and newborn child in South Shields in December 1937 also pushed him to settle permanently in Cardiff. At some point in 1938, al-Hakimi had secured property in Bute Street (a road running through the heart of Tiger Bay) for the 'Zaouia Allawia Friendship Society'. Al-Hakimi not only used it as a base for his operations and propagation of his teachings but also acted as a place of regular prayer for the Muslims (Halliday 2010: 30–2). In 1938 planning permission was submitted to build a purpose-built mosque on land purchased in the nearby Peel Street, though it was never built. Instead, they continued worshipping in the Bute Street *zawiya*. Britain had entered the Second World War, and in January 1941 the *zawiya* was hit by German bomb during the Blitz, destroying it entirely. A mosque however was opened in 1943 within the space in Peel Street, however rather than purpose-built, it was a prefabricated temporary 'Tarran Hut', a type of construction popular in Britain during the Second World War. It did however have a façade built at the street-level entrance, leading to the temporary huts (Saleem 2018: 48). This temporary set up was redeveloped again, as al-Hakimi secured the funds for a more permanent building that opened in 1947. This iteration of Noor al-Islam stood for nearly four decades, only being demolished in 1988 for a new two-storey construction.

For those familiar with the history of Wales, the phrase 'Welsh Revival' evokes very powerful images. It describes an era of intense religious fervour amongst Welsh Christian communities around 1904–5. The revival began with smaller movements in towns such as Ammanford but soon spread until all came to a climax as key preachers, notably Evan Roberts, went on tours across Wales. The Welsh Revival was an important part of Welsh history. It took place in a backdrop of other Christian revivals in Britain and Europe during the nineteenth and twentieth centuries. Abdullah Ali al-Hakimi's activism and work in Cardiff can equally lay claim to being a religious revival in Wales, one that is not included in the history books (yet) but still shaped the future direction of Wales powerfully. Cardiff during this era was a bustling port city, one of the largest in the UK. Thousands of Muslims working on ships found themselves in Cardiff, sometimes for short stays and sometimes for longer. Some decided to abandon the difficult life at sea and make a home in Cardiff. Most of these Muslims lived in the Docks area which became known as Tiger Bay. They came from diverse regions of the world, Somalis, Indians and Malays. By far however the largest contingent came from Yemen, specifically Aden. In the space of a few short years, Abdullah Ali al-Hakimi successfully transformed the local Muslim community in Cardiff (and, to a certain extent, South Shields, Liverpool and Hull). Al-Hakimi's work also extended to the wider community. He had a close relationship with politicians, the media and local leaders from other faiths, holding annual dinners where he would bring them all together. His diplomatic success is demonstrated by the attendance of the Mayor of Cardiff and future prime minister James Callaghan (then MP for Cardiff South) at the reopening of Noor al-Islam in 1947 after it was destroyed in the Blitz of the Second World War. Kenneth Little, a social scientist, carried out a survey of Loudon Square in 1944, a key area in Tiger Bay. He describes the Muslim community below:

> Mention should be made again of the strong body of Islamic faith. The adherents of this creed not only carry out their religious and ritualistic obligations with more fervour than the rest of the community, but are correspondingly surer both of their creed and of themselves. The various prohibitions enjoined by the prophet are on the whole rigorously observed, as are Ramadan and other fasts and festivals. In the celebration of the latter, ritual dress is worn by a large number of the Arabs and other Moslems. (Little 1942b: 139–40)

Al-Hakimi's early successes however were marred by the increasing political tension in his native Yemen and its impact in Cardiff. He was an opponent of the Zaydi Imam, both Imam Yahya (died 1948), and after his death, his son Imam Ahmad (died 1962), leading organizations in resistance to the rule of the family. His deputy, Hasan Ismail, however supported the imams. Fred Halliday describes their rivalry as 'bitter' (2010: 78), made more complex by the tribal affiliations involved. Al-Hakimi returned to Yemen in 1953, before passing away in 1954.

Today, there are two mosques in Butetown (what would once have been called Tiger Bay) that have lineage to al-Hakimi. Noor al-Islam Mosque still stands, though the 1947 construction was demolished and rebuilt in 1988. Another mosque, now the South Wales Islamic Centre was built by Hasan Ismail and his followers in 1969 (though rebuilt and reopened, with some difficulties in securing funds, in 1984). Colloquially, the South Wales Islamic Centre is referred to as the 'Yemeni mosque' by some locals and Noor al-Islam as the 'Somali mosque'. The congregations are much more mixed than such a name might indicate (see Chapters 3 and 5 for mosque discussion on the function of congregations and intra-religious diversity within British mosques). Despite the fracturing amongst leadership, it is not inaccurate to say that the South Wales Islamic Centre reflects the human and spiritual legacy of al-Hakimi, whereas the Noor al-Islam Mosque reflects the built legacy.

Three mosques

Considering these three mosques, we are presented with three important examples of the early period of mosque-building in Britain. They were often the result of charismatic Muslim leaders, such as Abdullah Quilliam, Khwaja Kamal-ud-Din and Abdullah Ali al-Hakimi. They operated in different spheres. Quilliam sought to set himself up as the most senior Muslim scholar and leader in Britain, through his title of Shaykh al-Islam of the British Isles. Shah Jahan Mosque, as a purpose-built mosque close to London, took on an important symbolic role. At one point a representation of a British Empire that value religious freedom and its Muslim subjects, and later, as an organizational home for a British Muslim elite. Cardiff's Noor al-Islam Mosque was established to help transform and revive the practice and knowledge of Islam amongst the Muslim seamen settling in Britain. Additionally, its complex history of building, bombing, re-building, off-shoot mosques and denominational change can be seen as a microcosm of how no institution can be entirely disconnected from the global picture (whether German bombing raid or political upheaval in Yemen). All three mosques are intimately tied to Britain's imperial role and the British Empire. The three mosques can also help underline how Muslim women have been involved in mosques from the outset. In the Liverpool as well as Woking, Muslim women were involved in their establishment and operation (Cheruvallil-Contractor 2020), and al-Hakimi sought to use his mosques to educate Muslim women and involve them explicitly. All three mosques are now celebrated for their historic status. The Liverpool Muslim Institute has a blue plaque commemorating the work of Abdullah Quilliam and has reopened for public and worshippers alike. The Shah Jahan Mosque has been the subject of television documentaries and books and is now a Grade I listed building (a site is of exceptional national, architectural or historical importance that requires local authorities to consider its significance before allowing any changes). The Noor al-Islam Mosque, along with the South Wales Islamic Centre, are both descendants of al-Hakimi's original mosque, and the role of Cardiff as an important city of Muslim organizing has become embedded in the city's self-narrative.

The mosque-building era

Despite a small number of exceptions, such as the examples give above, the bulk of Britain's mosques were established following migration from the Indian subcontinent after the Second World War. This period of migration and settlement is documented by researchers such as Caroline Adams (1987), Muhammad Anwar (1979, 1985, 1993) and John Rex (1991, 1994). The increase in the Muslim population of Britain led to a substantial growth in the number of mosques. Seán McLoughlin, writing in 2005, observes:

> In 1963 there were just 13 mosques listed with the Registrar General... estimates suggest that there may now be 1,000 including those that are unregistered... This mushrooming of numbers since the late 1970s and 1980s indicates that the reuniting of Pakistani, Indian and Bangladeshi families across continents was decisive in catalysing the reconstruction of Islam in diaspora. (McLoughlin 2005: 1045)

What prompted these migrants to begin establishing mosques? Settlement seems to be a compelling factor. There is a recurring theme in the literature that once the itinerant Muslim migrants settled in Britain long term, they sought to address their religious needs by establishing mosques. The link between the legal status of migrants and building mosques is indicated by Richard Gale (2008: 23) who describes how the Commonwealth Immigrants Act of 1962 had the unexpected result of encouraging migrants to establish families in Britain, which in turn led to mosque-building efforts. Andrew Geddes makes the same point, observing the irony that laws designed to limit settlement 'actually stimulated "beat the ban" migration from people who feared that they might be affected by the restrictions and separated from their family members as a result' (2003: 35). The link between migration law and the establishment of mosques was also observed by Gerdien Jonker (2005: 1069) in her study of mosque conflicts in Germany, as well as Ural Manço and Meryem Kanmaz (2005: 1107) in their study of mosque conflicts in Belgium. The mosque is a symbol of settlement. The more invested Muslim migrant communities are in their new homes in diaspora, the greater the likelihood they invest resources and capital into building institutions that meet their religious and cultural needs. The fulfilment of needs is a strikingly uniform motivating factor for the establishment of mosques in diaspora, something we will return to as a theme throughout this book.

This period is aptly described by Yahya Birt as a 'mosque-building-phase' (2006: 687). While the mosque is presented in the literature as a milestone in the settlement of Muslim migrants, clearly not all Muslims are migrants. The number of Muslims in Britain increased from 3.07 per cent of the population in 2001 to 4.83 per cent in 2011 (1.6 million Muslims to 2.7 million) according to the census. This growth, coupled with the revelation in the 2011 census that 47.2 per cent of Muslims were born in the United Kingdom (Muslim Council of Britain 2015: 22) indicates that this increase in the British Muslim population is likely to be fuelled by new births more than migration. This shift in demographics is an important part of the contemporary picture of mosques, as a young population increasingly takes up leadership of mosques established by their parents' generation.

For in-depth explorations of the process involved in building a mosque during the mosque-building era, very few works exist. This is perhaps because academics at the time were more interested in settlement and the implications of migration on wider society than the religious institutions they were building, the significance of which was more pronounced in hindsight. Acknowledgement must also be made of the small number of researchers who were involved in the study of British Islam, which naturally restricted the number of issues that could be explored. There are exceptions however, such as Simon Naylor and James Ryan's work (2002), which considers the politics of mosque establishment historically (in the 1920s) in comparison to a case in the 1990s. Gale (2005) also provides an account of the issues around planning permission in establishing a mosque in Birmingham, and Daniel Nilsson DeHanas and Zacharias Pieri (2011) explore a proposed 'mega-mosque' in East London.

Two scholars whose work is of interest are Pnina Werbner and Stephen Barton. Werbner's ethnographic and detailed accounts of Muslim women, Sufism and religious practice in Manchester amongst Pakistanis are insightful and have proven valuable scholarly contributions. They are published as a 'trilogy' (Werbner 1990, 2002, 2003) and paint a vivid picture of a Muslim community. In *The Migration Process*, Werbner (1990) turns her attention towards the issue of class distinction amongst British Pakistanis in Manchester. She draws on the work of Pierre Bourdieu to explain how gift exchanges, cultural celebrations and building religious institutions, operate to create cultural capital. She identifies the mosque as 'the central forum in which the elite competes to legitimise its status' and how 'intense rivalry characterised contributions for the mosque project, increasing the level of sums donated by elite members' (1990: 310–11). She, thus, provides us with an indication of how mosque building can establish status and primacy amongst nascent migrant communities. She contends that the mosque forms 'the highest locus of value and communal involvement' (1990: 310), and so is capable of distributing social capital. Stephen Barton's distinctively different approach from Werbner offers an important and valuable account of a mosque during an embryonic phase of Muslim settlement. He adopts the position of a self-reflexive scholar, considering his role as an outsider, a male and a non-Muslim (Barton 1986: 7–9). He also stated openly the ways in which his identity as a priest created tensions and opportunities during the research process (Barton 1986: 18–20), with some participants viewing him with suspicion on account of his interest in Islam, whereas others affording him the respect of a religious authority, albeit from a different faith. Barton's work is highly, and almost exclusively, descriptive. Space is also given in Barton's thesis to the role and function of the imam. The imam operates as a functionary of the mosque and the wider community, he leads prayer, officiates rituals, and is sometimes brought outside 'for the celebration of rites of passage within particular households' so as 'to bring blessing, baraka' (1986: 115). Barton draws out the contradiction of the role of the imam in that he is both leader and servant (1986: 189) – 'the imam who is respected in public may be ridiculed in private' (1986: 190). He observes that the Imam 'has virtually no part to play in relation with the wider, multi-cultural society of Bradford. It is not the Imam who represents the Bengalis to others, but the President of the Twaqulia Islamic Society' (1986: 191). Barton's observation that it is the president of the mosque who holds significant leadership authority highlights a key argument put forward in this book, that mosques are expressions of Muslim agency and power, that authority stems upwards from the congregation (and not necessary down from the religious authority, i.e. the imam).

These aforementioned works are only to set the scene for the contemporary period on which I focus. I approach in this and subsequent chapters the mosque as it is, and as it functions today.

The contemporary period

We can view the history of mosques in Britain as having three phases. The first phase can be thought of as the pioneer phase, being dominated by the energetic activity of activists and reformers. Its output can be seen in example of the Liverpool Muslim Institute, the Shah Jahan Mosque and Noor al-Islam Mosque. This period begins before the First World War and when the British Empire was an important global power and leads up to the Second World War. The second phase, the aforementioned 'mosque-building era' that stretches from the Post-

Second World War up to the early 2000s is when the British Muslim population was largely composed of first-generation migrants who established mosques, some grand purpose-built constructions but most humble converted dwellings, to meet their immediate religious needs. The third phase, the contemporary era, is one characterized by a changing-of-the-guard, and the coming-of-age of second- and third-generation Muslims who are assuming leadership of mosques established by previous generations, and the diversification of mosques to new and changing functions. The contemporary era has seen radical transformations of the activities of mosques, pushed them in new spheres, and had an undeniable impact on Britain as a whole. A typology to describe these dimensions of mosque function is introduced in the next chapter, 'The Interspatial Mosque'.

2

The interspatial mosque

Introduction

'What type of mosque is this?' The question is asked by a curious visitor to Shah Jalal Mosque in Cardiff, Wales, at which I am volunteering for an open day. Several dozen members of the public visit at pre-arranged slots for a tour of the mosque, and a crowd of fifteen guests sit barefoot in front of me on the thick patterned carpet. I mull over the question as it takes me by surprise. 'What type?' I repeat the question back to her in hope of some illumination. Does she mean 'theological' type? Or perhaps she means architectural? The questioner herself hesitates slightly, 'I mean, are there different types of mosques?' The simple answer is 'yes, of course there are'. Mosques are diverse. But are there 'types'? There are no agreed upon typologies to help navigate the diversity of mosques, and so I'm unsure how best to answer. I choose to give a straightforward answer. 'Well, there are a few types, you can get a church conversion, like this mosque. There are lots of houses that have been converted into mosques too. There are some, not many, purpose-built mosques too, which will often have a dome and minaret that make them more recognisable as mosques from the outside.' The questioner did not seem wholly satisfied by my answer but accepted it and we moved on. The question expressed a frustration I had felt for some time; the lack of vocabulary in English to describe the diversity of mosques. The Christian tradition in Britain has terms (sometimes legally defined or at least broadly understood informally, depending on the tradition) such as 'chapel', 'church' and 'cathedral' which convey a sense of the size, purpose and even denominational identity of the place of worship in question, there are no comparable terms in Anglophone Islam. In places where the presence of Islam is more historic, there is often a vocabulary that conveys distinctions between mosques and also other religious institutions (this vocabulary will be engaged with later in the chapter). That is not to say however that terms are not beginning to develop in Britain.

This is both at the level of mosque management, who may not only choose a name with a consciousness that it conveys something about the size and function of the mosque but also amongst the congregation of British Muslims, who are by necessity developing a vernacular to navigate British mosques. This chapter will present a three-tiered typology British mosques termed the 'the interspatial mosque', and then map the typology onto the emerging vocabulary used by British Muslims to describe mosques.

The interspatial mosque

A recent and notable addition to the literature on British mosques is *British Mosques – An Architectural and Social History* (2018) by Shahed Saleem. He offers a typology in his architectural study of British mosques. The typology outlines the 'house mosque', the 'non-domestic conversion' and the 'purpose-built' mosque (Saleem 2018: 11–13). While accurate in its descriptive function, Saleem presents the typology as one of linear progression, writing that the 'purpose-built' mosque is the

> culmination of the Muslim community's mosque-development trajectory, a journey that generally starts with 'a house mosque or converted building' that is eventually found to be insufficient to cater for the needs of a growing Muslim population, and is then replaced with a larger purpose-built facility. (2018: 13)

The determinative element of Saleem's model could be misleading. If it were true, then the purpose-built mosque in an area would make the house mosque and the 'non-domestic conversion' defunct. But this is not what we see in practice. Not only do house mosques and purpose-built mosques often exist close together, it is not uncommon that new house mosques are opened where there are already large purpose-built mosques nearby. Different mosque buildings provide, as we shall see, different, often complementary, functions. There is a necessity, then, to reconsider the differences between mosques and assess their purposes in relation to each other.

In the coming chapter I present a typology that captures the dynamic and shifting ways in which British mosques operate. Except for a few core activities (such as the prayer) the activities a mosque are not viewed prescriptively, either in the writings of theologians or the imagination of the contemporary congregation. Mosques provide a range of functions which are determined by the denominational and ethnic background of the leadership and congregation, their available resources (human, financial and material) and their context. The latter, the context, is where the interspatiality of the typology emerges. Mosque leadership will, as I demonstrate, locate themselves in a space in the widest sense of the word. This could be a geographic space, a symbolic space, a marketplace of welfare services or a denominational landscape. In relation to this space and broad ecosystem of other mosques and institutions, they will operate both competitively as well as cooperatively in developing a niche for the services provided by the mosque. Finally, it foregrounds the worldview of the mosque leadership and congregation in which every activity has religious significance (whether daily prayer or a foodbank).

The typology of the interspatial mosque provides a three-tiered dynamic description of British mosques, distinguishing between their priorities. It provides, in my view, a more coherent and accurate description of mosque activities so as to allow for assessing the differences between them. I have utilized the terms *fard, fard kifaya* and *sunna* to describe the three tiers. These are Islamic jurisprudential terms used to describe the status of obligatory acts of worship. I use them here not in the jurisprudential sense but rather adapt them for sociological analysis – to describe how the mosque's congregation envisage their role and function and how they class their actions.

First is the core function of the mosque, the *fard*, or the compulsory. The key activity at this tier are the five daily prayers. It is the function of the mosque without which there is no mosque. The second tier is the *fard kifaya*, the communal responsibilities, which are largely rites of passage and educational activities. These are the religious obligations that, rather than falling on the individual, fall on the community to fulfil as a social whole. The *janaza*, or funeral prayer, is one such example; it is not the family of the deceased who are responsible for organizing this but the whole Muslim community. In jurisprudence, if a *fard kifaya* is fulfilled by one individual, the responsibility of all is met. If it is left undone, all are blameworthy. The mosque is a key mechanism by which such communal responsibilities are fulfilled. And finally, the third tier is the interspatial *sunna*. *Sunna* means 'tradition', and more specifically the example of the Prophet Muhammad, and is used interchangeably with *mustahabb* as the legal classification of an action that is 'recommended' but not compulsory; essentially, such actions are within the spirit and ethos of Islamic teachings but, in terms of priority, are secondary to the *fard*. In the case of this model, I use the term *sunna* since it describes not only the 'optional, but encouraged' nature of the actions as conceptualized by the congregants but also the important link made with the Prophetic example (also called the *sunna*) indicated through the use of the word.

I adopt the emic language of congregants which emerged out of conversations about the purpose of mosques from management committees. They would use terms such as *fard*, *fard kifaya* or *sunna* to describe the importance or centrality of an activity undertaken by the mosque. The language is valuable in underlining that a mosque's activities cannot be easily divided into the secular and the sacred, since all the actions undertaken are made meaningful within an Islamic paradigm and through Islamic terms. A range of terms have been deployed in English to describe larger mosques with a broad range of activities, such as 'multipurpose mosques' or 'community centre mosques' and even 'cathedral mosques' (see Maussen 2009: 14, 214; Es 2012: 154; Zulfikar 2014: 176). Such terms fail to describe the self-conceptualizatfion of mosques, or to provide a coherent and meaningful insight into the activities of mosques. The interspatial mosque typology dispenses with these terms and provides instead a conceptualization produced from the ground up, through ethnographic data and the religious vocabulary of the congregations who attend the mosque and leadership who ran the mosque (while *fard, fard kifaya* and *sunna* are not used to describe mosques as a whole, they are used to describe the actions and activities of the mosque). The term also has the benefit of capturing the dynamic and shifting ways in which larger mosques operate. My argument is that all mosques in Britain can be classified as operating at the level of *fard, fard kifaya* or *sunna*. I refer to this three-tiered model as the 'interspatial mosque'.

The *fard*: A place of prostration

The first tier of the model of the interspatial mosque, as indicated, is the *fard*, or the obligatory. In this sense, the primary function of the mosque is the completion of the obligatory performance of the prayer. Up and down Britain, whenever I asked worshippers, imams, or mosque leaders, what the primary purpose of a mosque is, they would respond matter-of-factly that it's the *salah* (or the *namaz*) – the daily obligatory prayers of Muslims. Mosques are meant for the *salah* and without the *salah* no place can claim to be a mosque. In practice, mosques may be set up for countless reasons. I have come across examples of mosques set up because of theological or personal disagreements between congregations, or to provide a geographical centre for a dispersed community of rural Muslims, or sometimes even to create a job for a popular and well-trained imam. These practical motivations, however, exist parallel and subservient to the stated purpose of a mosque – as a place of prostration, the key religious obligation of the observing Muslim.

At the centre of Muslim worship, and indeed of any mosque, is the ritual prayer, the *salah*. This is indicated by the Arabic word for mosque, *masjid*, which means a place of prostration. *Salah* is to be performed five times a day by the observant Muslim, determined by the position of the sun during the day. *Fajr*, the first prayer, takes place at dawn. Then *zuhr* occurs just following the midday zenith. Next *'asr* takes place during the sun's descent, *maghrib* immediately following the sunset, and *'isha'* begins once twilight ends. In Britain, located as it is at an extreme northern latitude, the timings of these prayers vary significantly through the seasons. In the winter, the first will be around 7.00 am, and the last, 6.00 pm. During summer, the first can begin as early as 2.30 am and the last at 11.00 pm. (See Ali 2014 for an overview of these variations, and the theological issues they raise for British Muslims.)

While the salah is fundamental to the mosque, the mosque is not fundamental to the salah. In an oft-quoted hadith, the Prophet Muhammad instructed Muslims, 'whenever the time comes for prayer, pray there, for that is a mosque' (Sahih Muslim, *The Book of Mosques and Prayer Places*[1]). Provided a space is ritually clean (free from a list of specific impurities such as faeces or blood, and prohibited iconography, such as religious idols or any statue placed in the direction of prostration[2]), it can be used for prayer. That said, the allocation of a specific area for prayer in which these conditions can be met is common practice wherever Muslims are found in sufficient numbers.

Hence British Muslim can perform the *salah* in 'multifaith prayers' or 'quiet rooms' in institutions, airports and shopping centres. The *musalla* (literally, a place for the *salah*) is a common term for such a space in Arabic-speaking Muslim countries and is anywhere demarcated for prayer but one that is without a regular imam and not used (in most cases) for the Friday prayer. In other regions, such as South East Asia, the term *surau* (a Malaysian term) is used for a similar type of space. The distinction between a *musalla* and a small *masjid* in practice and colloquial usage is blurred. In some places a *musalla* can refer to large spaces allocated for the largest communal prayers such as those used to mark the major holidays). In other contexts, a *musalla* does not hold regular prayers whereas a *masjid* does. A common and useful definition from the legal tradition of Islam makes the distinction that the *musalla* is privately owned whereas a *masjid* is endowed by a trust or *waqf* in perpetuity; thus a *masjid* should never cease being a *masjid*, whereas a *musalla* indicates a temporariness (see Mangera 2004; Munajjid 2011). The temporality implied in the *musalla* applies well to hired and rented properties, and the absence of personal ownership implied in definitions of the *masjid* echoes Durkheimian descriptions of sacred spaces as 'belonging not to the priest or any other single person but to the whole tribe' (Pals 2006: 91). In the case of the *waqf*, it is God's property. Moving away from the legal descriptions, practice is less clearly defined. There are a diverse range of arrangements behind sites described as mosques in Britain; they may be rented space or privately owned, run as a charity, or sub-let from a larger charity or trust. The *fard* mosque typology includes the *musalla* and the small *masjid*, the rented properties and the institutional prayer rooms. The ritual prayer is the most important activity in any mosque; it gathers people together in the mosque – sometimes half a dozen, sometimes hundreds, fulfilling the description of the mosque as a 'place of prostration'. This gathering of a congregation is central to facilitating the next tier, the *fard kifaya*.

The *fard kifaya*: Communal responsibilities

The daily prayers are an individual responsibility that can be fulfilled communally, but there are certain acts of worship that require the involvement of wider Muslim society – either because of the financial capital necessary to complete them or due to the liturgical need for the presence of more than a single individual. While the prayer is an integral part of the mosque, the mosque's gathered congregation is an integral part of the *fard kifaya*, and such activities are seldom reproduced outside the mosque. So, while the daily prayers, in absence of a mosque, can be completed at home, many of the *fard kifaya* activities require a communal semi-public space. In a sentence, the daily prayers are fundamental to the identity of the mosque, but the mosque is fundamental to the completion of the *fard kifaya*. Mosques at this tier of the typology are larger, more focused on the communal religious responsibilities, especially the education of children.

Within the UK, supplementary Islamic education is one of the most significant of the *fard kifaya* activities. Jonathan Scourfield's project on Muslim childhood identified the central role played by mosques in religious upbringing (Scourfield et al. 2013), and the programme of almost every mosque has an educational element for young children. Prior to this, the more common method would be small group teaching by parents in domestic environments, a poorly researched area of Muslim education but one that has received attention from Farah Ahmed (2012) in consideration of pedagogical models in use by Muslim mothers educating their children through *halaqas* (a *halaqa* referring in this context to a semi-formal class with students sat around the teacher). The supplementary Islamic education offered by mosques include tuition in Quranic recitation, the basics of how to pray, and an introduction into the life of the Prophet Muhammad. They are often described in Britain as the *madrasa* (not to be confused with full-time Islamic seminaries), the *maktab*, the Quran School or Islamic School.

Rites of passage also form a large part of the *fard kifaya* activities. After the birth of a child, Islamic teachings instruct the parents to celebrate with a communal feast – the *ʿaqiqa*. Weddings, especially the *nikah*, the formal religious ceremony, are often held within a mosque, not only to facilitate access to an imam but also for the *baraka* or blessing associated with the space. Depending on the size and facilities of the mosque, the *fard kifaya* mosque may also offer the *janaza* prayer. All these actions fundamentally require communal involvement. In order for the *janaza* to be valid, public attendance is essential. Weddings must have at least two witnesses present, the union must be widely announced and the *ʿaqiqa* should involve sharing sacrificed food. Finally, the education of children is usually most effectively and efficiently delivered through group teaching, especially in relation to the social components of religion (how to pray collectively, for example).

Important to highlight too is the *jumuʿa* prayer. Historically, and indeed today in some Muslim-majority countries, many mosques do not host the Friday prayer. Pedersen et al. (2012: 657) comment that, with the advent of institutions such as the *jamiʿ* mosque (a large mosque intended for Friday prayer) and the *madrasa*, 'the use of the word *masdjid* becomes limited . . . [w]hile, generally speaking, it can mean any mosque . . . It is more especially used of the smaller unimportant mosques' which did not host the *jumuʿa* prayer. The Friday prayer also remains the prerogative, in classical Islamic *fiqh* texts at least, of a small number of *jamiʿ* mosques rather than everyday prayer spaces (see Calder 1986). By contrast, in Britain, the *jumuʿa* prayer is held in almost all mosques – especially the *fard kifaya* mosques (whereas prayer rooms may or may not host a *jumuʿa*). The symbolic meaning of the *jumuʿa* has also morphed in the diaspora and has become an important demonstration of religious commitment of the individual and the community. This meaning of the Friday prayer can be contrasted with the articulation provided by Norman Calder, who presents the writing of Muslim jurists of the classical period who conceptualized the Friday prayer as public-political ritual that can only be undertaken by a political authority at a single appointed mosque 'a ritual in which the whole Muslim (local) community, abandoning factional allegiances, expresses its adherence to universal Islamic values' (Calder 1986: 38). The status quo in Britain of multiple mosques offering Friday prayers with no overriding Islamic political authority overseeing them is in stark contrast to this exposition.

The *fard kifaya* mosques underline the importance of the *umma*, the religious community of Muslims but with a focus on the locality of the mosque. The responsibilities completed at the tier of the *fard kifaya* reaffirm the social responsibilities and relationships between individual Muslims. The next tier of mosque activity may extend beyond the immediate Muslim community and begins to conceptualize the mosque in a wider civic and public sphere.

The *sunna* mosque

The *sunna* mosque is the final and third tier. As mentioned above, the *sunna* is an action that is recommended but not obligatory. It is interchangeable with the term *mustahabb*, but the use of term *sunna* indicates a link to the Prophetic practice. *Sunna* actions are traditionally those that are not the essential pillars of Islamic practice but are exemplary. To pray the *fajr* prayer is obligatory. To pray the superogatory *duha* (a mid-morning prayer) or *tahajjud* (a late-night prayer) prayers is *sunna*. The *sunna* is effectively a way to denote the Prophetic ideal, and I should pause to stress that all mosques see themselves as being part of this ideal. Akel Kahera identifies the significance of the Prophetic mosque when he discusses the centrality of the 'spatial sunna' (2002a) in organizing modern mosques in America, stressing the importance of locating mosques in relation to the *sunna*. The importance of this tier is that it is not simply an adoption of Prophetic practice in a new context but often involves the mosque leaders engaging with, reflecting on and developing new ways of understanding the nature of the *sunna*. A mosque describing its environmental work such as litter-picking or supporting public health campaigns as *sunna* necessitates a discursive engagement with life of the Prophet Muhammad. Thus the *sunna* activities are not prescriptive but a creative process.

Activities at this level are *sunna* because they are not essential to a mosque's identity, but in the moral framework of Muslims jurists, a good Muslim fulfils the *sunna* when and where possible, and by extension, so too the mosque. Ismail Serageldin and James Steele (1996: 9) tie in the typology of 'the community centre complex mosque' as reminiscent of the Prophet's Mosque, which was 'more than a prayer space; it was the seat of temporal power, the place where people learned from the Prophet and the centre of civic activity in Madinah'.

The *sunna* mosque devotes its energies and resources beyond the fulfilment of the *fard* and *fard kifaya* duties and seeks to be of service in other additional ways. It is worthwhile to visit Seán McLoughlin's analysis of mosques from 2005 which, while focused on Pakistani-led mosques in Bradford, has applicability in contemporary Britain more broadly:

> Indeed, some mosques in the diaspora could be seen as re-inventing an Islamic tradition by slowly taking on a range of community functions that would be more or less unheard of in Pakistan today. So, while primarily being places of prayer and devotion, since the 1980s at least, some mosques in Britain have also functioned as advice centres for the unemployed, Members of Parliament's surgeries[3], homework clubs, youth centres, elderly day-care centres, and spaces to prepare food for communal gatherings such as weddings. (McLoughlin 2005: 1048)

Whereas the tiers of *fard* and *fard kifaya* are relatively fixed, the tier of the *sunna* mosque can and does adapt dynamically to suit the changing needs and circumstances of the congregation and the immediate community as McLoughlin describes. The leaders of mosques that can be categorized as *sunna* mosques may disagree semantically with McLoughlin that they are 're-inventing the Islamic tradition', however. Rather, every mosque sees itself as a 'revival' of the Prophet's Mosque as it functioned in his lifetime. The example of Prophet Muhammad confers a superlative religious sanction (and even a mandate) for the actions of Muslims and, thus, the Prophet's Mosque occupies a similar role in relation to how other mosques should operate.

The activities of *sunna* mosques in the UK are no doubt influenced by the British context, inspired by other faith groups and responding to new challenges of migration and diaspora, but they are understood and made meaningful on Islamic terms. The conceptions of *fard*, *fard kifaya* and *sunna* are staples in the lexicon of Islamic orthopraxis. The terms being deployed to describe mosque activity emphasize a worldview, in which every action has, religious significance. *Fard* mosques, *fard kifaya* mosques and *sunna* mosques are all found in Britain. Of the last, examples include the East London Mosque (see Eade and Garbin 2006; Ansari 2011), Birmingham Central Mosque, Edinburgh Central Mosque and several more across the country, all engaged in a diverse, shifting and complex range of activities. One important aspect of the *sunna* mosque is that the activities are rarely the same between two mosques. They are dictated by varying factors ranging from the denominational background of the mosque to available resources. These priorities will be shaped and influenced by the context of the mosque. British mosques are cooperative as well as competitive and will often seek to develop a niche for themselves in the marketplace of religious institutions and services provided.

An important point to note is that the typology presented is not tied to denominational identity in an explicit way. One can find mosques from each tier of the typology from a variety of denominational backgrounds. The intra-religious diversity of British mosques is further explored in Chapter 5. Having introduced the typology of the interspatial mosque, this will be mapped onto the landscape of British mosques and presented through a case study of three mosques in Cardiff.

The question of diversity

There are around twenty-six mosques in total (give or take a few ambiguities) in Cardiff, but I will focus on three locations for the basis of an empirical presentation of the interspatial mosque. I have chosen three mosques from one city for two reasons. The first is to demonstrate how the three tiers of the typology presented interact. It is not that *fard* mosques are deficient compared to *fard kifaya* mosques nor that the *fard kifaya* mosques necessarily aspire to become *sunna* mosques. Instead they can serve different functions and purposes and often do so in relation to each other. The geographic proximity of the three mosques thus highlights their complementary nature. The second reason, slightly contradictorily, is to stress their arbitrary nature. These are not mosques significant or noteworthy on a national scale; they are not mosques which are unique amongst Britain's 2,000 or so mosques. They have been chosen because they are sufficiently everyday and ordinary to demonstrate the dynamics of the interspatial mosque typology without resorting to generalizations. The first mosque described is one that operates at the level of a *fard*, according to my typology. It is one that may not be recognized as a true 'mosque' but nonetheless designates itself as one. The second is a house mosque that operates as a *fard kifaya* mosque, and the third is a *sunna* mosque.

The first mosque is located in Saray Restaurant, on Cardiff's busy City Road. Up and down City Road are a range of restaurants, takeaways and shisha bars, interspersed with fried chicken shops. One of the larger restaurants on this road is the Saray, offering mainly Turkish food. It differentiates itself from the several other Arab and Mediterranean restaurants on City Road by offering more uniquely Anatolian dishes (such as imam beyaldi), baklava made on-site, and the existence of a large room in the basement, accessible from the main floor, which it calls the *masjid*. Some might object to the description of this space as a *masjid*. It is privately owned; there is neither a committee nor a management structure in place and no appointed imam. Nonetheless, the owners have placed a sign that reads 'MASJID' on the door leading to the basement. The space itself is a large room ornately decorated. There is carpet on the floor such as one would usually find in a mosque, with the rows for prayer marked out, indicating the *qibla*. On the wall there is calligraphy, and in one corner, a *mihrab*. The *mihrab* is purpose-built and elegantly designed. There is a small barrier to allow division between the sexes, and there are heaters, fans and several shelves for keeping copies of the Quran. In total, the mosque can accommodate perhaps twenty worshippers at a time. In general, this is more than enough for the restaurant (which has a maximum capacity of about 120). The presence of a place for prayer makes the restaurant popular with diners during the summer months (when prayer times may run into the evening), and during Ramadan, when the restaurant offers a unique menu for the *iftar*, the meal with which Muslims break their fast. As mentioned, this self-described *masjid*, some might object, is more like a prayer room or *musalla*. As a privately owned space with irregular prayers, it fits the definition of *musalla* more neatly. Nonetheless, the basement is similar to many other spaces found across the UK – some institutional (such as the 'quiet rooms' in universities), others in commercial spaces (such as the 'multifaith prayer room' in shopping centres such as Manchester's Arndale), and those found regularly in airports and train stations. Its primary purpose is to allow customers to the restaurant to fulfil their religious obligation of prayer.

The second mosque in question is a common site in almost any Muslim community – a 'house mosque' in a residential area. Masjid Uthman was formerly the *Islami Shikka Pratisthan*. The *Islami Shikka Pratisthan*, or the Islamic Educational Foundation, was a mosque run primarily by Bangladeshis, serving the large Bangladeshi community in the Riverside area of Cardiff. Riverside is a stone's throw from the city centre, a small area tightly packed with terraced homes. On football match days, the roar of the crowd from the nearby Principality Stadium can be heard. The former *Islami Shikka Pratisthan* is a converted end-of-terrace residential property and, aside from historic mosques in Butetown, it is amongst the earliest in Cardiff. Before it reopened as Masjid Uthman, the congregation was almost exclusively made up of first-generation Bangladeshi migrants who largely worked in the catering trade, and it served this congregation's specific needs. During Ramadan, it offered the *tarawih* prayers (a recommended prayer of twenty cycles offered during the sacred month) twice in the evening. The first would be at its usual time after the *'isha'* evening prayer but, given that the majority of the mosque's congregants worked in restaurants and takeaways at this time, it was poorly attended. A second *tarawih* would be offered around 1.00 am, so that the men (and it only served men) could finish work, return home, eat, shower and travel to the mosque in time for the long prayer. Likewise, it was not unusual for a *wa'z* (sermon) by an itinerant preacher to be planned for past midnight, a suitable time for a congregation who largely worked in the service industry. In the early 2000s, the congregation grew large enough and wealthy enough to purchase a church that was for sale only a few hundred metres away. While it would have made financial sense to sell the existing property as a house or instead perhaps convert it back to accommodation so that it could be rented out to the congregation, the committee found it difficult to come to terms with the idea of their mosque no longer being a mosque. Instead, an arrangement was made with a local imam, a young Deobandi Darul Uloom graduate, to purchase and take over the administration of the mosque, and in the mid-2000s, the mosque reopened as Masjid Uthman. There were already a Masjid Abu Bakr and a Masjid Umar in Cardiff, named after the first two Rashidun Caliphs.[4] Uthman, the third Caliph, was thus the obvious choice, according to the imam, for the name of this new mosque. Both Masjid Abu Bakr and Masjid Umar are Deobandi[5] in orientation, as is Masjid Uthman, which is an indication of the wider landscape into which the mosque fits (a description of the denominational identities of mosques, and the value of such denominational labels, is offered in Chapter 5).

The mosque is in the same square-mile as Masjid Jalalia (the church converted into the mosque by leaders of the *Islami Shikka Pratisthan*), the al-Falah Centre, Markaz at-Tawheed, the Rabbaniyah *madrasa* and mosque and Masjid Abu Bakr. With so many mosques nearby, and indeed the primary congregation of the *Islami Shikka* moving to the newly refurbished church, what does Masjid Uthman offer and whom does it serve? The five daily prayers take place without fail, as do the Friday prayers, as it has a strong local congregation. It includes elderly men who prefer to walk to their local mosque rather than making a journey elsewhere by public transport or car. The after-school Islamic studies classes are also popular with parents in the area; the high proportion of Muslim homes near the mosque means local parents prefer their children to go to a mosque with a qualified *'alim* almost within earshot of their houses. On a weekday evening, it is common to see many young children walking to the mosque for after-school programme and back. In addition to educational programmes and the daily prayers, there are occasional additional classes. The most common is an introductory *fiqh* course, running through the religious literacy needed for Muslims to pray, fast and perform basic acts of worship and recitation of the Quran. Masjid Uthman provides a valued function in the locality and a base for the work of its imam. It is, however, like many other house mosques, small in capacity. It offers services needed and in-demand the local area (a place to pray within walking distance for Muslims nearby, a place to educate children in the basics of Islamic literacy). There are countless similar 'house mosques' with a similar scope of operation that fit the *fard kifaya* model across the UK, such as the Shah Jalal Mosque in Newcastle, Dawtul Islam in Glasgow, or the Lammack Prayer Room in Blackburn. It's worth stressing however that a converted domestic property or 'house mosque' is not by definition operating at the *fard kifaya* tier. The typology describes the activities and priorities of the mosque, not the architecture or building.

The last of the three mosques to be introduced in this sample is Dar ul-Isra. This is a converted church hall, located in the student area of Cathays. The deceptively large building was renovated in 2008, creating a second floor and doubling its capacity. The members of the mosque leadership are equally from South Asian and Middle Eastern backgrounds, though its congregation is more diverse, and drawn heavily from the university students who live and study nearby. In addition to the mosque building, there is a Scouts Hall and Activity Centre behind the mosque. The Scouts Hall was part of the original complex, and both buildings were used by St Mark's and St Teilo's churches. In 2006 the first Cathays al-Huda Muslim Scout Group was launched, operating out of the Scouts Hall behind Dar ul-Isra, providing a historic continuity to the building despite changing ownership from Christians to Muslims. The mosque also houses a large commercial kitchen, a front office, a library, a room for the ritual washing of the deceased, and a large ablution room with accessible toilets and a shower room. There is a large prayer space for women, though smaller than the men's prayer area. The congregation is large – informally estimated at about three thousand people who regularly visit the mosque and easily gather close to a thousand people for the weekly *jumu'a* prayer.

Dar ul-Isra's daily activities are sprawling and multiple, but it is the cycle of five daily prayers that structures all of them. The mosque's events fall into several categories. They may be educational, such as the daily Islamic school, which provides children between the ages of six and sixteen with instruction in reading and reciting the Quran. There are also a range of *halaqas* – study circles offering religious education. The mosque holds a youth *halaqa* on Friday evenings. In addition, there is an Arabic *halaqa*, an Urdu *halaqa*, a Malay *halaqa* and occasionally a Bengali *halaqa*. Alongside Islamic education, GCSE and A-Level tutoring is also offered on Saturday mornings in core subjects such as science and mathematics.

Social activities are common. The widescreen televisions used during *jumu'a* prayer to broadcast the imam's sermons throughout the mosque are often appropriated for video game competitions. During the World Cup and other major football tournaments, the televisions are also used to watch matches. Additionally, three parties are held after each Eid, a 'brothers' party', a 'sisters' party' and a 'children's party'. Other social events might be organized solely to foster opportunities to create new friendships between congregants, such as quiz nights, board game evenings and tea and coffee mornings. The mosque hosts regular fundraising activities led by national charities such as Islamic Relief. An example might be a lecture by a popular preacher, followed by a call for donations. Similar events are held by Human Appeal, Muslim Aid, Interpal and Syria Relief. In addition to the events led by the charities, there are opportunities for the charities to visit and raise funds during regular events at the mosque.

As for political events, politicians regularly make use of the gathered congregations of the mosque. Political visits are attempts at 'public engagement' by politicians and include holding open meetings with Muslims at the mosque on issues ranging from parking to organ donation. Dar ul-Isra generally has an open-door policy to politicians, viewing such visits as a civic duty and a key method of empowering its Muslim congregation.

Sporting activities within, or organized through, the mosque are common. The mosque is sometimes transformed into makeshift gym for various forms of exercise classes. The mosque has a football team that plays in the local league, and members of the congregation meet at an indoor football pitch (two groups meeting twice a week). One post-pandemic activity in 2022 encouraged congregants to join a several-mile bicycle ride (of various lengths for those of all levels of fitness) before meeting for a barbeque. There is an ethos of what can be described as 'muscular Islam' at Dar ul-Isra, comparable to 'muscular Christianity' (see Hall 2006) – an ethos of physical strength and an idealized masculinity entwined closely with spiritual piety. Being physically fit and active are woven into the mosque's activities and teachings.

Rites of passage also constitute a significant proportion of the mosque's events. The *'aqiqa*, a feast to celebrate the birth of a child, as well as weddings and funerals dot the mosque's annual calendar. This, alongside occasional interfaith events, the large Muslim Scouts group at Dar ul-Isra, and those informal events that do not fall easily into a single category make Dar ul-Isra one of Cardiff's most active and busy mosques.

These three sites, Saray's basement mosque, Masjid Uthman and Dar ul-Isra Mosque, demonstrate a significant challenge that is present when one discusses and studies mosques – the sheer diversity of them. All three places are referred to as mosques, and similar examples of all three can be found across the UK, but they are different from one another in significant ways. They are certainly related, but the growth of this diversity has increasingly put the term 'mosque' under strain. My argument is that it is helpful to consider each mosque in relation to the purposes it fulfils: the *fard*, the *fard kifaya* and the *sunna*. Such terms allow for a greater insight into the inherent diversity of mosques, recognizing the differences in size, scope and activity. Denominational descriptions, for example, might help reveal the character of leadership or provide some indication of the way in which worship in undertaken, they often do not tell us about the mosque's conceptualization of their role and activities. The typology, I propose, exists across denominational boundaries. Some mosques are locations for the fulfilment of prayer, and focused on the individual responsibility to pray only, the *fard* mosque. The second tier, the *fard kifaya* mosque, focuses on the communal dimension of Islam, specifically the prayer, the *jumuʿa*, and education and life cycle events. The final tier, the *sunna* mosque, expands to include a broader range of activities, the specific combination of which are determined by a range of global and local factors but are always tied into the vision of emulating the Prophetic mosque. We are thus able to discern how the mosque as an institution has stratified, providing different but complimentary functions.

The evolving *sunna* mosque

Sunna mosques consciously and conspicuously locate themselves in a diverse landscape (a space, in the broadest sense) of religious institutions, providing the services most needed in their local context. Alongside this, however, the larger and more successful of these mosques are looking beyond the local and city landscape and instead locate a niche for themselves in the national and sometimes international context. In the following section, I demonstrate how some contemporary British mosques are doing this by finding a niche for themselves on a national or international space. The aim of this section is to demonstrate how important the interspatial dimension is in determining how mosques determine their function.

What is the most important mosque in Britain? The question of the most important place of worship is not easily answered even in the more established Christian tradition, but Westminster Cathedral (the seat of the Archbishop of Westminster, the most senior Catholic clergyman in England and Wales) and Canterbury Cathedral (the seat of the Archbishop of Canterbury and the head of the Anglican Communion) are two potential contenders. I would argue that the East London Mosque is seeking to establish itself as the leading British mosque in terms of political significance (here I use the term political in the specific sense of related to parliamentary politics and current affairs). It has developed an informal relationship with the MCB, which is the largest British Muslim umbrella body that represents mosques, charities, schools and other Muslim organizations (Khan, Joudi, and Ahmed 2020). MCB is by no means universally accepted as the leading British Muslim organization, but few would question its place as one of the most prominent contenders. The East London Mosque has been fostering a relationship with the MCB over the last decade, producing joint press releases, running joint conferences and often hosting the MCB's annual general meetings. These events place the East London Mosque in a symbolic space as a site of national civic action for British Muslims. Its location in Tower Hamlets, which the mosque describes on its website as 'home to the UK's largest Muslim community', further cements its importance beyond the immediate locality. A dated but insightful article by John Eade and David Garbin highlighted how East London Mosque leaders sought to define it as the area's 'central mosque' (2006: 184) and more generally forged alliances with local governments and civic partners to achieve this. In the intervening twelve years, it has developed this further by forging alliances with national groups to become, if such a thing is ever possible, Britain's 'central mosque'. This is far from uncontested, but here I only intend to highlight the intention of the mosque rather than whether or not it has achieved this goal.

Two further mosques demonstrate how the symbolic significance of a city can also be adopted by a mosque within it. They are the Oxford Centre for Islamic Studies (OCIS) and the Cambridge Mosque Trust. Oxford and Cambridge are in the national imagination of Britain's foremost educational cities, a training ground for the elite and future leaders, and this, like London, has an impact on the national ambitions of the mosques there. The OCIS has built a multimillion-pound building to house its teaching and research. The ambitious project has received funding from nation states (Malaysia, Kuwait and Turkey) as well as royal families. It was designed in an architectural style that is inspired by existing Oxford colleges, with a quadrangle included. Where a traditional Oxford college would place its chapel, there is a mosque – and its grand design promises to make it a national landmark. As the home of the OCIS, it is making a statement about itself as being a leading institution for the academic study of Islam in Britain. In shaping its architecture to reflect both Oxford's tradition and Islamic norms, it is making a statement about integration and belonging. It is, quite literally, Islam in British stone.

The same can be said of the Cambridge Mosque Trust, another recently opened multimillion-pound project, with Shaykh Abdal Hakim Murad (also known as Timothy Winter) involved in the project and often fronting fundraising campaigns. The mosque undertook 'crowdfunding' campaigns online but was also sponsored by 'government agencies in the Republic of Turkey, together with a Turkish private company (Yapı Merkezi), and the Qatar National Fund'.[6] It claims to be 'Europe's first purpose-built eco-mosque' and argues on its website that 'as a major international city, Cambridge deserves a proper facility for Muslims which will enhance its prestige and provide an architectural focus attracting new visitors'.[7] Both the Oxford and the Cambridge mosques are appealing to the reputation and symbolism of the cities in which they are located and carving out a unique niche in the international Muslim landscape. The OCIS mosque intends to be part of a wider institution of learning, a landmark and a statement about Islam and Britain. The Cambridge mosque seeks to capitalize on the international reputation of the city and its eco-mosque innovation. What further distinguishes the Cambridge osque is its association with Abdal Hakim Murad, a Muslim scholar strongly associated with what Sadek Hamid (2016) describes as 'traditional Islam', a resurgent Sufism with an emphasis on the canonical legal schools, classical forms of learning and authority, and scepticism to other reform movements (especially Salafism). Should the mosque continue its association with Abdal Hakim Murad, it may also develop into a national denominational home for the emergent 'traditional Islam' movement Hamid identifies.

Two final mosques to consider are those of Darul Uloom Bury and Darul Uloom Dewsbury,[8] which contend with one another to be the foremost Deobandi seminaries in Britain. Both are primarily educational institutes, a full-time seminary or *madrasa*, educating *'ulama'* in Britain. The Darul Ulooms have mosques attached to them and are easily amongst the most influential Muslim institutions in Britain, yet they avoid the attention and publicity that the East London Mosque courts, and instead more quietly dedicate themselves to educational goals. Darul Uloom Dewsbury is also the European headquarters of the Tablighi Jama'at. The Tablighi Jama'at is a transnational Islamic movement that seeks to revive Muslim commitment to their faith, and while it has successfully appealed across the broad spectrum of Sunni intra-religious diversity, it remains closely associated with the Deobandi school out of which it first emerged (see Chapter 5 for more information). These two mosques-cum-madrasas are of inestimable importance to British Muslims, producing a large number of British *'ulama'*, contributing to the shaping of the Muslim scholarly class in Britain. By producing scholars who go on to establish their own mosques and educate lay Muslims, they have become important institutions in shaping the development of British Islam but are largely below the radar of the mainstream public discourse on Muslims. These mosque-cum-madrasas confidently embrace their Deobandi denominational identity. The role that religious denominational identity plays in the mosque is further explored in Chapter 5, including the argument that mosques are moving in two general directions. They are either operating in a broadly ecumenical way in order to cater for Muslims from a variety of backgrounds or adopting a pronounced and clear denominational identity in order to serve a much more specific audience. This strategy is, however, also interspatial in that they are responding to the context of the UK and the ecosystem of other mosques present. These centres of Deobandi leadership can be placed alongside other mosques of importance to other movements. The Green Lane Mosque in Birmingham and Masjid Tawhid in London, for example, are important centres for the Salafi Muslims in Britain.

All these mosques either have carved out or are carving out a role for themselves in the broader rather than just the local landscape. In a decade from today, one can expect there to be more clearly and less contested 'capital' mosques (such as the East London Mosque, and also for each of the nations of Scotland, Wales, Ireland and Northern Ireland). While most mosques in Britain focus on the local, serving an immediate congregation, some mosques are responding to regional and national needs and a wider, dispersed congregation.

Terminology: Describing the diversity

The typology presented of mosques operating at a *fard*, *fard kifaya* and *sunna* is perceivable in the words assigned to mosques. This section covers these words, many of them already introduced, and considers how they can indicate the size and function of mosques. It is valuable and insightful to demonstrate how the typology of the interspatial mosque is reflected in the vernacular terminology of British Muslims; doing so offers a potential for developing an Anglophone vocabulary for mosques (here I mean not necessarily words with English etymological roots, but words in common use and understanding by English speakers, even if loan words).

Musalla, prayer room, quiet room

I have already introduced the terms *musalla*, prayer room and quiet room. Mosques on the smaller end of the spectrum are often called *musalla*. *Musalla* is an Arabic term and is an allocated prayer space that is less formal than a mosque (though can in some uses also refer to a large prayer space used occasionally, usually on the outskirts of the city). 'Prayer room', or the alternative term 'quiet room' is often used by institutions to denote spaces of multifaith worship, especially at universities or hospitals. Quiet rooms are especially common in institutions keen not to break any appearances of secularism. These terms tend towards the '*fard* mosque', for which the performance of prayers is the primary function.

Masjid, centre, *markaz*

Moving towards the middle ground of the *fard kifaya* model, many more terms are available. Aside from the obvious ubiquitous mosque and *masjid*, the terms, centre and *markaz* are often used. There are a handful of institutions also called *zawiya*, a term that is associated with Sufi lodge and the centre for the communal activities of a *tariqa*. As the next chapter will detail in greater depth, the *tariqa* associated with Sufism has largely been replaced in Britain by the congregation, and so the *zawiya*, as it functions in places in North Africa, the Middle East and South Asia, is largely unheard of in Britain. Nonetheless, they begin to indicate the social and communal aspects important in *fard kifaya* mosques. A mosque described as a 'centre' or 'markaz' is a strong indicator of a *fard kifaya* mosque. They are commonly included in the titles of mosques and preceded by qualifiers that indicate their ambitions (such as cultural centre, welfare centre, Islamic *markaz*). The use of the term echoes Pnina Werbner's description of a mosque:

> In many respects the mosque represents the highest locus of value and communal involvement. It is the centre of religious debate and learning (and intense disagreement). It is controlled by the Punjabi Sunni majority within the Pakistani community . . . It is located between the central Pakistani residential enclave and the main Asian shopping area. In other words, it represents the ideological, regional, denominational, economic and social-cum-residential 'core' or centre of the community. (Werbner 1990: 314)

The *fard kifaya* mosque is importantly a place of communal activity, and so Werbner's term that 'the mosque represents the highest locus of value and communal involvement' is an apt description to underline how important the presence of a community is to the fulfilment of certain religious rites (namely the marriage ceremonies, the *janaza*, the *ʿaqiqa* and the religious instruction and education of children).

Jamia Masjid/central mosques

The largest mosques, those which are operating on the level of *sunna*, seek to identify themselves as a 'Jamia Masjid'. The term is used across the Islamic world (particularly countries from the 'Balkans to Bengal', a concept used by Ahmed (2015) to describe a social, geographic and historic period in which Muslims shared a paradigm, which included amongst other things a vocabulary influenced by both Persian and Arabic) and indicates physically larger mosques used when space is needed for larger congregations – such as the Eid prayers, the Friday prayers, and related festivities. The term 'jamia' has been adopted by many mosques in the UK and indicates a goal amongst the founders and mosque management to provide services above and beyond a 'standard' mosque.

Without question, however, the term which is the clearest indicator of a mosque which aspires to be a *sunna* mosque is 'central' – such as Birmingham Central Mosque, Glasgow Central Mosque, Manchester Central Mosque and so on. Central mosques also tend, more than other terms, to be associated with purpose-built mosques. A mosque that calls itself 'central' claims to be the primary mosque of a city or locality, rhetorically placing other mosques as 'peripheral' to their centrality. This rhetorical action will be read and understood differently by a non-Muslim audience than by a Muslim audience. For the latter, they will be more than aware of the contested nature of such claims, and that there is no religious merit that distinguishes a central mosque from a 'house mosque'. To the wider non-Muslim public, however, such claims hold more weight, and will act significantly to establish and place that mosque as a key mosque for those wishing to engage with Muslims. This distinction underlines the forward-facing attitude of the *sunna* mosque, which often places a greater emphasis on public engagement.

The terms above provide shades and inflections to the mosques that are present in the British religious landscape, and how British Muslims themselves are formulating a vocabulary to navigate these differences.

Conceptualizing functions

The question posed at the beginning of this chapter was how academics can conceptualize the diverse functions and activities of British mosques in a coherent way. The answer provided is the typology of the interspatial mosque, with its three tiers: the *fard*, the *fard kifaya* and the *sunna*. It is interspatial in a way that the mosque fits into and locates itself in a space, in the widest sense of the word. This could be a geographic space, a symbolic space, a marketplace of welfare services or a denominational landscape. It is tiered since mosques in Britain follow a system of priorities that structure the activities they house. It begins first with the prayer, the fundamental religious duty which brings the mosque into purposeful existence. The second tier, that of the *fard kifaya*, are those religious obligations most effectively met communally. The final tier, that of the *sunna*, is dynamic and shifting, but it's always tied back to the Prophetic example and the Prophet's Mosque. Case studies of mosques fitting each model were presented to the benefits of using these categories and how a diverse range of mosques coexist in a single context. With thousands of mosques across Britain and indeed Europe, the need to see them as they are, diversity and difference up front, is an important first step to recognizing these places of worship more accurately.

3

The congregational mosque

British mosques are congregational, and Islam in Britain is congregationalist. This chapter intends to evidence and elucidate this claim. To say mosques are congregational is not merely a description but a statement about how they are established and sustained, about where authority and power are located and about the nature of Islam in Britain. This chapter argues that the congregation has become the primary means by which British Muslims are doing religion together. The congregation in the Muslim context is an undefined and loose voluntary association, bounded predominantly by their practice of the daily prayers, sometimes but not necessarily attached to a physical space, which determines and acts collectively in advancing the religion. It functions as a means of supporting, nurturing and socializing religion amongst its members. It is often local but not exclusively. It is usually unbureaucratic and informal but not exclusively. To congregate is also an action, and in studying congregations, attention is directed to an active dimension of religion.

Thinking congregationally about British Muslims, British Islam and British mosques helps elucidate a model of practice that in its ubiquity is often overlooked, and thinking congregationally is what the following chapter will seek to do. To demonstrate the congregationalism of British Islam is challenging for a few reasons. First, it is ubiquitous. With no clear contrasting mode of communal behaviour amongst Muslims, it can appear mundane, commonplace and unremarkable. Furthermore, in the British context, the congregational model is also shared by other religious traditions, making it even less visible. Finally, the congregation within British mosques is often unstructured, loose, tiered and organic in a way that resists that tangible and concrete terms that might be expected if one looks for congregational behaviour using a Christian model. Grasping the nature of congregational organizing by Muslims however is important to understanding how mosques operate. Congregational mosques are run from the ground up (from the local immediate community and then tying into larger national bodies) rather than hierarchically (with a larger body dictating or determining the choices on the ground). In other words, the locus of authority in congregational mosques is located in the mosque and its attendees. This in turn has far-reaching consequences for the organization and development of Islam in Britain.

'When Muslims come together, they pray together'

Ishtiaq Ahmed has been involved with the Bradford Council of Mosques for over four decades, an umbrella body representing and working with Bradford's 130 or so mosques. In that time, he has lived through controversies ranging from the Salman Rushdie Affair (in which Bradford became a key point of discussion after protestors burned a copy of the book in the city) to the riots that took place during the summer of 2001. The Bradford Council of Mosques predates the largest national Muslim body, the MCB. Ishtiaq explains the significance of Bradford's mosques. He tells me what he told a room full of councillors and politicians in Bradford one day, that when they see the city's skyline, 'now adorned with domes and minarets', 'it means this is our home'. This positive embrace of mosques and the role they play in society runs through his comments to me – 'mosques are our future, if we want a bright future, we need to have vibrant mosques'. Ishtiaq is reflective over the role of mosques in Britain and his own through the Bradford Council of Mosques. When we speak, there is a clear sense of him looking back over a long career, and he was keen to remind me before we spoke that he had now retired. I ask him about the 'early days' of his work, the period described as the 'mosque-building era'. He responds pithily, 'when Muslims come together, they pray together'.

Of course, for Muslims to pray together, a mosque as a built location is not a necessity. Any space can be used for worship in the Muslim tradition. Muslims can gather, appoint an imam and face the *qibla* (the direction of Mecca) and that worship is considered communal. Ishtiaq speaks of the strategy the first Muslims in Bradford use, 'people would pray in living rooms of each other's homes, sometimes they might hire somewhere for the *jumu'a*, but the need for a mosque was clear'. He links it to the life of the Prophet Muhammad, 'when he settled in Medina, the first thing he did was build a mosque, so when Muslims settle in a new country, they do the same'. This basic factor of Muslim communal religious behaviour then determines the way in which mosques operate subsequently once founded. To phrase it differently, the congregation – a community of Muslims who pray together – precedes the mosque.

The first purpose-built mosque in the city, according to a report issued by the Bradford Council of Mosques to celebrate their fortieth anniversary, is the Tawakullia Islamic Society in Manningham (Ahmed and Ali 2021). In the case of Tawakullia Islamic Society, there is a unique opportunity for an insight into its early formation. The previously cited study by Stephen Barton titled *The Bengali Muslims of Bradford* (1986) focuses specifically on the 'Twaqulia Islamic Society' (the spelling was later changed by the mosque leaders). At the time it operated from a converted terraced property. There are desperately few accounts of early mosque formation, and the experiences are increasingly lost as the generation of mosque founders passes away. Barton recounts the thoughts of mosque congregants of the period before there was a mosque. 'If several men were together at the time for prayer and the subject was mentioned, then they prayed, but not otherwise' (Barton 1986: 79), he also notes that 'public halls were hired for the celebration of major festivals' (Barton 1986: 80). A group of Bangladeshi Muslims, who were part of the Pakistani People's Organization (Bangladesh was, at this point, part of Pakistan) set up an organization, the Twaqulia Islamic Society, and 'from their own funds and public subscription, purchased two houses in Cornwall Road, in the main area of Bengali habitation, which they immediately began to use as a mosque' (Barton 1986: 81).

The collection of funds through subscription and donation indicates a part of the process of congregational formation in the view of Ishtiaq: 'there is an Islamic teaching that if you collect funds for a mosque, it has to be used for that mosque and not anywhere else, and so it creates an attachment'. The strategy of subscription also highlights another aspect of the congregation that they are spaces serving an immediate geography.

'Mosques are local initiatives'

The first mosque in Bradford was the Jamia Masjid on Howard Street, a house mosque opened in 1958, a clearly *fard kifaya* mosque providing 'rudimentary facilities for collective worship and basic Islamic education for children' (Ahmed and Ali 2021). It began as a single property (30 Howard Street) but then expanded to include the adjacent houses (28 and 32). Within a mile of Jamia Masjid there are several mosques (all of course established after Jamia Masjid): Doha Mosque, Salahadin Mosque, Shah Jalal Mosque, Noor-ul-Islam Mosque, Jamiyat Tabligh ul Islam, Millat Islamia Islamic Cultural Centre and Suffa-tul-Islam Central Masjid, a large purpose-built mosque with a capacity of nearly eight thousand.

These mosques do vary in terms of the ethnic and denominational background of their leadership (see Chapter 5 for a more expanded consideration of this), but it would be in Ishtiaq's view a mistake to consider each mosque solely an issue of theological or ethnic divergence. 'Walking congregations are always a mosque's primary constituency', Ishtiaq explains to me, 'mosques are local, they are local initiatives'. The term 'walking congregation' refers to those attendees who can attend the mosque on foot. The centrality of the 'walking congregation' is difficult to gauge, because it varies from mosque to mosque. The *fard* and *fard kifaya* tier mosque, offering a space for prayer and education, certainly serve a smaller geographic area. Larger mosques can have a 'gathered congregation', visiting regularly from across the country or even internationally. What remains constant is that they are 'local initiatives', but how that locality is defined varies. In Bradford, as we've seen, there can be several mosques within one small area, each othering a distinctive function in the ecosystem of mosques, but sustained through a walking congregation they serve.

Oadby is a borough outside of Leicester served by a single mosque, Masjid al-Ameen. One of the mosque founders was happy to tell me the story of the mosque but requested not to be named directly: 'better leave it anonymous, people can have a lot of jealousy'. He had moved to Oadby from closer to the centre of Leicester. 'After I moved here, my priority changed, there is no mosque here. This is not acceptable.' He gathered other Muslims in the area about his concerns, and started meeting with them regularly for prayers, classes and to plan how to secure a mosque: 'so the whole process started from my house at that time'. Soon after the group started hiring premises from the council for worship, 'and we used a church for the *tarawih* prayers in Ramadan' until finally they identified a property the council was willing to sell to the Muslim community. 'It took us three years to buy that place', he tells me, 'so sixteen years in total from when we decided to open a mosque to getting the building, and now it's been running for twelve years'. This long journey, from inception of idea, securing the funds, establishing a meaningful and organized congregation and securing the premises is repeated for many mosques. For some, the journey may have been even longer, for others shorter. Regardless, the centrality of the efforts of a local congregation remained paramount.

The founder of Masjid al-Ameen continues to tell me about the necessities for a mosque. 'You need to have a community before a mosque for lots of reasons, including that the local authority will ask for evidence who will run it, what the need is.' The mosque's ethos is one of welcoming he insists, 'we are a Sunni masjid, right, we are non-sectarian, we allow everyone in anyone to come to read them. That's including men and women and children'. This inclusivity is important 'because we are the only mosque for a radius of five miles or so, and some outside of Leicester might even travel seven miles or more to visit our mosque on Friday'. I ask if the membership is clear to him; does he know who is in the congregation and who is not? 'Yes, of course, you have the regulars, but also the ones who come every now and again or just for jumuʻa'. Ishtiaq also underscores this point:

> Membership of mosques is pretty stable. You have regulars. There are some who might visit across mosques, but people do travel to go to the mosque they want to attend. The sharia ruling too that a mosque that collects funds can only use that funds for itself, and not another mosque, is important. So people give to their regular mosque and they become attached to it.

The congregation of mosques are usually known, stable and local.

'Mosques are sustained by their congregations'

'There is a myth', Ishtiaq tells me, 'of millions or billions of pounds of money coming to mosques from abroad'. It is a myth he considers to be misleading: 'mosques are sustained by their congregations'. Mosque finances are publicly available in most cases as almost every mosque is also a registered charity. While this isn't only strategy available for mosques in terms of how they legally establish themselves, it is the most common due to the advantages conferred by charitable status in the UK (an exemption or reduction on certain forms of tax, as well as a tax rebate on donations). Charity status requires a mosque to provide accounts of income, expenditure and other financial transactions annually.

Reviewing these public financial documents, a predictable pattern emerges. The largest, most regular and most reliable source of funding for a mosque is direct donations from the congregation. Donations are usually listed as 'unrestricted funds' in charity accounts, indicating they can be used for general mosque activities. They are raised through a number of sources: the collection buckets on a Friday, more focused fundraising during the month of Ramadan, a regular subscription payment from members is also common (and often identified as a separate category on accounts) and linked to the subscription model is 'door-knocking'. The strategy of door-knocking is less common in recent years but not unheard of in towns and cities with a sufficiently large Muslim population.

Hajji Habibur Rahman (a pseudonym) used to accompany a well-known Bangladeshi *pir* on his journeys to the UK and would help instruct followers of the *pir* on how to fundraise for a mosque in their locality. 'The neighbourhood', he tells me in the Sylheti dialect of Bengali, 'want a mosque, so we would go to houses of the Muslims we knew and ask them to make a donation now, and a promise of an annual donation'. He emphasizes the importance of setting a date for the annual donation, 'make it an important date, Ramadan is best'. It was important 'to ask each person for the address of any other Muslim families locally. They don't have to be Bengali, any Muslim would give for a mosque'. This simple method of fundraising would help pay for the regular costs of a mosque, from bills to hiring the imam.

After donations, the second source of income is services and foremost amongst them is tuition fees for the education services offered by the mosque. This can be the *madrasa* or after-school Islamic supplementary education, but there are also more specialized classes such as those to teach memorization of the Quran in its entirety. This income stream is usually then funnelled into the employment of teachers but can also be substantial enough to support the functioning of the mosque. Other income generating activities include funeral services, marriage services and hiring of the mosque (though the latter is rare). Some mosques have also sought to develop means of generating regular income through partially commercial activities. This can be through the rental of space to other businesses (who might run a bookstore, café or restaurant or similar) or by establishing an ancillary business run by the mosque itself.

The final source of income, which is only found with the larger and more organized mosques (those operating at the *sunna* tier of the interspatial mosque typology), is grant funding. These grants may be from charitable foundations to run projects or activities, from the government as part of a scheme to deliver services, or indeed through Islamic philanthropic foundations who have a variety of motives for investing into a mosque (promotion of a particular denominational approach or the social capital gained through investment in Islamically focused projects).

Speaking to Kamran Hussain, the general manager of Green Lane Mosque, one of the largest mosques in Birmingham and one which will appear more than once through this book, he lists to me the funding strategy used to support their broad range of activities. Green Lane Mosque in Birmingham is a firmly *sunna* mosque; Kamran explains this in his own words: 'the evolution of mosques in general, if you look when they were established in the early generation, at that time their fundamental focus was to establish somewhere to pray, somewhere to go *jumu'a*, and the *madrasa*'. He continues, 'their attitude was "lets get the fundamentals in place, get the bricks and mortar, get the basic services established"'. This was funded simply, he tells me: 'you remember the old days when people were going door-to-door to do collections to establish the *masjid*'. The early days, however, have given way to new practices according to Kamran:

> Now, we're second and third generation, we got those foundations in place. We're looking at the next stage of evolution, and people are asking, what is the purpose of the *masjid*? Looking at the Prophetic model of the *masjid* where the Prophet Muhammad would house the homeless, collect and distribute the *zakat* and *sadaqa*, take care of people, feed them, education classes, meetings, a place of congregation for people, all those things the typical *masjid* isn't doing, but we're thinking, we need to be emulating the model of the Prophet's mosque.

Green Lane Mosque's activities are indeed broad, their annual report for 2020 lists their six priority areas of work: 'youth and social activities', 'welfare services', 'dawah and outreach', 'humanitarian and social campaigns', 'masjid activities' and 'education', and under each are numerous projects, regular events and services. Unlike many mosques, they regularly apply (and are successful, as far as British mosques go) for grant-based funding. Even then, they received only £46,405 from grants in 2020 compared to £3,109,591 from donations, the bulk of which are from their congregation. Unlike the 'walking congregations' Ishtiaq refers to however, Green Lane Mosque has a larger appeal. Kamran explains that 'Green Lane Masjid is one of the bigger masjids here in Birmingham and the UK, and people perceive us due to our attachments to certain *'ulama'*, people see us as an authority religiously amongst the *salafiyya*,[1] so that garners an international and national influence'. This in turn leads to financial support from individuals who support Green Lane Mosque but may not be local. 'Our reach is much wider than our Birmingham perimeter, we're able to get money from all over by going online in terms of fundraising, especially through direct debis, sometimes just £20 a month'.

Kamran walks me through their funding strategy.

> When it comes to youth work, it is predominantly funded by grants or the fees we might charge for youth club, for kickboxing or boxing classes, we try and keep things as low as possible when we can.

> When it comes to welfare services, they are predominantly funded by grants, or just run by volunteers at nil cost. So we have counselling services, so they're provided by volunteers, we just provide a room every week.

> Our outreach work, like school visits, conferences, the talks run from the masjid, organisational visits, presentations, videos we put on Youtube, that is funded by the congregation. The Friday collections, the donation boxes around the masjid. That way it is not funded by a group, it remains independent, it has no ulterior motives.
>
> Education is funded by fees, we charge for our courses, the madrassa has 600 kids online and on-site, all fee-funded, but really we're just trying to break-even to keep things as affordable as possible.
>
> Masjid activities, the religious activities, the daily prayers, the Friday *jumu'a*, the *iftar* during Ramadan when we feed two or three hundred people daily, that's all from the congregation, collections, online donations, and direct debits.
>
> The social campaigns are grant funded, or if we have the funds, by ourselves. Humanitarian projects, especially internationally, is congregationally funded, *sadaqa* and *zakat*.

Green Lane Masjid has been successful in diversifying their income streams as a strategy, even listing £19,688 for the year 2020 as having come from investments, but it is still predominantly congregationally funded. This underlines Ishtiaq's contention – 'mosques are sustained by the congregation', not just in terms of the financial support they offer but the volunteering and human resources that provide to the mosque.

'Mosques are independent'

'Mosques are very independent. It is a complicated picture very few people understand, especially if they're not familiar with mosques', states Ishtiaq. I question him further, 'can any external organisation exert their will on the mosque?' I present the example of the Anglican Church, in which there are examples of local rural churches closed by the hierarchy to the protestation of the local congregation. Ishtiaq responds, 'there are authority structures for mosques, but these are all voluntary affiliations'. He continues:

> So it might be that UKIM (the United Kingdom Islamic Mission) give some guidance on where a mosque is needed or how or when. There are also networks based on *'aqīda* or *fiqh* mosques are part of. They might connect to scholarly networks. There are also spiritual schools to which mosques subscribe. But this is always voluntary. The locals are ultimately the ones who decide.

Ishtiaq's thinking is reflected in the approach of the Bradford Council of Mosques, which on their website and publications state that 'the role of the CFM (Council for Mosques) has always been advisory with a strict policy of non-interference in the internal affairs of member organisations'.

The closure of mosques during the pandemic is an illustrative example that highlights both the broad ecosystem of authority and national organizatifons mosques may be part of as well as the independence of mosques in making decisions. On 20 March 2020 the UK went into 'lockdown'. By this stage, there were numerous cases of the coronavirus recorded in Britain, the government had advised against 'non-essential' travel, and a few days prior schools had announced their closure. The speed at which the new virus had become a global pandemic took many by surprise, but Britain was late in comparison to other European countries in announcing 'lockdown' measures. It was, as has now become clichéd to state, 'unprecedented'.

After the announcement on 20 March 2020 by Prime Minister Boris Johnson, it became clear that mosques, as all places of worship, would need to close by Monday 23 March. This raises the question: 'who has the authority to close mosques?' One answer is of course the UK and devolved governments, under whose legal authority all British mosques operate. However, well in advance of this announcement, several mosques had already closed in anticipation of the pandemic and the worsening situation. The Hujjat Islamic Centre in Stanmore, London was amongst the earliest to close on Friday 13 March. The Edinburgh Blackhall Mosque in Scotland, Birmingham Central Mosque in England and Dar ul-Isra Mosque in Cardiff, Wales, followed thereafter on Monday 16 March. Soon, spates of mosques were closing across the country. The Green Lane Mosque in Birmingham and the Cambridge Central Mosque were closed on Tuesday 17 March, the East London Central Mosque and Manchester Central Mosque on Thursday 19 March. All this was before mosques were required to close on Monday 23 March. The mosques in question neither waited for the state to close them nor did it require a wider body or authority to approve its closure. When an individual mosque wished to close, it did. While the independent congregationalism of mosques allowed for cautious mosques to close in response to what they perceived to be an imminent disaster, it also meant some mosques resisted closure until legally mandated.

There was an accompanying emergence of organized bodies, some new, some old, who fought for legitimacy and authority with mosques during this same period. On 12 March, the British Board of Scholars and Imams issued a statement highlighting that mosques should 'prepare' for closures. The Muslim

Council of Britain called for the suspension of all congregational worship at mosques and Islamic Centres on 16 March 2020.[2] On the same date, the British Islamic Medical Association encouraged mosques to close,[3] and the Mosques and Imams National Advisory Board issued their closure notice on 19 March.[4] One of the most reticent closure statements came from *Wifaq ul ulama*, a Deobandi collection of scholars. On 17 March, they issued a statement advising mosques to wait, before conceding to closures on 19 March 2020.[5] One of the last national organizations to issue a call for closures was Faith Associates.[6] The list does not include smaller councils of mosques or regional bodies.

The bodies listed above range from scholarly boards that issue religious edicts (the British Board of Scholars, Wifaqul Ulama) to specialist organizations (the British Islamic Medical Association), training bodies (Faith Associates), and of course, councils of mosques with affiliates (the MCB being foremost amongst them). Yet none of them hold direct authority over any single mosque in Britain. Usman Maravia and colleagues produced a critical discourse analysis of the plethora of documents issued by Muslim authorities in the early days of the pandemic (Maravia et al. 2021). They classified the documents as 'fatwas', 'others' and 'guidance' and argued that the 'fatwas' had the greatest authority. Yet even in this case however, the authority is unenforceable. The mosque is independent and all statements issued, bar that from the state, were unenforceable.

This complex marketplace of authority has been a part of the Muslim religious landscape of Britain for decades. The pandemic did however act as a catalyst for centralization of authority. The British Board of Scholars and Imams (BBSI) had launched in early 2020, seeking to create a more unified platform for various religious authorities and denominations in the UK. The platform was able to locate itself as an effective and successful cross-denominational (though exclusively Sunni) authority through its religious and medical guidance around the pandemic (Wyatt 2021). Without the complex history of more established organizations such as the MCB, it was also able to act more successfully as an interlocutor with government, joining a 'reference group' for reopening places of worship with the Westminster Government.[7] Yet even the BBSI is not in a position to dictate the decision of any mosque.

In a similar position is the MCB. It is the largest Muslim umbrella body with around 500 affiliates the majority of which are mosques. The representative model utilized, however, means that the MCB derives authority from mosques and their participation, rather than reverse. The MCB has however had to compete with local councils of mosques. Some of these are well-established, even predating the founding of the MCB, such as the Bradford Council of

Mosques. Some however emerged during the pandemic or became more active and formalized as a result of it. These local councils of mosques tended to work on smaller scales, with a select number of mosques, and thereby acted with a more consensual authority. As such, when local councils of mosques announced closures, they would often be speaking on behalf of a significant number of mosques. A joint statement by United Council of Mosques Pendle and the Lancashire Council of Mosques issued on 20 March 2020 listed twenty mosques closing, and reflected the more cooperative decision making of the bodies involved. In 2022, the MCB published a report titled 'Local Muslim Representation Empowering Council of Mosques & Local Umbrella Organisations' based on interviews with various local umbrella bodies. The findings added further evidence to the increasing prominence of local bodies in organizing mosques and the importance of engaging with various levels of state authority.

The pandemic highlighted a need to decisively close mosques. The current structures of authority, independent mosques sometimes participating or aligning themselves with larger bodies, demonstrated the broad ecosystem of authorities in operation, as well as the moves to establish broader bodies capable of acting regionally, and at times nationally. The choice of national bodies stresses too the options available for mosques to choose an authority that reflects their own concerns in decision making.

The answer to the question of who has the authority to close mosques remains, for the time being, the mosque itself and the relevant government authority. The mosque generally consists of the imam, the committee and the congregation. The imam's authority is contingent on the committee, who appoints and employs him. The committee's authority is contingent on the congregation, whose financial and human resources allow for the functioning of the mosque (and sometimes more directly through elections). In Muslim-majority countries, some mosques are part of the state structure or embedded within a wider, sometimes transnational, hierarchy. Rizvi (2015) provides several examples of such state-sponsored mosques that play a role in the national and transnational ambitions of nation states. In the United Kingdom, it is the congregation who are largely responsible for the upkeep of the mosque, the salaries of imams and general finances. While committee members and imams may be influential, they negotiate this power with the congregation. There are sometimes external funders of mosques, but it is rare for a mosque to be solely funded by a single organization or source, and in many cases external donations are used for capital costs rather than functioning costs (which thereby limits their influence on the day-to-day activities of the mosque). The congregational focus and authority of the mosque is explored further in Chapter 6.

It is notable that, in much of the literature on mosques in Britain, the congregation is absent from considerations of power and authority and are overshadowed by reference to the mosque committee and imams. Philip Lewis (2006b: 175) speaks of the way in which some imams seek 'freedom from control by conservative mosque committee elders', while Stephen Jones et al. (2014: 216) state that, in the UK, 'the majority of mosques are run by local lay committees, with the imam sometimes being a minor functionary'. Ron Geaves (2008: 103) also focuses on these two agents when he reflects on the conditions that lead to mosques recruiting imams from abroad and concludes that it 'may reflect the desire of young imams to seek employment in Britain but also their amenability to the control of the powerful mosque committees', and Dervla Shannahan (2013: 1) discusses how 'UK Mosque management committees privilege male involvement'. While all the examples cited are no doubt accurate, the absence of other mosque actors in the literature is notable, especially the congregation. If the committee is as powerful as the literature suggests, how does it achieve and manage this power? Are there any ways in which their power is resisted or challenged? Werbner (1990: 310–11) sheds some light on how a mosque committee might cement their influence over the congregation through her example of competitive charity, but the tendency to simplify authority in the British mosque and see it as restricted to imams and a committee is still prominent. The congregation is not a minor partner in the mosque; it is in many cases a precursor to the mosque itself as seen in the examples presented earlier in the chapter. The congregation therefore needs to be re-centred into academic conceptualizations and understanding of mosques. Mosques are the most numerous Muslim institutions in the UK, but it is the congregation that is the mechanism by which Muslims engage with these institutions. It is the congregation who provide the financial, human and spiritual capital to make Britain's contemporary mosques viable.

The Muslim congregation

Thus far I have sought to demonstrate how mosques are congregational institutions. The congregation often precedes the physical mosque. Mosques are locally grounded. The mosque is the product and established through the efforts of the congregation. The mosque is sustained through the financial and human capital of the congregation, and finally, the loci of authority within a mosque is the congregation. I believe that we have moved from the 'mosque-building-era' into the era of the congregation, in which a new and emerging form of religious association is taking prominence in Britain. I expand on this argument further here. It is worth restating that the congregation should be understood as more than just those who attend the mosque, but rather as the primary means by which Muslims in Britain communally perform, engage in and share religion. It is being utilized in favour of other forms of organization (discussed later), and is accompanying the home as the primary location for socialization of Muslims.

I make the case that the term 'congregation' is valid for describing Muslim communal religious activity and not simply a case of carelessly applying a Christian term to other religions. Rather, the concept of the congregation is present historically as well as in the contemporary period amongst Muslims. The congregation is a particular form of religious organization that has been present from the very inception of Islam but has varied in importance and prominence throughout history. Ammerman (2009: 564) sees the congregation as something that emerges whenever and wherever 'religious communities are in diaspora' and says that 'something like a congregation can stand alongside families to sustain a religious tradition that gets little support from the rest of culture'. The Prophet Muhammad and his followers in Mecca were organized much like a congregation, meeting regularly and often secretly, to preserve and pass on the new religion. The Prophet Muhammad and his followers did not establish a mosque until they left Mecca for Medina. This provides a period of thirteen years in which the early Muslims in Mecca organized as a congregation without a physical space, making use of private homes to meet.

Following the death of the Prophet Muhammad, Islam became a dominant religion in the Arabian Peninsula. Mosques continued to be established, evolving various functions and inflections as they developed into institutions such as the *zawiya*, the *khanqa*, the Jamia Masjid and the *madrasa*. One particular form of mosque is what are called 'tribal mosques' (Rasdi 2014: 85). The tribe was the dominant means of social organization in Arabian society during early Islamic history, so many mosques, unsurprisingly, were established along tribal lines, even to the extent that 'the people of your masjid' became a term meaning 'your tribe' (Pedersen et al. 2012: 649). The 'tribal mosque' presents an interesting historical counterpoint to the congregational mosque. Pedersen et al. (2012: 649) argue that Muslims in the early period were expected to attend the 'chief mosque' of an area for the Friday prayers, a practice that continues in many places in the Muslim world with the Jamia Masjid, a specific larger mosque allocated the responsibility for the Friday prayers. Mosque affiliation amongst Muslims, then, has always had the potential for being multiple, ranging from a local or tribal mosque to the larger Jamia Masjid.

The mosque has remained a key part of Muslim expression throughout history well into the modern period, but its role in religious organization and communal activity is varied. It could be central, such as in the case of the time of the Prophet Muhammad in Medina, or more peripheral. The advent of the *tariqa* or Sufi orders, for example, created a new paradigm for the communal expression of religious worship. Huseyin Yilmaz (2018) argues that Sufi *tariqa*s emerged as dominant form of religious organization in Anatolia during a period of political upheaval following both the Crusades and the Mongol invasions in the twelfth century. The religiously competitive environment of Anatolia itself, in which no religious epistemological framework held monopoly, created an opportunity to redefine key concepts amongst Muslims. The *tariqa*s grew in importance in this context and became a significant form, of religious communal activity – ostensibly associated with Sufism and a means of organization that could be super-local or even transnational (Knysh 2017; Sedgwick 2017).

In Britain, where Muslims have found themselves detached from the historical institutions of the Muslim-majority societies and within a minority diasporic context, Sufi groups have struggled to maintain the *tariqa*, which, though remaining important, has required reinvention (van Bruinessen and Howell 2013). This has led to what has been described as 'post-tariqa Sufism' (Geaves and Gabriel 2014; Sedgwick 2017), in which the authority of the pir or sheikh has been lessened and other models of organization have become more important. The 'Barelvi' movement is a useful example, with Marcia Hermansen arguing it represents a form of Sufism that is 'now centred in mosques and madrasas' rather than 'functioning as an initiatory Sufi order' (2009: 29). That Post-*tariqa* Sufis in the West can in many ways be argued to behave much more like congregations than the *tariqa* of the past in that they are collectives bound by shared practice and place, rather than collectives bound by an individual. Other forms of communal religious institutions include the *madrasa*s – educational institutions of varying degrees of formality. Brannon Ingram (2018) has documented the Deobandi networks of *madrasa*s and their activity as a form of 'revival' of Islam, an account that highlights how central the institution is for teaching, continuing, supporting and maintaining religion. A very basic form of religious association is the *halaqa* (Hairgrove and Mcleod 2008; Bhimji 2009), a 'circle' of students seated around a teacher. In Muslim contexts, *halaqa* can be a regular part of religious instruction, an occasional gathering or part of the activities of charismatic leaders. Certain denominations and movements employ their own idiosyncratic means of *doing religion together*, such as the Muslim Brotherhood, who have a formalized system called the *usra* or 'family' (Anani 2016: 87), a group of five to six individuals who meet regularly for *tarbiyya* (spiritual and moral development). The *usra* operates as part of a wider network, creating a hierarchy of membership and authority.

The summary of these forms of religious organization is intended to demonstrate how Muslims in Britain have, at their disposal, a broad array of means of communal organization, used by Muslims throughout history. The emergence of the congregation, operating within and through British mosques, is by no means a certain conclusion of Muslim migration to a new location or even following the establishment of mosques.

While maintaining the legitimacy of the term 'congregation' in the study of Islam, it is worth considering what Niels Vinding (2018) describes as the 'churchification' thesis. This is a range of processes that include 'pedagogical, analogical or rhetorical' mobilization of comparison between Muslims and Christians, mosques and churches, imams and priests; the implicit assumption that Islam in Europe should operate in the same way as Christianity in Europe; the unavoidable influence of churches and Christianity on Muslims in Europe; and finally, the deliberate co-option or rejection of Christian models by Muslims. It could be argued that I have committed the first error, by using a Christian term (congregational) to describe Muslims. I have outlined within this article several reasons why congregations are an element of Muslim practice (though the extent to which contemporary congregational practice is influenced by Christian congregational practice remains to be explored). The third and fourth category of 'churchification', however, might be in operation. Congregational behaviour by Muslims might be unintentionally or intentionally adopted because of its familiarity in the Western European context. The congregation is recognized by the public and the state as a mode of religious organization, which confers several informal advantages on Muslims seeking to undertake activities. Likewise, congregations help provide a framework through which to cooperate and communicate meaningfully with other faith groups, foremost amongst them, of course, Christians. Examples of these advantages are discussed in Chapter 6. Ammerman (2009: 566) also refers to this, writing that religious minority groups are 'shaped both by the dictates of religious traditions and by each society's cultural and legal expectations as to how religious organizations are supposed to work – what sociologists might call an 'institutional template'.

In summary, the congregation, I argue, is a form of religious communal behaviour that can be found amongst Muslims historically, but that it has taken on a new prominence and relevance amongst Muslims in the diaspora. Part of this can be explained by 'churchification' (Vinding 2018) and Europe's 'institutional template' (Ammerman 2009: 566), but there remain other factors unconsidered and hitherto unexplored.

Defining the Muslim congregation

In Christian congregational studies, a number of conceptualizations and definitions of the congregation have been put forward. This section presents three of these, selected for their clarity and concise articulations, which allow engagement and critique. It then outlines a definition developed primarily with Muslim congregations in mind. Hopewell (1987: 13) proposes the following:

> My working definition of the congregation is this: *A congregation is a group that possesses a special name and recognised members who assemble regularly to celebrate a more universally practised worship but who communicate with each other sufficiently to develop intrinsic patterns of conduct, outlook, and story* (emphasis original).

Another definition is offered by Cameron et al. (2005: xiii), who describe the congregation as a 'group of people with varying interests and backgrounds who meet because they have something in common; who share fellowship, a sense of vision for the world'.

The third definition is proposed by Ammerman (2009: 563):

> Congregations, in their prototypical American form, are locally situated, multi-generational, voluntary organizations of people who identify themselves as a distinct religious group and engage in a broad range of religious activities together. They are usually, but not always, associated with some larger tradition and its affiliated regional and national bodies (i.e., a denomination) .... The space where they meet may or may not be an identifiably religious building, but congregations do typically have a regular meeting place and regular schedules of religious activity.

Notably, all three definitions omit any emphasis on belief or theology. This is expected, given that these scholars will have interrogated a reductive notion of religion as primarily or exclusively about belief, but it also raises an important aspect of the congregation: to congregate is an *action*. In studying congregations, attention is directed at an active dimension of religion.

The second notable feature of the definitions is their implicit foregrounding of relationships. Congregations are people who relate to each other either through 'intrinsic patterns of conduct, outlook, and story' (Hopewell 1987: 13), via their 'fellowship' or 'vision for the world' (Cameron et al. 2005: xiii), or through their identity as a 'distinct religious group' (Ammerman 2009: 563). This relationship is not only horizontal (with each other) but also vertical (present in Hopewell's and Ammerman's allusions to the universal or larger traditions). If a congregation is a group of people *doing religion together*, it follows that they share some conception of orthopraxis. Orthopraxis is a fundamental part of the congregation. Gary Quinn and James Davidson (1976: 350) argued that such a conception might further develop the relationship between sociology and theology: 'orthodoxy-orthopraxis can be understood, not only as believing, but as doing religious faith in a social context'. They wrote as theologians, considering how the church might benefit from emerging sociological studies of Christians, so their call for a focus on orthopraxis was unlikely to reach or have impact on sociologists. However, the argument highlights that, when scholars research people 'doing religious faith in a social context', they are also researching conceptions of orthopraxis, whether or not they choose to acknowledge it.

Critiques can also be made of the proposed definitions. Hopewell's definition is potentially reductive, or at least can overlook how congregations can be locally rooted but within a more universal paradigm. He asserts the importance of a Geertzian understanding of religion as a unique and particular expression of symbols, meanings and significance. Defining the congregation as having *'intrinsic patterns of conduct, outlook, and story'* (Hopewell 1987: 13), however, precludes the potential universality of that symbol, meaning and significance. His identification of the congregation having a 'special name' is also debatable, as many congregations (including Christian ones) may not see themselves as congregants at all, but as Christians, Muslims or Buddhists – part of their worldwide fraternity of co-religionists. It is possible, I'd argue, to both look congregationally at a religion without separating it from the larger community of which it is a part. Cameron et al.'s definition is also potentially too broad. It could include a local football league, an environmental campaign group or the local chapter of a political party, which inevitably leads back to the well-trodden debate about 'what is religion?' Ammerman's definition benefits from being situated geographically as typical of the United States and, implicitly, of Christian groups. It does, however, raise questions. Can an online group of religious worshippers be considered a congregation if they are spread across the world? This question took on more than theoretical salience during the course of the Covid-19 pandemic, in which many religious congregations turned online and many individuals joined congregations now accessible to them digitally. Can groups of people who come together 'irregularly', such as in the rituals performed domestically by Muslim women (Mazumdar and Mazumdar 2004), but who nonetheless maintain all other aspects of the definition, qualify? All definitions look towards the people participating and downplay the importance of the buildings in which activities take place. But do buildings such as institutional prayer rooms that attract regular worshippers, albeit of different religions, who (in a place such as an airport) may only ever pray together once in their entire lives, have a congregation? Or are they 'congregation-less'? These critiques, however, are not fundamental failures of the definitions; rather, they open a juncture of analysis and prompt consideration of the role, nature and function of the congregation amongst British Muslims and help further examine the ways in which communities form around mosques.

Thinking congregationally and also looking at relationships, how do people relate to one another, and on what terms? When they disagree, how do they disagree? How does the congregation relate to those outside of it, whether other congregations, the nation-state or larger denominational hierarchies? Thinking congregationally requires a constant shift between the individual and different types of communality (congregational identity, religious identity, national identity, local identity etc.).

Finally, to think congregationally is to think about 'orthopraxis'. There is no dearth of studies foregrounding the importance of orthodoxy in studies of religion, despite a turn away from a belief-centred conceptualization of religion towards one that is open to multiple alternatives (Spickard 2017). Thinking congregationally is therefore to consider the ways in which *people do religion together*, with attention to the *doing* and considering religion as diverse activities (beyond rituals and prayer). Here it is possible to emphasize the importance of locating the *doing* temporally and spatially: how, where and when do people *do religion*? Thinking congregationally also entails looking at the relationships involved in this activity, horizontally and vertically, the immediate relationships and the global ones. Finally, thinking congregationally is an exploration of *orthopraxis*, which opens an avenue of analysis that considers the role of text, dogma and normative teachings.

The term 'congregation' has also been employed in a limited way by numerous other scholars of Islam, usually sociologists, in describing the activities of mosques and those who attend them, yet often without much theorization behind why the term is deployed. This includes European studies (Ebaugh and Chafetz 2000;

Bartels and de Jong 2007; Borell and Gerdner 2013; Kors 2018) as well as similar works in the United States (Lotfi 2001; Wang 2017). None of the aforementioned scholars, however, have provided a description or rationalization of this term or reflection on their choice to use it. This does not necessarily entail criticism, as in a purely etymological sense, the term congregation has parallels with the Arabic word *jamaʿa*, which is synonymous with the word congregation and is used in a similar way by many Muslims. There are plenty of reasons for scholars to utilize the term without feeling the need to problematize it or provide a more developed conceptual framework. That said, if the attention and focus of a study is the social and communal dimension of religious practice or the operation of mosques, there is a need to more fully describe what a Muslim congregation looks like. Ammerman (2009: 565) offers this description of the Muslim congregation:

> The Friday prayer service in Muslim territories falls somewhere between the pattern of occasional ritual gathering and settled religious community. Mosques do not routinely have membership rolls and rosters of social programming; the faithful are simply expected to stop (at the nearest mosque or at home or work) when they hear each day's calls to prayer. Communal prayers, however, are highly valued, and the Friday prayers and sermon express both devotion to Allah and the ideals and concerns of the gathered community. Being a good Muslim requires these local gathering places for prayer and study, even if in Muslim cultures the faith is sustained by an entire social fabric of institutions beyond the local mosque. Outside Muslim territories, mosques often take on fully 'congregational' forms, with imams who function much like other professional clergy.

Ammerman notes the difference in operation of the mosque within and outside of 'Muslim territories', emphasizing that, in Muslim-majority countries, Islam is practised, expressed and sustained through 'an entire social fabric of institutions beyond the local mosque'; here we can point to the *tariqa*, the *halaqa*, the *usra* and other forms of communal organization introduced earlier, as well as schooling and the family.

Ammerman also defines the Muslim congregation in the negative, referring to the absence of 'membership rolls'. This is not universally the case. It is common practice in British Bangladeshi mosques of the Fultoli-orientation (see Ahmed and Ali 2019) to maintain a public list of fee-paying members of the congregation, who contribute annually to the mosque and for its functioning. The membership rolls include either families (e.g. the Miah Family, the Akbar Family) or businesses (usually takeaways or restaurants). These lists, however, may have very little correlation with attendance. There is a significant degree of social capital and *baraka* (blessings) for a business attached to supporting a mosque through subscription, and so many do so even if they do not attend the mosque or attend a mosque elsewhere more regularly. Yet Ammerman is correct that membership in and out of a congregation is porous. The previously discussed definitions of the congregation all allude to some sort of collective; Hopewell's (1987: 13) phrase 'recognised members' provides a more concrete description than either Ammerman (2009) or Cameron et al. (2005), who avoid the difficulty of membership by simply referring to a 'group'. Nonetheless, the question of membership of a congregation and the form it takes has received the attention of numerous academics (see Guest, Tusting and Woodhead 2004: 12, for a consideration of the 'typologizing' congregational studies works that explore this).

Paul Hiebert's (1978) application of the mathematical concepts of bounded sets and centred sets proved influential in considering the question of religious belonging in congregational studies. He argues the direction of travel (towards or away from the centre) is more significant than proximity to the centre in terms of assessing congregational belonging. Adapting the same framework, Muslim congregations operate more like the 'fuzzy sets' of computer programming language, in which there are clear insiders and clear outsiders, but degrees of membership for others. A mosque congregation will have the 'regulars', the 'mosque-uncles', 'the brothers', 'the sisters' – all part of the core of the congregation – but also the 'Friday Muslims', the 'Ramadan Muslims' or the 'Eid Muslims'. The terms sometimes have connotations of religiosity (with the latter terms usually being a used disparagingly), though there are many who might be a 'regular' at one mosque but a 'Friday Muslim' at another. Putting aside membership, congregations take different forms in different spaces. There is what might be called the 'standard' tiered mosque congregation, but also the congregation of rural Muslims with no regular place of worship, domestic congregations that move between different homes, the congregations of institutional prayer rooms and so on. There is also the complex area of inter-congregational relationships. In several cities in the UK, for example, Deobandi mosques coordinate their recitation of the Quran in Ramadan so that they complete its recitation on different days in the last week of Ramadan. The congregations from these mosques will all gather in the relevant mosque completing the Quran on the night in question. This is but one example of many types and forms of inter-congregational cooperation and competition, all of which compose the varied communal religious life of British Muslims.

Another relevant question to consider is the salience of denominational and theological differences to mosques and their congregations. The discussion hitherto has attempted to be general enough to cover the entirety of Muslim diversity in Britain. There are, however, significant differences in communal religious practice between denominations that have consequences for the congregation. Shia institutions take a different form and structure from Sunni ones, with 'congregational halls' that host distinctively Shia rituals (Scharbrodt 2019). The leadership of Shia mosques is also more closely connected, with a clearer hierarchy or authority – though still congregational in that the locus of authority remains within the mosque. The most hierarchically organized 'mosques' are the Ismaʿili *jamatkhanas*, though as an institution, these are significantly different from the mosques of Sunni Islam or other denominations of Shiʿism. Likewise, post-*tariqa* Sufism of the more Sunni variety is organized congregationally, but in ways unlike the mosque congregation. Instead, adherents may meet in local chapters or annual retreats, such as the Threshold Society, or in spaces overtly designed to be unlike a mosque, such as Rumi's Cave in London.

Ammerman introduces another phrase that needs unpacking – what does it mean to be 'fully congregational'? – especially in a Muslim context, lest we contribute to 'churchification' and impose a Christian form of the congregation on Muslims. In the following, I offer a description of the British Muslim congregation, one that is far from conclusive and comprehensive but nonetheless provides some orientation.

The Muslim congregation is a voluntary association of Muslims meeting regularly for the purpose of practising Islam together. The association is loose and tiered, with some strongly associated with the group and others only participating occasionally. The Muslim congregation's locus of authority is within the congregation itself, so even when the congregation does affiliate with a wider movement, denomination or leader, this affiliation is voluntary and the congregation can choose to disaffiliate itself. The congregation meets physically, and the location may be fixed or shifting. Muslims can participate in more than one congregation, and likewise, a single congregation can be spread over multiple sites. The core practice of the congregation is the ritual prayer, but a wider variety of other activities can be and are undertaken by the congregation.

The size of the Muslim congregation

The initial part of this chapter opened with a description of the significance of congregational behaviour to the establishment, maintenance and authority of mosques. It then outlines the features of the Muslim congregation in more abstract terms. Both of these sections have been concerned primarily with the concept and function of the congregation in relation to mosques. There are certainly many other questions that can be asked about the congregation and Muslims, amongst them, how large is the Muslim congregation numerically? This question may, in part, be driven by the prevalence of estimates of the Christian congregation, and its use by some in gauging the vitality of Christianity in Britain.

Statistics and estimates on Muslim congregation sizes are sparse. A 2015 survey indicates that 60 per cent of British Muslims visit a mosque once a week (ICM Unlimited 2016). However, as the survey focused on Muslims living in areas where at least 20 per cent of the population are Muslim, these are likely inflated figures (since such places have a higher concentration of mosques, making them more accessible). If we accept these figures as indicative (with a dose of scepticism), 60 per cent of Britain's 2.6 to 3.9 million Muslims[8] attending a mosque at least once a week would translate as an overall weekly gathering of at least 1.6 million Muslims, dwarfing Anglican figures of 756,000 weekly congregants (Wright 2018). A contrasting survey, conducted through YouGov, indicated that 48 per cent of British Muslims never attend a mosque (Wells 2006), which does not tell us much about congregation sizes, but it raises the question of how many British Muslims are part of a congregation at all. The datedness of these surveys is also revealing. Very few individuals or organizations have considered the Muslim congregation worthy of inquiry or examination. It is unclear why this turn away from the congregation has taken place, though the broader changes in religious affiliation in Britain more generally (with religious institutions arguably becoming less important) may be one answer why British Muslim institutions have not been given appropriate attention.

There are several difficulties in using a 'weekly attendance' figure to calculate the size of the congregation. First, mosques may overestimate their congregation, both out of simple bias and wishful thinking, but also due to the need to justify expansion projects that may be underway. To add to the complication, the fact that Muslims attend more than one mosque means there is a potential for double-counting figures. Likewise, the influence of social desirability makes it difficult to ascertain mosque attendance from self-confessed attendance patterns, as Muslims may again over-report how often they visit.[9] These often-contradictory factors have been well documented in Christian congregational studies. Peter Berger (2005: 113) observes that American survey respondents often overestimate their religiosity, with real attendance at churches much lower than surveys might indicate, whereas European survey respondents often overestimate their secularity. The issue of church attendance, and its relative (un)reliability, has been a notable subject in the sociology of religion throughout the decades. This stretches from debates and comments in the pages of the *American Sociology Review* (Hadaway, Marler and Chaves 1993; Hout and Greeley 1998; Smith 1998; Woodberry 1998) to analysis and (re)evaluation of church attendance and its significance today (Brenner 2012; Rossi and Scappini 2014; Kortt, Steen and Sinnewe 2017). Despite challenges in assessing quantitative measures of congregational activity, it remains common practice to do so. In Britain, various churches regularly collect and publish 'Statistics for Mission' or similar reports, including the Church of England (Church of England Research and Statistics 2019), Church of Scotland (2013) and the Methodist Church (2019).

Congregations are also stratified. There is often a small contingent that attends a mosque daily (sometimes even more than once a day – many mosques have a small group of worshippers who attend all five of the daily prayers). There are then those who may attend occasionally. In the same vein, attendance is rhythmic. People may attend mosques more often during holidays than on workdays, more often on a weekend than a weekday. Local and mundane factors have an influence too. Some might attend more often in the summer months, when the long evenings allow them to walk to the mosque. Others may attend more in winter, when they visit the mosque for *fajr* before the working day and *'isha'* on the way home from work. Add to this trans-congregational movements, foremost amongst them the Tablighi Jamaʿat, whose attendance at a mosque is difficult to quantify; they are not regularly part of a single congregation, but the movement's use of mosques nationally is so significant that discounting them entirely would fail to give a comprehensive picture of mosque usage and attendance. These factors, especially when taken cumulatively, make a simple numerical gauging of the congregation difficult. That does not mean it is impossible but that new measures may need to be developed.

In considering the size of the congregation, it is necessary to also consider its breakdown by gender. We know it is predominantly male, reflected in the fact that around 28 per cent of British mosques do not have spaces for women (Naqshbandi 2017). Considerable attention has been given in both academic literature and journalism to campaigns for greater access and representation of women in mosques (see Chapter 8 for further consideration of women's use of mosques). It is important, in pursuit of comprehending the British Muslim congregation, to understand the heterogeneous ways in which individuals conceptualize their relationship to mosques. Muslim women are involved in many of the behind-the-scenes activities entailed in functioning of a mosque, many of which are easily overlooked since they often take place 'backstage', in Goffmanian terms (Goffman 1959), a point made by Sophie Gilliat-Ray (2010a: 202). In other words, if what counts as 'participation' in a mosque or congregation is restricted to attending the mosque for prayers, the intensive labour and contribution of women (usually first-generation migrants) supporting the functioning of the mosque in ways such as preparing food, providing childcare and supporting in administrative and regulatory duties (accounts, paperwork and finances) can be erased.

In 2019, I worked with the MCB on a survey of women's perceptions of the mosque.[10] The survey received 1,034 responses from women across Britain and included questions on mosque attendance. Fifty-five per cent of women responded that they attended a mosque 'regularly' (at least once a month), while 45 per cent of the respondents indicated that they never attended a mosque. Of those who did attend regularly, 57 per cent regularly attended a single mosque, and 41 per cent regularly attended between two and four mosques. These figures, which I am cautious to generalize from, gives us an indication of practice on the ground. The full picture of Muslim women who attend mosques is most probably much lower than the 57 per cent of the survey respondents, who are predominantly British-born, young and self-selecting (having taken an interest in answering the questionnaire) and so hold different conceptions of orthopraxis from first-generation Muslim migrants. It does, however, underscore two things. First, that younger Muslim women are taking a more active role in worshipping at a mosque and, second, with 40 per cent of the respondents having affiliation with more than one mosque, we are reminded of how fluid congregational belonging is.

Before concluding, however, it is important to contextualize the quantitative element within the sociology of religion and critiques of it. James Spickard (2017: 13) writes that, according to

> the default sociological view, one measures both religiosity and religious identification organizationally. Survey research, in particular, takes such items as a frequency of church attendance, one's agreement or disagreement with established church doctrines, and the like as indications of one's religious commitment.

As Spickard himself and many others have recounted, this can easily miss religion that does not fit into tidy institutional boxes and is less easily quantified. In some sense, numbers give us an indication of importance and scope, which is my intention in presenting the data provided earlier. Religiosity is rarely quantifiable in any meaningful way but what attendance figures can help us observe is the rhythms of 'institutional' religious practice, the factors affecting congregational growth amongst Muslims and, most importantly, whether or not Muslims will become 'secularized', or adopt a more privatized religious expression like some of their Christian and 'No Religion' fellow citizens, and thus abandon regular attendance at a religious institution. Attendance can help us build a picture of a specific type of religious expression and little else.

The British Muslim congregational turn

There is, I believe, a clear case for approaching the mosque as a site of congregational activity, foregrounding the actions, relationships and orthopraxis that make the mosque what it is. This chapter has sought not only to outline the importance of the congregation to mosque operation but also as a form of doing religion together that is a product of the British context and its 'institutional templates'. The role of the congregation in shaping the mosque is picked up in later chapters, for example in sacralizing mosques (Chapter 4), in the negotiation of intra-religious diversity (Chapter 5), and perhaps most significantly in the mosque as a site of civil society (Chapter 6).

Within Islamic studies, there is scope to bridge the gap between sociological studies and the philosophical, theological and historical. Congregational studies is a broad field that has brought together a variety of disciplines, both confessional and non-confessional in approach. The congregation offers fertile ground for bringing together the various disciplinary approaches within Islamic studies. It has demonstrated the capacity to bridge the worlds of text and practice in Christian congregational studies (Guest, Tusting and Woodhead 2004) and is capable of doing the same for Islamic studies.

For British Muslim studies, it can address a dimension of contemporary Muslim life in which understanding is lacking. Research into the religious practice of Muslims, when placed alongside existing studies of identity, ethnicity, denomination and public policy, will provide a fuller and richer account of the British Muslim experience. Furthermore, I would argue that the growth of British mosques is not yet understood, the congregational daily lives of British Muslims have not been well documented and the mechanics by which the congregation develops and functions is only beginning to be traced. Until this blind spot is addressed, British Muslim studies will have a patchy and partial understanding of the role of institutional religion in the daily lives of Muslims. To fully understand this, it is necessary to move from viewing the 'mosque' as a taken-for-granted concept to interrogating the various ways in which Muslims understand, engage with and establish mosques. In other words, the congregation needs to be taken into account.

Finally, for the sociology of religion, considering Islam congregationally allows for the development of new tools and methods. As Spickard relates, the 'default' view of sociology has been one that has considered institutions as the sole expression of religiosity, before developing alternative frameworks such as lived religion, which Ammerman ponders may have too strongly disregarded institutions. Thinking congregationally, I believe, offers a new frame. Here, the work of lived religion is drawn upon but, as thinking congregationally entails thinking about how people do religion together, it focuses on the communal aspects as much as the individual. It relates the experiences of the congregation back to the institutions they are part of and participate in. I also believe an exploration of orthopraxis as a term and concept will benefit the sociology of religion, religious studies and our conceptualizations of religion in general.

The apparent success of a minority religion and its institutions, in the face of a presumed secularism, presents an important case study in documenting and tracking the changing forms of religion in Britain, a shift that has been highlighted by numerous sociologists of religion (Woodhead and Catto 2012). The findings will provide a basis for further scholarship and debate about religion in modern Britain. The growth of Muslim congregations in Britain ties directly to questions of secularization. Linda Woodhead (2012: 5–6) cites declining church attendance as an oft-used indicator of secularization; it is an indicator she ultimately rejects, arguing instead religion is morphing into new, individualized and less institutionalized forms, and that 'secular' and 'religious' are losing their analytical power (Woodhead 2016). How do we, in the context of a society at times described as 'post-secular' (Habermas 2008) or 'post-Christian' (Guest, Tusting and Woodhead 2004), understand British mosques? The natural question, which British Muslim congregational studies can address, is what role do and might the institutions of religious minorities play in Britain? The answer will help us understand much more about contemporary society, politics, modernity and, of course, religion.

I referenced earlier the work of Yilmaz (2018) and his contention that the political and social upheaval of twelfth-century Anatolia led to the emergence of the *tariqa*, a form of association and organization that would shape the trajectory and development of Islam for centuries. As Muslims in diaspora establish themselves in Britain and elsewhere, the congregation is, in my view, emerging and asserting itself as a key mechanism for religious organization, especially in what can be described as Anglophone Islam. This too, I believe, will influence the trajectory and development of Islam globally for generations and so stands as a worthy area for academic exploration.

4

The sacred mosque

Anyone who has visited a mosque will know the custom of removing one's shoes before entering, but it is a ritual that has always fascinated me, in part because of the diverse justifications offered by worshippers for the practice. For nearly a decade, I've informally sought out opportunities to ask my co-religionists 'why do you take your shoes off when you come to the mosque?' The responses are far from uniform but generally fall into three camps. The responses usually begin with bewilderment; it is an odd question to ask, and few will have self-consciously reflected on it, with the exception of those who often show non-Muslim visitors around the mosque who will usually have a rehearsed response ready to roll out. The most common answer is 'it is *sunna*', the practice of the Prophet. There are some debates about how accurate this is. The Salafi position on the issue is that the Prophet only removed his shoes if there was a reason to and otherwise wore his shoes during prayer. I once had the experience of being shown around a British Salafi mosque with Saudi Arabian visitors, all of us wearing our shoes in the carpeted prayer hall. For the Salafis, a ritualistic removal of shoes could be an innovation, something to avoid. Following the lead of my hosts, I didn't remove my shoes as I entered the mosque, despite a lifetime of socialization that it is nigh blasphemy to walk wearing shoes in the prayer hall. Some responses to the question of why shoes are removed explain it simply as a matter of practicality: 'we take our shoes off to keep the carpets clean'. So while there is nothing preventing one from wearing shoes, the dirt, grime and potential ritual impurities (faeces, blood and alcohol) that could be brought into the mosque by wearing shoes is reason enough to remove them. The next reason follows on from this but with more explicit spiritual reasoning: 'You must be *pak* to stand in front of Allah', *pak* (an Urdu word for purity) referring to the bodily purity achieved through *wuduʿ*, one which is undermined through the dirt potentially on one's shoes. Another response focusses on the question of sacredness: 'Musa took off his shoes in front of Allah, and we're about to stand in front of Allah'. In Moses's first encounter with God, as narrated in the Quran, he is told 'Verily I am your Lord! So take off your shoes; you are in the sacred valley, Tuwa' (Quran 20:12). The worshipper, much like Moses, is entering a sacred (*muqaddas*) place, and much like Moses, is about to spiritually enter the presence of God. 'It is about *adab*', I was told by a congregant on one occasion, 'you would not enter someone's house with your shoes on, so how can you enter God's House in the same way?' Thus, for those who responded in this way, removing shoes is a mark of respect for the significance of the space being entered. It includes a recognition that part of what makes the mosque unique is that it belongs to God (it was 'God's House') and as such, one should observe the proper decorum of a guest (to remove one's shoes before entering a person's home, though not universal etiquette, would be unquestioned in many Muslim cultures).

This chapter attempts to wrestle with the significance of the space of the mosque. Significance is itself an open and ambiguous term capable of describing positive or negative connotations. Things can be significant in a broad range of ways and sacredness can be thought of as a religious significance. Muslim sacredness can also be described as *baraka* (blessings, or to be blessed). I will attempt to map these conceptions together through examination of Ghamkol Sharif Central Jamia Masjid, a mosque in the suburbs of Birmingham tied to the influential British Muslim saint[1] Sufi Sahib Abdullah. I intend to demonstrate some of the ways in which mosques are imbued with meaning, how they are made significant, and the ways in which that significance is negotiated. This chapter also presents, through the case of Ghamkol Sharif, how the mosque is imbued with sacredness (through an account of the origins and building of the mosque), how the sacredness is encountered by Muslims (through the negotiation of *adab* or etiquette), and how this sacred is temporal as well as spatial.

Baraka, blessing and sacredness

The study of the sacred is a category of anthropological, sociological and religious studies research that can be dated back to the earliest works in each field (primarily Émile Durkheim and Mircea Eliade). Sacred has in its etymological origins the notion of something set apart and distinguished due to its significance. Contemporary usage is much broader, encapsulating all which is inviolable, important, cherished and valued. The word sacred has also been less regulated in everyday and academic usage than its conceptual cousin, 'religion'. While religion is tied inescapably to the word 'secular' and has thus been reified and particularized (Asad 1993), sacred has been broadened, being applied both in popular parlance as well as academia more freely to a broader range of human experiences. Adrian Ivakhiv argues that the signifier 'sacred' is a means of distributing 'significance across geographic spaces' and 'involving the distinction of different kinds of significance from among those being distributed', such as 'ideological', 'cosmological', 'political' and so on (Ivakhiv 2006: 171). For the purposes of this chapter, sacredness can be understood as an open-signifier of significance, under which the distinctly Muslim expression of *baraka* can be placed. However, mapping Islamic conceptions onto Anglophone ones rarely creates a perfect fit, and so it is necessary to return to some of the key conceptions in the Islamic tradition and academic literature in order to locate what is meant by *baraka* in the context of the contemporary British mosque.

In the textual sources of Islam, drawing from the Quran as well as the Arabic preserved in *hadith*s, words such as *qudus* and *muqaddas* are in operation. Both can be translated as 'holy' or 'sacred'. The term *ruh al-qudus,* for example, refers to the Holy Spirit, though in Islamic cosmology it refers to the Archangel Gabriel rather than a member of the Trinity (Quran 2:87 is one example). Alternatively, there is the word *haram*. Depending on conjugation and context, this can refer to prohibited actions in Islamic law or an inviolable space. Thus the Prophet's Mosque in Madina and the mosque around the *Ka'ba* in Mecca are described by Muslims as The Two Sacred Sanctuaries.[2] Yet the most common Arabic word, now a loanword in many languages spoken by Muslims, to describe the transcendental, divine, and otherworldly qualities of a space or time is *baraka*, or blessings. The word *baraka* has connotations of 'any good that is bestowed by God; *and particularly* such as continues and increases and abounds' (Lane and Lane-Poole 2003). Significantly, unlike the word sacred, it does not operate in a binary (as sacred does with profane or mundane) but instead implies a spectrum of strength and intensity. Things can be more or less blessed. *Baraka* can be found in actions, texts, people, places and times. In people, the presence of *baraka* can be likened to concepts like that of charisma in Weberian terms (for a sociological analysis of charisma see Turner 2001, for its operation in an Islamic context see Searcy 2010). In places, it is closer to the concept of sacred space (Cormack 2013). *Baraka* is a broad concept with a range of meanings, and its utility relates to this abundance of meaning. Similar to Cohen's (1993) argument that communities form around open and contested symbols or Bauer's contention that pre-modern Islam can be characterized by a high tolerance and cultivation of ambiguity (Bauer, Biesterfeldt and Tunstall 2021), *baraka* serves as an open, ambiguous term to describe a wide range of positive religious connotations.

What is the 'sacred'?

As I locate the mosque as a site of sacred space, as considered in the broadest sense, it is necessary to elaborate what sacred space is, and how it relates to *baraka*, a commonly used term to describe religious significance in terms of space, place and action. The two most influential theorists in the development of theories of sacred space are the aforementioned Durkheim (d. 1917) and Eliade (d. 1986). For Durkheim, the sacred was used to provide a definition of religion in The *Elementary Forms of Religious Life* (1915), in which he stressed the importance of the profane and the sacred in ordering human activity. The sacred are 'those things set apart and forbidden' (Durkheim 1915: 47). A different definition of the sacred was utilized by Eliade, who was one of the earliest advocates of a phenomenological approach to the study of religion. In *The Sacred and the Profane* (Eliade and Trask 1959) and *Patterns of Comparative Religion* (Eliade 1958) he puts forward a theory that positions sacredness as the result of 'kratophony and hierophany', which 'transforms the place where it occurs, hitherto profane' into 'a sacred area' (1958: 367). Between Durkheim's 'things set apart' and Eliade's transformations, two divergent approaches to the sacred emerge. Durkheim identifies the sacred as the product of human endeavour. Eliade argues it is the product of divine intervention. David Chidester and Edward Linenthal name these two approaches as the 'situational' and the 'substantive' (1995) definitions of the sacred. The situational is characterized by Durkheim's theories and many subsequent scholars of sacred space, including Jonathan Z. Smith (1987), Kim Knott (2005) and Lily Kong (2001), as well as Chidester and Linenthal themselves (1995). Substantive approaches, by contrast, are 'attempts to replicate an insider's evocation of certain experiential qualities that can be associated with the sacred', thus 'the sacred has been identified as an uncanny, awesome, or powerful manifestation of reality, full of ultimate significance' (Chidester and Linenthal 1995: 5). Alongside Eliade, it is possible to place Rudolph Otto, who also adopted the 'substantive' approach in his theorization of the 'numinous' (Otto and Harvey 1958). Situational and substantive approaches to sacred spaces are essentially answers to the question of whether sacred space is made or encountered, and as the chapter will go on to demonstrate, the answer need not necessarily be one or the other, and it is possible for Muslim sacred spaces to be conceptualized in a way that combines both.

Accepting sacred space as an umbrella term for significance, one can locate Muslim sacred space within it. Muslim sacred space is tied, in most cases, to the Quran. Edited works by Patrick Desplat and Dorothea Schulz (2012) and

Margaret Cormack (2013) highlight the various notions and nuances of Muslim sacred space, which invariably centre around *baraka* or 'blessings', a transient quality of otherworldliness experienced through places, people, and things. This echoes another definition of sacred space proposed by John Eade and Michael Sallnow who 'suggest that the triad of "person", "place", and "text" might provide the co-ordinates' for the construction of sacred space in Christianity and perhaps for 'other scripturally based religious traditions as well' (1991: 9). Muslim sacred spaces are spaces of *baraka*, then, received through an engagement with the divine.

There is also a question of 'where' sacred space is, and where scholars look to explore sacred space. Lily Kong speaks of 'official sacred space' (2001), a helpful term to discuss those places clearly marked as reserved for religion, such as mosques, churches and other places of worship. In contrast, unofficial sacred space is found in unexpected places, which Kong believes demands greater attention and research (2001: 228). These might be found in nature or public institutions. Sheryl Reimer-Kirkham et al. draw on Kong's distinction to explore unofficial spaces in the healthcare setting, describing them as 'thirdspaces', unique and meaningful places 'carved out' of otherwise 'banal' surroundings (2011: 205–6). Another approach is offered by Kim Knott in *The Location of Religion* (2005). She explores where religion manifests in ordinary landscapes, such as the street. Knott's examination stresses the role of the body as a key location for where religion is centred, and thus a contingent part of sacred space. Chidester and Linenthal agree and identify that 'the human body plays a crucial role in the ritual production of sacred space' which 'revolve[s] around the axis of the living body' (1995: 10). The subtle but important conclusion is that sacred space can be found everywhere, and scholars have developed a vocabulary to describe these various locations, which underscores the importance of looking at the practices and processes around sacred spaces.

The literature on Muslim sacred space also looks at a diversity of locations, but with an overall tendency to overlook 'institutional', 'traditional' or 'official' sacred spaces of mosques. Qureshi looks at the domestic rituals of *milad*, *dhikr* and *Qurankhwani* (1996) amongst South Asians in Canada. She observes that the rituals are domestic. Desplat claims that their co-edited collection (Desplat and Schulz 2012) 'moves beyond interpretations that focus exclusively on the ritual character' of Muslim sacred spaces and instead looks at the more 'subtle and routinely everyday activities and interpretations by people who may not participate in ritual activities' (Desplat 2012: 10). The authors of the chapters locate Muslim sacred spaces in the city, from doorsteps to the entire city layout.

Perhaps the most studied site for Muslim sacred space has been the shrine, with a large number of studies identifying the boundary-breaking/identity-crossing nature of such sacred places (Strothman 2012; Samuel and Rozario 2012; Damrel 2013; Gross 2013). To utilize Kong's terminology, the study of Muslim sacred space is inclined to what can be called 'unofficial sacred spaces'. This inclination can be attributed to an interest in the exceptions often found amongst researchers, the relatively challenging nature of gaining access to the 'official' sacred space of a mosque (for non-Muslim researchers especially) which is more tightly regulated than shrines, as well as a general trend amongst certain anthropologists to study Sufism (McLoughlin 2007: 281). In this wider context, the importance and value of understanding the sacredness of mosques are pronounced, and even more so for British mosques. Failing to appreciate the meaning attached to mosques by Muslims will always provide a blinkered and partial perspective of contemporary Islam.

Building *baraka*

There is no universal ritual for sacralizing a mosque or consecrating the ground upon which it is built. The *hadith* 'the entire earth is a masjid' establishes the principle that prayer can be undertaken almost anywhere, and so a mosque can be established almost everywhere. So how does a mosque mark itself out as different from any other site? I will answer with the strategy adopted by one mosque founder, Sufi Sahib Abdullah, who was instrumental in the building of Ghamkol Sharif Central Masjid. Junaid Akhtar, the grandson of Sufi Sahib Abdullah, continues to serve and work as a prominent teacher in Birmingham. He currently leads the Sufi Abdullah Foundation. He has strong memories of the work of his grandfather Sufi Sahib and the founding of Ghamkol Sharif. 'It was in 1962 that Sufi Sahib was instructed by his Shaykh to go and spread the remembrance of Allah and the Prophet Muhammad ﷺ in the UK', Junaid tells me. He spent several years in Britain, working as a labourer while simultaneously growing a community of Sufi devotees. 'People at that time, they didn't know which way qibla was when you asked them, they didn't pray, and they had lost their connection to Allah and his Rasul', Junaid recounts. Pnina Werbner was amongst the first to study Sufi Abdullah and his movement in Britain, and narrates in her work *Pilgrims of Love* the same motif of the Sufi saint 'taming the wilderness' (2003: 45) in her work (especially in rural Pakistan, though by no means exclusively found there). If there is a hagiographical motif associated with

British Muslim pioneers, it is not taming the wilderness but religious revival amongst the urban working class. The framing of Muslim men, disconnected from their homelands and religion, lost in a disenchanted industrialized world, who have their religious birth right returned to them through the activism of an early Muslim leader is a common one when discussing Sufism in Britain. Re-enchantment of the secular is the mission of the contemporary Muslim saint.

The origin of the mosque came about after a search for a more mundane location, a car park. Sufi Sahib had secured properties in the Small Heath area of Birmingham, using it as a base and centre. As it expanded, they sought to purchase land nearby simply for visitors to park.

> They wanted a car park, and there was space in the land opposite the centre, and when Sufi Sahib inquired, the council said we will give not just the car park, we'll give you the whole area, at the third of the price, but that is if you build a mosque. The council said that. And Sufi Sahib said, this a sign from Allah, Allah wants a mosque here, that Allah has given us the ability now to establish a mosque for the community. And a purpose-built one, not a converted one.

Just as the Muslim pioneer reintroducing religion to Muslim migrants is a common motif in origin stories of Muslim communities in Britain, so too is the idea that a mosque founded by Muslims was in response to God's will. Islamic creedal statements on the nature of fate (*qadr*) make this a forgone conclusion; everything is ordained by God, but there is a particular emphasis placed on God's intervention in bringing about the mosque in the narrative of Ghamkol Sharif Central Masjid. This prompts the question: is the mosque made significant through the actions of worshippers who built it? Or is it ordained as sacred by God? Referring back to the two approaches to the study of the sacred space introduced by Eliade and Durkheim, the question can be rephrased: is the sacred space of the mosque situational or substantive? Is it constructed or is it encountered? My contention is that such a binary can only ever provide a partial account, and the dominance of a situational account in scholarship can overlook the way in which sacred space is conceptualized by communities. The theories of Durkheim (and the situational school) and Eliade (and the substantive school) provide two narratives on sacredness. They are not inherently conflicting narratives: sacred space can be both viewed as constructed by the actions of its inhabitants as well as containing within it transcendental qualities that illicit response in those within. I adopt James Beckford's (2003: 29) view that a social constructionist approach to the study of religion 'leaves open the possibility that divine or supernatural powers may affect human life directly' while the researcher focuses on the social implications of religion. In the case of Ghamkol Sharif, its significance is a product of its appointment as a place of worship by God, chosen as such in the scope of the primordial and eternal destiny of all created things. It was also imbued with *baraka* through the actions of the attendees, as will be explored further subsequently. A strictly situational account of the founding of the mosque would recount that the land was purchased by Muslims, a mosque fundraised and established on the site, and ritual worship took place with regularity, imbuing the place with the *baraka* encountered. Muslim worshippers at any mosque, including Ghamkol Sharif, would not disagree, but such an account would overlook an important aspect of the mosque, the substantive element. God has chosen the site to be a mosque; it was God's will, not the people's, that it should be a place of worship. It is not an arbitrary location. Thus worshippers encounter the *baraka* of the mosque not just due to their own worship at the place but also due to God's intervention.

The building of Ghamkol Sharif was carefully attended to in order to make the mosque itself a site of *baraka*. Junaid recounts that his grandfather had learned that when the Ottomans had reconstructed parts of the Prophet's Mosque in Medina; they had recited the Quran in its entirety over every brick. In the building of Ghamkol Sharif, however, an alternative strategy was adopted:

> Sufi Sahib said we didn't have the ability to recite on every single brick, but what Sufi Sahib did, was from day one of construction, he made sure that Quran was recited on site, every single day, an entire Quran was recited. For the four or five years of construction, Quran *khatm* was done every single day.

Barbara Metcalf contends that 'Clifford Geertz has elaborated on this point by noting that Islamic buildings are primarily spaces where the faithful engage with sacred words, whether in prayer (the mosque), education (the *madrasa*), or meditation (the *khanaqah*)' (1996: 5), which serves to underline the importance of text in the construction of Muslim sacred space. Here it can be seen in practice, the recitation of the Quran imbuing *baraka* into the mosque. In addition to recitation of the Quran, Junaid states that 'all the people who were to help, all the volunteers, were to be on *wudu*'. No volunteer could start work until being on *wudu*', that is where the *baraka* comes from'. Junaid stresses that all the volunteers involved in the building of Ghamkol Sharif were students of Sufi Sahib, thus part of a spiritual chain. The building of the mosque was an embodied practice, treated similarly to other acts of formal worship such as prayer, which require the individual to be in a state of ritual purity.

The intentionality of seeking *baraka* can be observed in even decisions about commissioning services:

> Sufi Sahib, with happiness, would say that we didn't commission any international or non-Muslim companies. He would be stern and remind people about this. It would be our own Muslim community, especially the volunteers, who helped make the *masjid*, giving their day and night towards building. That is where *baraka* comes from.

This intentionality can be found in other stories Junaid shared with me about construction. He tells me emphatically that 'cement, bricks, nothing went to waste'. '[Sufi Sahib] would do that in everything, even if we were washing dishes he would make us aware not to waste water.' The conservation of water is a regular Islamic ethic, but Junaid stressed how this extended to building materials. 'In England, you know, in the morning it's sunny and the evening it's wet, so you could lose a batch of cement to that, but Sufi Sahib would also find a way for it to be used, insisting nothing could go to waste.'

As mentioned, there is no ritual of sacralization universally accepted by Muslims. Rather, there are strategies for building *baraka*. Every action in the process of deciding to build the mosque, the material, the recitation of the Quran on the work site, preventing waste, being on ritual ablution during work, and the use of volunteer labour, sought to invoke God's *baraka* onto the site.

Sacred time

Ammerman argues that 'lived religion' has been defined by its exclusions, 'it includes attention to laity, not clergy or elites; to practices rather than beliefs; to practices outside religious institutions rather than inside' (2016: 1). While I do not strictly locate my approach as 'lived religion', it nonetheless shares a concern and focus on what people (in this case Muslims) do and an interest in the everyday. I pick up the challenge outlined by Ammerman, who continues her argument writing that if 'scholars exclude actions that are tied to traditional religious institutions, they not only exclude much of what most people would think of as religious practice, but also much of what people are actually doing' (2016: 1). In attempting to provide an account of sacredness in the institution of the mosque, I seek to provide a perspective of lived religion and sacred space often overlooked. In the Islamic tradition, the Prophetic teaching, 'actions are by intentions' (Bukhari 1 1), is often used to emphasize that all actions can be considered worship and have sacred character. The binary, of sacred and profane, that has been central to the theorization of religion by scholars such as Durkheim (1915) is less pronounced in the Islamic tradition. In an engaging article in *Sociology of Religion*, Nancy Ammerman outlined the challenge of 'finding Waldo', or rather religion, and the various approaches scholars and academics of religion have utilized to do so (Ammerman 2014). Ammerman encourages the reader to see religion both in the places traditionally associated with it (mosques, temples, gurdwaras and churches), but also outside of it (in the workplace, at social gatherings, in the street). 'Just as we should not expect religion to be everywhere' she argues, 'we should also not expect it to stay in its predictable corner' (Ammerman 2014: 196). This works in reverse also, as she writes, 'conversations inside the religious community are full of the stuff of everyday life, with mundane and sacred realities intermingling here no less than they do everywhere else' (2014: 201). It is a view that reflects the varied activities of British mosques. As Ammerman argues, I found that the mosques I studied, though an ostensibly religious and sacred space, are also host to discussions about the economy and sports, they housed activities around education and employment and are places where experts came to warn about the dangers of diabetes, or where councillors visited to negotiate tensions about parking. 'It is not just that people take religion into everyday life; they also take everyday life into religion' (Ammerman 2014: 201). It is a point made in similar words by Shahab Ahmed: 'the production, constitution, and operation of truth[3] in the bulk of human and historical Islam has been conceptually, discursively, socially and spatially *diffuse*' [emphasis in original] (Ahmed 2015: 191). Few religions it should be noted operate a clean binary between religion and non-religion. As such, when discussing activity in the mosque all of it has the potential to hold some sacred character. Yet it would be deeply misleading to imagine that Muslims, no less than any other religious community, do not distinguish between the nature of ritual prayer (the *salah*) and a GCSE tuition class, no matter how religious the intention behind the latter. This distinction can be found in Islamic law where actions are divided into *'ibadat* and *mu'amalat*. The former, literally 'acts of worship', refers to actions of ritual obedience to God and thus are theocentric. The *mu'amalat* refer to the interactions between creations of God, namely between humans, so they are anthropocentric. Both are subject to the *shari'a*, but they are two different categories of action. The *'ibadat* hold a different sacred significance than *mu'amalat*. While both might be considered acts of worship and obedience, *'ibadat* are particularly infused with *baraka* or blessings. It is that the mosque is a space marked out for *'ibadat*, regularly and repeatedly so, that makes it sacred, a site of *baraka*.

To understand the operation of the mosque as sacred, one needs to consider not just the spatial dimension but the temporal. Kim Knott (2005: 43) agrees with Jonathan Z. Smith, writing that 'sacred space is not the stimulus for ritual; ritual, as sacred making behaviour, brings about "sacred space". Ritual takes place, and makes place in this sense'. It is a sentence that only partially describes the way in which space can be engaged with. Knott's view does not account for the temporal. Time is a stimulus for ritual, and given the tightly embedded nature of space and time, this needs to be considered, especially in the Muslim context where the 'time for prayer' is a central part of 'everyday religion'. Time prompts ritual. Ritual, as sacred-making behaviour, can equally bring about sacred time.

A feature of classical studies of sacred space is the idea of sacredness as a stable category. Spaces can be made sacred or desacralized, but in between, the sacredness is imagined to be held almost monotonously. In the context of the mosque, time is a vitally important factor. Sacredness waxes and wanes throughout the day, week and even year. It comes in waves, oscillating between a tangible intensity and an imperceptible passivity. It is between moments of intensity that the mosque hosts the social, educational and more everyday affairs of human life. This sacred rhythm that dictates the activities of the mosque is one of many rhythms that structure human life, according to sociologist Henri Lefebvre. In a posthumously published book, *Rhythmanalysis* (2004), he outlines the way in which rhythm structures and underlines human activity on an individual and communal level, pondering whether there are differences between lunar cities (ports in which the lunar tides dictate trade and the flow of people) and solar cities (dependent on the agricultural produce from farms, dictated by the seasons). His own application of his theory aside, there is an undeniable link between the sun and moon and its patterned movement in the sky (the subject of numerous Quranic verses) and the ritual worship of Muslims, as will be explored in further depth. Rhythmanalysis of the mosque then provides an appropriate and fitting theoretical approach by which to analyse the sacredness of the British mosque. This will be demonstrated by considering an important weekly sacred time, the Friday prayer, in Central Jamia Masjid Ghamkol Sharif.

The Friday prayer at Central Jamia Mosque Ghamkol Sharif

Central Jamia Mosque Ghamkol Sharif is large, purpose-built and located such that there are dramatic views of it as one approaches. It has a prominent dome but an even more prominent squat minaret. The building is an odd-shape, one side is almost a square, whereas the other curves around like a hexagon. I'm visiting on a cold Friday in March 2022 for the congregational prayer in the afternoon; the pandemic restrictions have largely eased, and crowds are returning to mosques in numbers not seen for nearly two years. The mosque is located in Small Heath, Birmingham, and sits between a heavily residential area on one-side and a dual-carriageway (the A45) on the other. As I approach the mosque, the *bayan* (pre-prayer sermon) can be heard over speakers broadcasting it. The wind is strong and so loud that most of the broadcast speech is unintelligible until I'm well within the mosque car park. In the Hanafi *fiqh* of the South Asian variety, the Friday sermon in full must be in Arabic, and so the *bayan*, a sermon, is delivered in a more accessible language before the ritual Friday congregational prayer (the *jumu'a*) begins in earnest. My walk to the mosque took me past the everyday sights of a city like Birmingham; busy roads, construction work, a garage, terraced homes and double-parked cars, but the mosque stands singularly as a landmark in the area. It is hard to miss, either driving past on the dual-carriageway or walking. It is an undeniably impressive work of architecture, intended to be beautiful, eye-catching and grand.

I am part of a stream of individuals entering, none walking with urgency but all clearly with purpose. There is a quiet exchange of *salam* amongst some congregants as they enter, but most are reverent and silent. A few enter the downstairs prayer hall directly in front of the entrance, most walk upstairs to the toilets to make ablution or enter the main prayer hall on the first floor. In the toilet, there are rows of stools in front of taps, running along the wall and a shared drain carrying the water away. There are dozens making *wudu'* and dozens more waiting for a free space. The mosque is clearly at capacity. There is no impatience as individuals wait their turn. After making ablution myself, I enter the main prayer hall, leaving my footwear on the shoe shelves lining the corridors and foyer space between the *wudu'* facilities and the prayer halls. There are hundreds of pairs of shoes, some neatly placed on the shelves, others stuffed into free spaces and corners and some left haphazardly on the floor.

The prayer hall is awe-inspiring. A low ceiling in the front gives way to a sudden rise to the inside of the dome. Multiple chandeliers provide illumination in addition to the sunlight streaming through the windows. The carpet is thick and decorated with lines for prayer. The most eye-catching feature is the *mihrab*, however. The imam is delivering his sermon from the middle of three arches. The entire wall is a green marble tile. Calligraphy with the declaration of faith runs across the wall like a ribbon. Directly above the *mihrab* is a replica of the golden doors of the *Ka'ba* (smaller than the real thing, but still large); on the left is a framed picture of the Prophet's Mosque in Medina, on the right, a framed picture of the *Ka'ba* itself. Everything about the hall, the tiled walls, the decoration, the chandeliers, the calligraphy, the visible dome that adds an almost vertigo-inducing height to the room, conveys a sense of importance and significance. There is a suspended ceiling composed of polystyrene tiles, the type more often found in office buildings and school classrooms, the only underwhelming element of an otherwise impressive location.

I take a seat on the floor, cross-legged. Others are sitting like me, some on their haunches, a handful on chairs dotted around the edge. Soon the imam finishes his *bayan*, which was delivered on the importance of caring for one's parents, and the appointed muezzin stands and delivers the call to prayer (*adhan*). The congregants were already quiet before this, though with some exchanging greetings, a few hushed conversations, some casually browsing through their smartphones and others using prayer beads to count their *dhikr*. This all stopped with the *adhan*, however, and attention was focused towards the *mihrab*, sometimes bodily, with individuals shuffling or orientating themselves towards the *qibla*. Once the call to prayer is complete, the congregation individually offers two units of prayer. The prayer is unsynchronised, with the actions of bowing, prostrating, sitting and standing all taking place under the individual rhythm of the person. After a few minutes, the Arabic *khutba* begins with the imam greeting the congregation with *salam*, the words are melodic song, more like poetry than prose. The *khatib* recites *hadith* describing good conduct, kindness to parents, love for the family of the Prophet Muhammad and the importance of offering prayers. He concludes the first part of the sermon and sits silently for a minute before standing and beginning the second part. The second sermon is shorter and is largely focused on prayers for the family of the Prophet, the Prophet himself, the companions of the Prophet, notable saints including 'Abd al-Qadir al-Jilani (d. 1166), and finally the founder of Ghamkol Sharif, Sufi Sahib Abdullah.

As soon as the *khutba* begins, another *adhan* is given, and the congregants rise for the *jumu'a* prayer itself. Two cycles of prayer are led by the imam, with the Quran recited loudly (the usual day prayers of *zuhr* and *'asr* prayers are recited inaudibly or silently). The prayer is completed and there is a moment's pause. This is followed by a gentle wave of quiet recitation and prayer. The individual words aren't intelligible; instead, it is more like the sound of the tide on a beach. The collective hum of hundreds of congregants whisper their personal words of devotion.

A few minutes later, or perhaps even less, the imam then leads the congregants in collective *du'a'* (supplication to God, which can be both formalized through the use of specific Quranic words, for example, or informal and undertaken in a vernacular language). Hands are raised and the imam begins by praying in Arabic, then Urdu, then English, code switching regularly, to Urdu and Arabic words peppering the English. Prayers are made again for the Prophet and his family, the congregants, the entire Muslim umma, and then notably, for the families of two deceased individuals whose janaza or funeral prayers will be offered subsequently. After the *du'a'* there is another pause, and this time more routine announcements are made. A reminder of the *janaza* prayers to be offered shortly, that food will be served downstairs following this, an exhortation for congregants to visit and make use of the newly opened library on the ground floor boasting over 'six thousand titles'. Finally the congregations are encouraged to attend an event, 'The Sufi Tradition of Serving Mankind' taking place the next day. By now, many congregants are leaving, presumably back to their places of employment or education. A sizable minority remains however for the funeral prayers.

This account of a *jumu'a* prayer in Ghamkol Sharif is a snapshot of an hour during a single day, but it is part of a wider liturgical calendar of Islam, one that shapes the days and weeks of the year. It provides an insight into the mosque as a site of religious activity, but it also provides an example of sacred time, perhaps the most significant moment in any week for the mosque. Upon entering the mosque, the pleasant smell of bukhoor or incense greeted me. Burning incense before important rituals is a common practice amongst some Muslims, and it serves well to illustrate the concept of *baraka*. The diffusion of the bukhoor mirrors the diffusion of *baraka* and the arrival of a sacred moment. The immediately identifiable fragrance of burning and scented woodchips tells the arriving congregation that today the mosque is hosting something religiously significant. The bukhoor also works to mark out the time as sacred: it is transient, it lingers but not for long, and soon enough only the lightest traces of it remain. Similarly, the blessings of *jumu'a* are not a permanent fixture but will pass. It is currently increasing in intensity as the climax (the moment of *jumu'a* prayer) approaches. Sacred space is not static, and the burning woodchips provide the most appropriate means of marking both its temporal and spatial brevity. And just like with *baraka*, the smell of the incense will add, accumulate over time and linger so as to be almost permanently accessible (if not as strongly). This transient, oscillating nature of sacred time is something best understood through rhythm, which I consider next.

The sacred rhythm

The model of how Muslims pray remains remarkably universal. Whether from Morocco or Indonesia, Sarajevo or Johannesburg, Muslims can pray together. Denominational inflections can determine some components of prayer, but in general, when Muslims gather, there are few barriers to them praying collectively. During the Friday prayer at Ghamkol Sharif, this almost universal pattern of prayer could be observed. The actions of the canonical prayer are cyclic and each unit is described as a *rakʿa*. Each cyclic unit comprises of standing, bowing, standing again, and then prostrating twice with a sitting in between each prostration. The announcements of the *imam* provide a verbal cue to follow.

The prayer times are also set with regularity. The prayers are determined by the position of the sun in the sky. *Fajr*, the first prayer, takes place at dawn. Dawn is when the first light of the sun can be seen (morning twilight), and sunrise (when the disk is visible on the horizon). Then *zuhr* occurs just following the midday zenith of the sun. The Friday *jumuʿa* usually takes place at this time, replacing the *zuhr* prayer itself. The *ʿaṣr* prayer takes place in late afternoon (the canonical schools offer methods to calculate it using shadows cast by an item and differ on the length the shadow must reach). *Maghrib* is immediately following sunset for Sunnis and after the disappearance of the glow of the sun for Shias (importantly, sunset itself is a time forbidden for prayer in both traditions). Finally *ʿisha* begins generally when twilight ends (though again, there are differences in how this is calculated between canonical schools of law). In Britain, located as it is on extreme northern latitude, the timing of these prayers varies significantly throughout the year. In the winter, the first will be around 7.00 am, and the last, 6.00 pm. During summer, the first can begin as early as 2.30 am and the last at 11.00 pm. The midday prayer, however, largely remains in the same time period. At Ghamkol Sharif, during the winter period, the *bayan* (pre-*jumuʿa* sermon) would begin about 12.30 pm, with the formalized *khuṭba* (considered part of the *jumuʿa* prayer itself) beginning around 1.30 pm. This would be pushed an hour later during the summer months and the associated British Summer Time (from the last Sunday of March to the last Sunday of October).

Given this variation, communication between any mosque and congregants about the time for prayer is important to the functioning of the *salah*. In Muslim-majority countries, the call to prayer is broadcast via loudspeakers. In urban centres, it is common to hear a dozen mosques or more all within earshot announcing their calls to prayer, creating a euphony (or cacophony, depending both on the opinion of the listeners and the skill of the muezzin) across the cityscape. In Britain, this method is rarely an option. While most local authorities do allow leeway on this issue during the daytime, it would be prevented for early morning and night-time prayers. On a more practical note, the call to prayer is less practical in Britain. The ratio of Muslims to mosques means few congregants are within earshot even of their local mosque, and the constraints of work and education mean that even fewer would be able to respond to the call to prayer. Nonetheless, the call to prayer is not entirely unheard in Britain. Ghamkol Sharif's minaret-mounted loudspeakers broadcast the call to prayer as well as the sermon on Fridays.

Given that mosques in Britain were unable to rely on a traditional call to prayer in order to gather worshippers, they have needed to innovate other means and methods. One of the first methods adopted has now largely been eclipsed by new technologies but remains a hidden staple in the everyday life of first-generation Muslims – the private radio transmitter. Ghamkol Sharif broadcasts on the radio frequency 454.4125. The earliest mosques in Britain, seeking to maintain the same type of verbal communication used in Muslim-majority contexts historically, introduced the use of the transmitters. Which mosque was the first to adopt this method and how it spread has been largely lost to history. The mosque broadcasts prayers through a one-way transmitter on a private channel. Congregants purchase dual-band receivers to tune in to the mosque's frequency, leaving it plugged-in and somewhere central in the home. The calls to prayer, the prayer itself, Friday sermons and any lectures, and any announcements of deaths or births are thus announced. There is a geographic limit on the range of the transmitters, usually a few kilometres, but they generally serve the majority of their congregants. In the era before the internet, social media, and even mobile phones, the private radio transmitters allowed for mass-communication by the mosque. During the pandemic of 2020–1, the importance and utility of the transmitter re-emerged. The 'digital turn', to account for Covid-19 restrictions, certainly took place within mosques, but it was also accompanied by a return in the use of this more analogue technology largely amongst older and first-generation migrants. Local councils of mosques issued lists of radio transmitter frequencies in their area to support congregants wishing to access the channels. There is remarkably little research or public understanding of this seemingly popular mosque service.

A more low-tech option used by mosques is printed timetables. Ghamkol Sharif's mosque timetable includes the beginning of prayer times for each of the canonical prayers but also for when the actual congregational prayer takes place. There is also the Gregorian and Islamic date listed along with the row for Friday highlighted. Timetables inform worshippers when to pray at home or work and also when to arrive at the mosque to pray in congregation. The wait between the prayer time beginning and prayer in the mosque can vary but for *fajr* and *maghrib* they are normally offered immediately after the time for prayer begins.

As mentioned, the seasons dramatically change prayer times. Stornoway Mosque, the northernmost mosque on the British Isles, would pray *fajr* at 8.19 am and *maghrib* at 3.36 pm on the shortest day of the year (around 21 December). On the longest day of the year (around 21 June), *fajr* is at 3.02 am and *maghrib* at 10.35 pm. The changes in other places in the UK are no less dramatic. The Cornwall Islamic Community Centre is located in the historic Quenchwell Chapel, formerly a Methodist place of worship that was purchased by local Muslims in 2008. It is the southern-most mosque on the British mainland. On the winter solstice, the Cornwall Islamic Community Centre would pray *fajr* at 7.37 am, and *maghrib* at 5.20 pm. On the summer solstice, *fajr* begins at 2.25 am and *maghrib* is 9.35 pm. Winter months would see prayers in quick succession as short days squeeze together the daytime prayers, and summer months scatter the daily prayers across the entire 24-hour period. The variations between prayer times affect the character of attendance at the mosque. In winter months, it would be common to see smartly dressed office workers attending *fajr* prayer before starting work. A summer *fajr*, which is in the middle of the night, is more likely to be attended by university students yet to go to sleep and the most committed attendees. In winter, parents might bring their children for a few hours in the afternoon on the weekend. They would sit, recite Quran and collectively pray the afternoon prayers, socializing children in the environment of the mosque. The summer evenings can often be busy with activity on weekdays, as the later *maghrib*, and *'isha* draw out attendance. Just as whether a mosque is located in the suburbs or the city centre has an impact on who attends, whether a prayer is in the early morning or late evening has an impact. Timetables provide a way for the mosque to communicate these seasonal changes in prayer times to congregants. Most mosque websites host annual timetables, since while the prayer times change from day-to-day, month-to-month, they remain the same from year-to-year (being kept from drifting too much out of sync thanks to the February leap day). The prayer timetable may be handed out as a booklet with all twelve months, printed onto a calendar issued annually, or simply provided month by month on photocopied pages.

Modern technology has provided new means to connect worshippers with their chosen mosque. Timetables are regularly distributed through social media channels, such as Facebook, Twitter, and more recently, WhatsApp broadcast lists. More digitally literate mosques offer smartphone applications with daily prayer times, notifications, a '*qibla* finder', and direct access to live-stream broadcasts from the mosque in question. You would find all of the above services in East London Mosque's application. The Shahjalal Mosque in Manchester has an application that goes further, with resources such as *duʿaʾ* lists and a section dedicated to learning the ninety-nine names of Allah, as well as a tool for calculating *zakat* payments, in addition to the above. The Bradford Grand Mosque (also known as al-Jamia Suffa-tul-Islam Grand Mosque) application includes poems and odes to the Prophet Muhammad for the congregants to recite. Almost all mosque applications include a means to donate to the mosque, usually through PayPal or GoCardless (the latter a British company that allows direct debit payments). While Ghamkol Sharif doesn't have a smartphone application, it does have a varied digital presence. Their aforementioned radio broadcast channel can be found on their prayer timetable, listed alongside their website address, their Twitter and Instagram handles, and the links for their YouTube and Facebook pages. While far from prolific, each channel is generally updated with site-specific content regularly, and recordings of sermons and activities of the mosque are available on their Facebook and YouTube pages.

The traditional *adhan* and the innovative technologies (from radio broadcasting to prayer timetables and social media) are all used by Muslims in order to recreate the connection provided to a sacred rhythm, the rhythm of prayer, in a context when a modern industrial reckoning of time is hegemonic. Such attention to it is necessary as the sacred rhythm established by ritual prayer runs contrary to other routines and rhythms of the day, most explicitly, the working day and commitments of employment. Congregants gather at the mosque to observe this rhythm. In between these moments, however, are the times when the mosque hosts activities with less explicitly sacred connotations. These rhythms formulate the way in which sacredness is invested into space and encountered.

The weekly rhythm

Friday is the most significant day in terms of the Islamic week, and the example covered provides an insight into why it is marked out for a specific act of worship, the *jumuʿa* prayer. Mondays and Thursdays are also given special status as marked out for optional fasts that especially devout Muslims may observe, but no other day within the week is given a status like that of Friday. The instruction for the *jumuʿa* prayer is directly from the Quran:

> Believers! When the call to prayer is made on the day of congregation, hurry towards the reminder of God and leave off your trading – that is better for you, if only you knew – then when the prayer has ended, disperse in the land and seek out God's bounty. Remember God often so that you may prosper. (Quran 62: 9–10)

In Britain, it is not uncommon for the Friday prayer to fill the mosque to capacity; worshippers gather and the space between rows is shortened in order to accommodate the numbers in attendance. While this didn't take place in Ghamkol Sharif when I visited, it was nonetheless close to entirely full – an impressive feat in a mosque that estimates it can hold up to 6,000 worshippers. In mosques that do fill up, it is a common sight to see congregants who arrive late to pray on the bare ground outside the mosque rather than to miss it, and mosques with car parks or courtyards readily use the available space for attendees.

Wider rhythms

Perhaps the largest rhythm that structures the use of the mosque is the oscillation of the solar and lunar calendars. The solar year is the basis for the Gregorian calendar. By contrast, the Islamic calendar of worship is calculated according to the lunar year, which is linked to the lunar phases. The lunar year is eleven or twelve days shorter than a solar year and so each lunar year shifts in relation to the solar calendar. In practice this means that key festival dates, such as Ramadan, begin ten to twelve days earlier every solar year, travelling backwards through the seasons. Ramadan in 2013 started on 9 July, in 2015 it began on 18 June, in 2018 it began on 16 May and in 2021 it began on 12 April. Ramadan during these years fell on the longest and warmest days of the year, and the length of the fasts can reach twenty hours due to their proximity to the summer solstice. The generational timespan of this rhythm was succinctly summarized by a mosque leader in Cardiff, who addressed the congregation during *tarawih* prayers with the following:

> The last time we broke our fasts at this time, we were young like you. The next time you break fasts at a time like this, you will be old like us.

The relationship between the solar calendar, the lunar calendar and Ramadan presents a generational narrative. It takes thirty-three years for Ramadan to travel through an entire year, a rhythm that can only ever be experienced through a lifetime, at most two or three times. Why are these larger rhythms important? They show how the big rhythms construct the small differences of a single day and how meanings are attached to time and to space. The calendars, industrial and religious, represent a wider human activity of codifying time, identifying patterns, and attaching (or interpreting) meaning to them. These rhythms stretch from the everyday to the generational, from the immediate to the cosmic. Ultimately, to adequately perceive and understand the sacred-making activities of the mosque, one must be conscious that the local and specific actions of prayer and worship take place in a timescape that stretches into the past and into the future through the cyclical rhythms they are nestled within.

Sacred time

Central to my description of sacredness in the mosque is that it is not just space which is at stake, but time also. Any consideration of spatiality must also consider temporality. Space is experienced temporally, and time is experienced spatially; the two dimensions of human experience are tied together in our language, metaphors and expressions. A mosque is host to 'sacred moments' that punctuate the day, the week and the year. These moments are constructed collaboratively through the synchronicity of particular times and particular spatial practices. The term 'moments' is taken again from Lefebvre, who speaks of moments that pierce the ordinary routines of life (Butler 2012: 27). The combination of time and space in moments requires us to think about space and time in more interrelated ways. Within certain sciences, spacetime has already become a familiar concept, becoming a way to express the interrelatedness of space and time. The term spacetime, in the study of human society, can be an important remedy for failing to consider how space and time are intertwined. Lefebvre and Regulier (2004: 89) contend:

> In each of social practice, scientific knowledge and philosophical speculation, an ancient tradition separates time and space as two entities or two clearly distinct substances. This despite the contemporary theories that show a relation between time and space, or more exactly say how they are relative to one another.

When describing sacred space, many scholars adopt a Durkheimian definition of the sacred, which is that the sacred are 'things set apart' (Durkheim 1915:

47), the approach discussed earlier in the chapter. Rituals, as Jonathan Z. Smith indicates, delineate and demarcate space as important and special (1987). They do this for time also. The ritual activity of mosques does not just mark out space as separate but time also. The five daily prayers are the best example. The sacredness waxed and waned, creating moments and places rich with significance that were set apart and delineated through verbal thresholds and shifting spatial practice. Congregants attending the mosque eat, play and talk jovially in the mosque, yet when the time for prayer is marked with the *adhan*, the atmosphere changes, conversations diminish and they still themselves are in preparation. This is the same place, but the time has changed. Verbal thresholds are important in marking sacred times: words, doxologies, prayers and invocations that mark the beginning or end of blessed times. Sacred time is what matters here. The varied activities and uses of the mosque are placed in relation to this sacred rhythm. Lefebvre and Regulier argue in their rhythmanalysis of Mediterranean cities that

> [T]here is a tendency towards the globalising domination of centres (capital cities, dominant cultures and countries, empires), which attacks the multidimensionality of the peripheries – which in turn perpetually threatens unity. In rhythmanalytic terms, let us say that there is a struggle between measured, imposed, external time and a more endogenous time. (2004: 99)

There is likewise a struggle in British mosques between a form of endogenous time of the sacred rhythm (at least endogenous to the congregants while within the mosque) and the time of the space outside, which functions according to the working day. Accommodations are made to bring the routine of the working day and the sacred rhythm into harmony. The sacred rhythm and the working day both demand dominance from the congregants, who negotiates the competing demands.

The significance of the sacred rhythm, however, is more than just organizational. Borrowing from Eliade, who argues that 'rhythms are seen as revelations – that is, manifestations – of a fundamental sacred power behind the cosmos' (1958: 388), sacred rhythms provide a connection between the divine and the worldly (*dunya*) – a connection which is perceived as *baraka*. Paden (1994: 101) theorizes that reoccurring ritual helps support the 'religious worlds' of believers, writing that '[a]t relentlessly regular intervals – every day, every week, or year – the "great thing" that life is based on, that happened in the mythic past, happens again'. Rhythmic rituals are a way of mapping religious meanings into otherwise everyday occurrences. In fact, this everydayness forces a reconsideration of classical definitions of sacredness. The two grandfathers of the study of the sacred, Durkheim and Eliade, agree one can contrast the sacred with the everyday and mundane, whereas I argue there is something everyday about the sacred, and there is something sacred about the mundane.

Religious worship fits into an everyday rhythm, and everyday activities are incorporated into a wider religious paradigm in the mosque, as presented and discussed in terms of the interspatial mosque. The rhythms are, in fact, a key way in which the diverse activities of mosques are maintained. Rhythms allow space to be malleable. Quoting from Chidester and Linenthal's work, if all places are sacred, 'where in the entire universe can I find a place to shit?' (1995: 11). Muslims, for whom prayer can be undertaken almost anywhere, face a similar challenge of managing defecation and other acts that defile or challenge sacred meanings in a world where everything was filled with religious significance. Rhythms are a way in which this sacredness is managed. The whole world is a masjid, and the masjid is sacred, but sometimes are more sacred than others. In between sacred moments are times when classes, exercise sessions and political meetings can be held. Rhythm allows the mosque to manage sacredness and *baraka*.

The sacred mosque

This chapter introduces and discusses a key concept in the mosque – that of sacredness. It advances existing literature on sacred space but argues that in order to understand the sacredness of the mosque, time and space must be considered together – which leads to an appreciation of the sacred rhythm structuring all mosques. The conclusions can be drawn wider still in the study of human society, as it presumes rhythms (whether industrial or mechanical, cosmic or ritual) shape the activity of individuals and communities. Viewing sacredness (or *baraka*) as rhythmic, something which ebbs and flows, also provides an important reorientation of how mosques in the UK provide services that are less overtly spiritual or sacred in character. The moments in between prayer and worship provide opportunities for mosques to host other activities, such as education, sports, charitable work, without detaching them from their sacred context. The British mosque is a place of divine connection – failure to appreciate this dimension of the mosque will always lead to a partial analysis or a blinkered, narrow understanding. This chapter, perhaps more than any other, seeks to ensure that the British mosque is not stripped as a site of *baraka*, a site of sacredness.

5

The diverse mosque

This chapter will explain two things. The first is to provide an insight into the diversity of British mosques in terms of denominational identities but also to argue that these identities are negotiated and in tension with an ecumenical impulse. This ecumenical impulse leads to ecumenical mosques that subsume their overt denominational identity in favour of welcoming a diverse congregation.

In 2014, journalist Innes Bowen published a book that sought to lay bare the 'sectarian' identity of British mosques. *Medina in Birmingham, Najaf in Brent: Inside British Islam* (Bowen 2014) described itself as the 'definitive guide to the ideological differences, organisational structures and international links of the main Islamic groups active in Britain today'.[1] Bowen's book represents an interest in the forces and affiliations within Islam. Any sectarian overview is far from straightforward, however. Hassan Joudi has been the Assistant Secretary General of the MCB for two-year terms and has been at the forefront of projects such as the previously mentioned 'Visit My Mosque'. His work has taken him to mosques across the country. We spoke about his work at length, an oddly formal conversation with someone with whom I've had a working relationship for several years. Reflecting on the question of sectarian identity in mosques, he recounted the following:

> I remember actually on my way to school, when I was very young, on a road that we used to drive through with my parents in Willesden in Brent. On that road there's a big Catholic Church, and then just down the road from it, then there's a Methodist church, and then further down there is Brent Baptist Church, and I'm sure there as a Church of England church too. So same road, four different churches, all very big buildings.

The denominational background of a mosque is less clear than, in the case of, these churches but it is nonetheless discernible through doctrinal choices in worship, the biography of the leadership and the wider networks the mosque is connected to. Mosques are rarely so forthcoming with their denominational identity. Hassan continues:

> There are some mosques, well actually relatively few, to be honest, which will specifically say something-mosque, like Salafi Mosque or whatever. It's not like the Christian community where most churches that you come across they'll have the word Methodist or Catholic in the name. I haven't done a survey, but you know finger-in-the-air,[2] probably only about one in ten or less mosques

There are three reasons for mosque management to be reluctant to identify themselves on denominational terms. The first is no doubt the influence of instructions in the Quran and hadith against sectarianism. So even when Muslims do maintain a strong link with a denomination in terms of practise and teaching, they may not identify themselves in such terms. Secondly, there are very few theological or denominational differences preventing Muslims from praying with the canonical prayers collectively. A well-informed Muslim would be able to detect the practises that differentiate Hanafis from Shafiʿis or Sunnis from Shiʿis, but in general, Muslims all pray, and do so in similar, mutually compatible ways. In more local terms, this means Muslims can and often do pray their *salah* in any mosque available to them. A mosque that focuses on offering a place to complete the daily prayers will rarely have a need to make visible their denominational identity. A final reason is that mosque congregations themselves are diverse. This is especially true of mosques serving a small Muslim community. Muslims in Britain are in general more denominationally diverse than one would find in the Muslim-majority world. A rural mosque, serving a large geographic area and a population of Muslims in the hundreds, despite their small numbers, would likely include South Asians working in the service industry, Middle Eastern students from a nearby university and North African doctors from the community hospital, all in one place. Each member of the congregation would hold some denominational identity, but would need to negotiate their religious practice with the other members of the congregation. Such arrangements are common, leading to the emergence of broadly ecumenical mosques, that subsume strong denominational affiliations in favour of welcoming a diverse congregation. As will be explored later, this ecumenical approach is not the only strategy adopted by mosques. Mosques both reflect and emerge out of denominational networks and practices.

Before continuing, there is an important issue of vocabulary. I have opted to use the term denomination for this analysis, over other terms such as sect. This is in part because denomination can avoid the negative connotations of terms such as sect. Denomination, in its etymological roots, has an emphasis on the name people may ascribe to themselves or others. This is also valuable. The description of diversity that follows is largely based on the self-description of Muslims, which can be more instructive and revealing than a focus on doctrinal issues. The Deobandis and Barelvis, for example, share many similarities theologically, methodologically, linguistically and historically but have traditionally had an antagonistic relationship. A denominational approach which emphasizes the collectives and terms used by Muslims themselves helps underscore these modes of difference.

The ecumenical mosque

There is already a process underway in British mosques that I argue indicates their future direction. Mosques adopt, with varying degrees of intensity, one of two strategies with regards to their denominational identity. The first is that of becoming an ecumenical mosque. That is to forgo any overt claims to denominational identity or religious particularism. They seek to create a space in which Muslims of all identities feel like they belong. Religious leadership in the mosques will have a denominational identity and be trained in a particular approach, but in their activities, sermons and teaching; they will emphasize the shared beliefs and actions that unite Muslims. This could be done passively, simply by avoiding denominational markers, or actively, by stressing the importance of Muslim unity.

The second approach is that of the denominational mosque. In this case, the mosque clearly adopts a particular approach. Its leadership advocates for the benefits of their theology, creed and approach over others. They will be clear in their denominational identity to others. Examples of this can be found across the UK. In Chapter 2, I discussed the way in which certain mosques adopted the role of being denominational headquarters for a movement and examples will also be discussed in this chapter. They exist on smaller scales too with denominational mosques and ecumenical mosques in close proximity to each other. Historically, there is precedent to this also. The relationship between the *zawiya* and the *jami' masjid* was somewhat similar, so too the shrine and the *masjid*. The dichotomy between a public orthopraxis and a denominational or local orthopraxis is a valid one worth exploring further. The beginnings of this reification are only just emerging in Britain, but if the development continues along this line the British mosque may have a more distinct division between the mosque serving all Muslims and the mosque serving some Muslims. This chapter will include examples of how denominational mosques (mosques with a clearly identifiable identity) negotiate that identity within a more diverse landscape of belief and practice amongst Muslims.

Rather than ecumenical mosques and denominational mosques being mosques in opposition, they are better understood as mosques specializing to provide a collective service to a wider body of Muslims. In this sense, they are interspatial mosques of the type discussed in Chapter 2. Denominational mosques can only exist when there is a broad and sufficiently capable ecumenical mosque serving the Muslim community. This dynamic is easily identified when visiting rural mosques. Mosques in the countryside, small towns and villages are almost always ecumenical mosques. The Muslims in the vicinity, diverse in ethnic and denominational identity, must cooperate to be able to purchase and maintain a space. No single denomination or approach can be given privilege or precedence in order to maintain the integrity of the Muslim community. However, once numbers and financial capacity increase the establishment of a denominational mosque is common in order to meet the specific religious needs and wants of the denominational mosque.[3] An example of such a rural mosque will be presented shortly.

Stornoway Mosque

Cardiff, where I am based, is located on the southern tip of Wales, a country itself based in the south of the British Isles. To drive to Stornoway would take in the region of fourteen hours heading north with no breaks. Practically then, it would be closer to a two-day trip across over 600 miles and a ferry ride to the Outer Hebrides (also known as the Western Isles or Eilean Siar). Nonetheless, I made the plans and preparations for the journey several times between 2019 and 2021, and each time pandemic restrictions stopped me from making the journey. Eventually I gave up, and instead interviewed one of the mosque's founders and committee members, Dr Abdul-Ghaffar, over the phone. I was interested in Stornoway Mosque for two reasons. First, its symbolic status as the northernmost mosque in Britain, and second, because it exemplified the characteristics of rural mosques. There are many places across the UK where one can find a handful of mosques all within walking distance of each other (both Chapters 2 and 4 provide such examples), rural mosques, by contrast, operate in a different dynamic, usually being the only mosque to serve a number of Muslims spread across a broad geographic area. Stornoway is located on a rural and somewhat isolated island of the northern coast of Scotland, and as such, for all the Muslims of the Western Isles, it is the only mosque available. According to the Scottish census of 2011, the Western Isles has a population of sixty-one Muslims. Abdul-Ghaffar indicates in our conversation that this has increased over the decade, with new migrants from Syria being settled on the island. For these sixty or so Muslims, if they wish to worship at a mosque, it must be Stornoway Mosque, and as such, there is an ecumenical approach by default.

The opening of the mosque in May 2018 received media coverage from al-Jazeera (Macguire 2018), BBC (BBC News 2018), the *Guardian* (Sherwood 2018a), and of course the local paper the *Stornoway Gazette* (Stronoway Gazette 2018). The coverage celebrated the mosque's small community and their challenges in opening a mosque somewhere so rural.

My congratulations to Abdul-Ghaffar on the opening of the mosque was met with a mixed reaction by him. He was critical of the notion that a new mosque, by default, should be something to celebrate. 'It is good, but you know, you have to actually also look on the other side of the coin, that it [new mosques] had become the main source of conflict as well.' He was referring to the conflicts in and between mosques, 'in Scotland, we don't have that kind of a problem yet'. He recounted his own upbringing:

> But in England, I grew up in Rochdale, there was a time, I'm talking about I'm going back to 60s now, when I first came to Britain, I was there I was in Rochdale. You know, we used to have one mosque, at that time, one mosque and everybody, irrespective of their nationality, or you know, the language or whatever, you know, all Muslims, they will actually congregate in that mosque. And we never had any issues. Never a problem. If you're familiar with Rochdale now, maybe it has 30 or so mosques, but now they're always in dispute with each other.

The growth of mosques, in Abdul-Ghaffar's view, also led to a type of factionalism that places with smaller Muslim communities could avoid. Abdul-Ghaffar jokes, 'I'm sure if we had a larger community in Stornoway we will probably say we will have two Eids as well, you know, but we just don't have that many Muslims to fight'. Stornoway, despite being atypical in its remoteness and isolation, is similar to many other rural mosques, where there is a necessity to provide a service to a broad range of Muslims, and where the limited resources of the community require a degree of cooperation and coexistence. Rural mosques are often the most ecumenical, but as we'll see, even in urban centres with large Muslim populations, there is an impulse to cater for British Muslim diversity.

British Muslim denominations

There is a joke I have heard numerous times in mosques. A Sufi, a Salafi, a member of the Tablighi Jama'at and a member of Hizb ut-Tahrir are in the mosque when the lightbulb goes out. A meeting is called to determine how to resolve the situation. The Sufi gathers everyone's attention and suggests 'we should all engage in worship, and then the light of Allah will fill this darkened mosque'. The Tablighi Jama'at member chimes in that they cannot change the lightbulb until 'we purify ourselves by going out on *khurooj* for at least forty days'.[4] The member of Hizb ut-Tahrir says it is futile to change the lightbulb and 'the priority should be to work to re-establish the Caliphate, who can then determine how best to change the lightbulb'. The Salafi silences everyone and in the darkened and silent mosque asks, 'brothers, where is the evidence from the Quran and the Sunnah that the lightbulb has gone out?'

I was told this joke over ten years ago in my own local mosque and provided you're vaguely familiar with the religious diversity of British Muslims, and the individual quirks of each group, the joke is a funny one. Without that prerequisite knowledge, the humour falls flat. It does, however, introduce the diverse landscape of denominational groups amongst Muslims in Britain. From Geaves's seminal work *Sectarian Influences Within Islam in Britain* (1996) to more contemporary works from journalists (Bowen 2014) and academics (Hamid 2016), the study of Muslim theological diversity in Britain has received sustained attention. While there is insight that can be gained from understanding the landscape of Muslim religious diversity, there is a danger too. The first is that British Muslim theologies are both complex and shifting – any description is partial, incomplete and open to criticism. Especially now, when British Muslims are redefining the terms on which they form their identity, anything written is only a snapshot of a moving picture. The second reason is that a focus on religious diversity can over-exaggerate the role of theology as an explanatory factor for human behaviour.

An overview of the denominations found amongst British Muslims is simple enough. The three overarching historical divisions are Sunni, Shi'i and 'Ibadi (with a modern schism, the Ahmadiyya). The most significant difference between Sunnis and the Shia is that the Shia believe authority remains in the hands of the family of the Prophet exclusively. This fundamental difference in authority is the schism which led Sunnis and the Shias to develop their respective traditions on parallel paths. The ʿIbadis are a less well-known tradition; there are fewer than 3 million worldwide (barely registering as a single percentile amongst the global Muslim population of 1.6 billion). Nonetheless, ʿIbadis constitute an early third schism, neither Sunni nor Shia (see Hoffman 2012 for an extended English language treatise on the group). In Britain, and indeed globally, Sunnis are the majority. There are very few reliable estimates of the number of Shiʿis in Britain, though they run about 6 per cent of British mosques (Elshayyal and Rajina 2021). The ʿIbadi is a minority everywhere but Oman, with adherents found in North and East Africa.

The Ahmadiyya are a more recent movement. They recognize a spiritual Caliphate begun by Mirza Ghulam Ahmad (died in Lahore, 1908). The Ahmadiyya believes Mirza Ghulam Ahmad to be a promised Messiah and Mahdi. The Ahmadiyya movement's fifth Caliph is based in London, from where he serves about 10 million Ahmadis globally. There is a significant (but small) population in the UK, second only to Pakistan, though there are no estimates on how many exactly but likely to be in the tens of thousands (see Ross-Valentine 2008 for an ethnographic account of the movement). The Ahmadiyya is keen on propagation of their faith. Muhammad Ali translated the Quran into English in 1917, predating the more famous translations by Marmaduke Pickthall (published in 1930) and Yusuf Ali (published in 1934). They were also involved, via missionary Khwaja Kamal-ud-Din (1870–1932), in the Shah Jahan Mosque (Salamat 2008). The Ahmadiyya also opened the first mosque in London, what was at first called the London Mosque and is now often called the Fazl Mosque (Naylor and Ryan 2002). In contrast to other Islamic movements in Britain, they are 'bureaucratically sophisticated' (Balzani 2010), something reflected in the structures of authority within their mosques which align themselves closely with their Caliph, Mirza Masroor Ahmad through a hierarchical structure (Moles 2009: 132–4). Mohammed Nasser Khan is a committee member for the Baitul Futuh Mosque in London and was involved throughout its construction. He describes the structure of the Ahmadiyya movement in Britain as follows:

> We have a very active Property Department Centre here in Morden. So the headquarters is here. But each mosque has its own mosque manager and secretary who's in charge of that mosque, he reports back to the centre with any repairs maintenance that he has to do, obviously, the routine maintenance, which is part of the budget for that mosque, but if there are extra repairs, or if this new capital project that is presented that committee looks at it, passes it, or rejects it, or whatever they need to do to oversee, committee that oversees all major projects, to make sure we're getting transparency, value for money.

The spiritual centre and headquarters of the Ahmadiyya movement is Baitul Futuh Mosque in London, one of the largest in the UK with a capacity of 13,000. The Ahmadiyya movement sustains itself despite the challenges of being few in number through strong networks of support (Balzani 2020). The centralized structure of the Ahmadiyya mosques in Britain means Nasser Khan is able to provide unambiguous answers about the number of mosques: 'we have 23 purpose-built mosques, 47 in total, the others are mission houses, converted mosques'. Aside from the forty-seven mosques, he continues, 'we've got 140 branches in the UK, not all of them have mosques, but they will have branches and meet in Scout halls and people's homes, but it's all structured.' The recognition of the Ahmadiyya by other Muslims has been a contentious issue, particularly in Pakistan where the Ahmadiyya face both social and political discrimination. The Ahmadiyya are not recognized as part of the Muslim faith by most other British Muslims on account of their heterodox views on Prophethood, and as such, generally operate independently.

Amongst Sunnis, there are the Deobandis. Deobandis are a South Asian Muslim tradition with origins in colonial India. They are arguably the most important actors within British Islam, especially today. They manage about 41.2 per cent of mosques in the UK according to the only available statistics (MuslimsinBritain.org 2017). The Deobandis, more than any other movement, invested in and opened the first British-based Darul Uloom, Muslim religious seminaries, educating imams and religious scholars in the British Isles as far back as the 1970s. Their prominence and influence in Britain has had a varied reception. Journalist Innes Bowen in a work on mosque leadership in Britain (2014) and Ed Husain, a self-described former 'extremist'-turned-intellectual (2021) both argue the Deobandis promote an isolationist, austere and subversive Islam at odds with wider Britain. Others, however, have highlighted their role in producing Muslim religious leaders (Birt 2005; Geaves 2008; Gilliat-Ray 2006, 2018; Mahmood 2012), and the importance of Deobandi seminaries in producing British-born and raised religious scholars (Geaves 2015; Sidat 2018, 2019). Explicit considerations of Deobandi mosques are rarer and with the exception of King (1997).

The Tablighi Jama'at are often associated with the Deobandi tradition. Its founder, Maulana Muhammad Ilyas Kandhlavi (d. 1944), was a graduate of a Deobandi Darul Uloom. But Kandhlavi felt the values and virtues of the Darul Uloom needed to be brought out of the seminaries and into the lives of ordinary Muslims, and so the Tablighi Jama'at took the scholarship of the Deobandis to the masses. The Tablighi Jama'at stress personal religious piety achieved through 'khurooj', short trips ranging from three days to four months, in which members of the group visit mosques, spending the night, preaching to local

Muslims, and engaging in personal worship and study. The Tablighi Jama'at has been described, with good reason, as the largest Islamic movement in the world. While numbers are hard to assess, its global membership is estimated by Peter Mandaville to be between 12 and 80 million, and in Europe, more than 150,000 (Mandaville 2010). Kuiper (2019: 111) lists conservative global estimates of 10–20 million. The difficulty in assessing the group's membership is in part due to its low barriers to entry, which may very well be part of their success. The Tablighi Jama'at population of Britain is nestled within the Deobandi, but its success has attracted members from outside the Deobandi tradition also.[5] The movement became embroiled in a controversy in the run-up to the 2012 London Olympics when they planned to build a new mosque on land they purchased near the Olympic Park site. The proposed mosque would have become the largest in Britain and potentially one of the largest in Europe. The project, dubbed the 'London mega-mosque', became a focal point for debating the identity of modern Britain and the rights of religious minorities. The entire affair is documented by scholar Zacharias Pieri (2015) who explores both the Tablighi Jama'at and the wider British population's response to the controversy. The mosque was never built.

Markazi Masjid in Dewsbury is often referred to as the European headquarters of the Tablighi Jama'at. The masjid is also a *madrasa*, vying with the Darul Uloom Bury to be the foremost Deobandi institute in Britain. The key activity associated with Tablighi Jama'at is the aforementioned 'khurooj', trips of 3, 10 or 40 days of visiting mosques (usually in the UK, but excursions to Europe and globally are also organized by and for more committed members), and simultaneously delivering a message of religious revival to Muslims both at the mosque and living nearby. The Tablighi Jama'at presents an interesting movement for creating links between mosques and operating within mosques but not in the traditional congregational form of local attendance. While some mosques, particularly those of a Barelvi background, refuse to host Tablighi Jama'at excursions, many other mosques from a wide denominational background do.

Also originating from South Asia are the Barelvis. On the surface, they are remarkably similar to Deobandis. Both follow the same school of Islamic jurisprudence (Hanafi), both celebrate many of the same figures, both trace their origins to the Indian subcontinent and both lay claim to Sufism. Their close proximity to each other – in terms of theology and geographic origins – often leads to a tension between the two movements, and Barelvi versus Deobandi polemics have been a feature of South Asian Islam for over a century. A superficial reading would place the division as being one of binaries, Deobandi legalism versus Barelvi mysticism or even Deobandi radicalism against Barelvi moderation. Tareen (2020) challenges these simplistic dichotomies, however, arguing that their competition is located around their respective response to colonialism. The polemic between Deobandis and Barelvis exists in Britain too, where Barelvis make up a significant remainder of the South Asian mosques. In Britain, one of the most successful branches of the Barelvi movement is Minhajul Quran (Morgahi 2015), which arguably holds the widest influence over Barelvi mosques. The Ghamkol Sharif Mosque in Birmingham (established 1992) is largely seen as a prominent national Barelvi mosque, though with no strict hierarchical position to describe it as a denominational headquarter.

An often overlooked tradition is that of the Fultolis. The Fultoli tradition emerges from Sylhet in Bangladesh and has been brought to the UK through the migration and settlement of British Bangladeshis who largely hail from the Sylheti region. The founder of the tradition is Shaykh Abdul Latif Chowdhury Fultoli, also known as 'Fultolir Saheb', 'Saheb Qibla Fultali' or 'Shamsul Ulama', who was a Bangladeshi Sufi *pir* hailing from the northeast region of Bangladesh known as Sylhet. He was born in 1913, in the Bengal region of British India and died in 2008. Academics have mistakenly identified Fultolis as Barelvis (Garbin 2005; Brown and Talbot 2006: 129) or classified their mosque as Barelvi-orientated (Eade and Garbin 2006: 189). The origins of this confusion are likely that both Fultolis and Barelvis engage more prominently in historic practices associated with Sufism (for example, the *mawlid* and communal circles of *dhikr*). Another reason for the confusion is the founder of the Fultoli movement traces his religious lineage (*silsila*) back to Sayyid Ahmad Barelvi (d. 1831, a student of Shah Muhammad Ismail, d. 1831), not to be confused with the founder of the Barelvi movement, Ahmad Raza Khan (d. 1921).[6] Shah Muhammad Ismail represented a scholarly tradition, separate and distinct from Muhammad Qasim Nanautavi (d. 1880, the founder of the Deobandi movement) and Ahmad Raza Khan. Fultoli Islam is the contemporary manifestation of that tradition. The link shared between Fultolis, Barelvis and Deobandis is that they emerged out of the vibrant and highly charged religious public sphere of India under the Raj, in which calls for religious reforms had both urgency and political relevance.

Fultoli mosques are often keen to include 'Shah Jalal' in the title of the mosque. There are thirty-four Shah Jalal mosques in the UK, with the majority in England but with two in Wales and one in Scotland. Alternative names include Jalalia (meaning 'of Jalal'), of which there are five (all in England bar one in Wales) or Jalalabad (meaning 'the place of Jalal') – there are seven such mosques, all in England. There are also similarly named Shah Poran mosques (a disciple of Shah Jalal), with one in Wales and four in England. This naming convention means that Shah Jalal is the Muslim figure with the most mosques named after him (forty-six in total, and a further five named after his disciple Shah Poran). No other figure comes close, including the Prophet Muhammad or famous companions (Abu Bakr, 'Umar, 'Uthman, 'Ali, or Bilal). Naqshbandi identifies thirty-two mosques belonging to the Fultoli tradition in his database (Muslims in Britain 2019), only some of which overlap with the eponymic naming convention discussed above. Likewise, Garbin (2005) identifies a handful of mosques in Birmingham with Fultoli-links (such as the Jalalabad Sunni Jame Masjid and Islamic Centre or the Muslim Association of Salisbury).

A comprehensive list of Fultoli mosques is however difficult to compile. The movement in Britain is going through a generational crisis, with few younger Muslims (even those raised in Fultoli families) maintaining an affiliation with the movement (Ahmed and Ali 2019). As such, mosques established by Fultolis can change ownership and identity. An example is the Jamia al-Jalalia, a madrassa and mosque based in Oldham opened in the early 2000s though officially incorporated as a trust in 2008. The Bangladeshi Fultolis found themselves unable to maintain the functioning of the madrassa, both financially and following a series of controversies involving trustees. In 2011, the trustees eventually handed over control to Jamia al-Karam, the flagship madrassa for the Barelvis in Britain, to continue the functioning of Jamia al-Jalalia, which was eventually reopened in 2012 as Oldham Islamic College. One of the best-known mosques with a Fultoli heritage is the Brick Lane Jamme Masjid. The establishment of the mosque was ostensibly a reaction to the more reformist tendencies of the East London Mosque nearby, leading to congregants purchasing the building, originally a chapel and subsequently a synagogue, and converting it to a mosque (Saleem 2018: 71). Indeed, Eade and Garbin observed how the commitment to Fultoli Islam amongst the mosque congregation was a stumbling block for the recruitment and growth of reformist movements amongst Bangladeshis in East London (Eade and Garbin 2006: 189). It remains staunchly Fultoli and annually hosts an 'urs on the anniversary of Fultolir Sahib's death.

More distinct from Deobandis, Barelvis and Fultoli Muslims are the Jama'at-i Islami, an Islamic reform movement, once again with links to colonial India, that consider the personal religious and spiritual devotions of Deobandis and Barelvis lacking and instead advocating an anti-colonial movement with a focus on political activism. The Quran has a social mission in their view, one which should bring Muslims out of the mosques and into public life. To revive Islam, in the view of the Jama'at-i Islami, is to engage to reform and improve social welfare and government (Kamran Bokhari n.d.). In this regard, they share much with the Middle Eastern *al-Ikhwan al-Muslimun* (or Muslim Brothers). The founder of the Jama'at-i Islami, Maulana Abu 'l-A'la Mawdudi (d. 1979), introduced a distinctive idea that amalgamated the thoughts of many others prior. He had witnessed the success of the nation-state and reasoned that the only way to truly achieve success against colonial imperialism was the establishment of an Islamic nation-state (Adams 1983). Jama'at-i Islami has grown beyond Mawdudi, however, taking their vision worldwide (Hartung 2014). In Britain there is no official branch of Jama'at-i-Islami, but its vision and teachings have been pursued by organizations described varyingly as 'Jamaat-related' or 'JI-inspired' (Nielsen 1992: 136; Ansari 2004: 350). The United Kingdom Islamic Mission is foremost amongst these, which 'was effective in creating a network of mosques in most British cities and towns with significant Muslim populations' (Hamid 2016: 19); however its more recent influence has waned, being overtaken by other national bodies such as the MCB. Other groups often linked with Jama'at-i Islami, for example the Islamic Foundation in Markfield, have become 'more circumspect about publicly announcing its ideological inspirations' (McLoughlin 2014: 213), confounding the decrease in influence of the movement in Britain. Over half of British Muslims have a South Asian heritage but Middle Eastern reform movements such as the Muslim Brotherhood play a significant role amongst British Muslims of Arab heritage, and by gaining new followers from other backgrounds. The Muslim Brotherhood I have already compared to Jama'at-i Islami. The founder, Hasan al-Banna, led a religious revival in inter-war Egypt, attracting young followers through preaching an egalitarian vision of Islam that appealed to the increasingly stratified Egyptian society. The Muslim Brotherhood's vision was always diverse and often far-reaching, and so the Brotherhood in Britain is largely represented through welfare organizations, youth groups and educational institutions.

The Jama'at-i Islami, Muslim Brotherhood and other groups such as Hizb ut-Tahrir are often grouped together as 'Islamists', though they represent a broad spectrum of views on the relationship between Islam, power and society. There is an added complication in recent years, 'Islamist' has taken on a more generalized meaning in public discourse that equates it with 'bad Islam'. These two factors have led some to argue that it is time to abandon the term entirely (Qureshi 2022). Hamid's (2016) work *Sufis, Salafis, Islamists* is one of the valuable accounts particularly of Islamist activism and organizing in Britain, with an articulation of a coherent framework for understanding the term. Hamed argues Islamism's presence can be mapped not in a strict hierarchy of authority but through a network of people and organizations with varying degrees of influence over one another.

The final, and significant, Sunni religious denomination to mention is the Salafis. Salafis differ from their co-religionists through the stress on recreating a pure Islam, free from any cultural influences or innovation, with a heavy textual emphasis. The simplicity of the Salafi message and its stress on scripture resonate well with Western-educated and literate young Muslims. The complex lives of Salafis in Britain, negotiating hostility and suspicion from outsiders, intra-religious tensions, and adherence to a counter-cultural religious orthodoxy are explored in a rich ethnographic account by Inge (2017) who focusses on converting women to Salafism. The descriptor 'Salafi' is itself debated and contested (Dawood 2020). Some adopt it as a pious goal, while others reject it in favour of more universal language (such as *ahl al-sunna wa-l-jama'a* – the term used historically to contrast with the *shia't 'Ali* or 'the partisans of 'Ali'). There are several distinct traditions of Salafism (Wiktorowicz 2006), some of which are strongly associated with a politically quietist approach (particularly that emerging out of Saudi Arabia), whereas others call for violent resistance to state powers (see Maher 2016 for an in-depth study of Salafi Jihadism as it is often termed). A further significant dimension of Salafi diversity is the *ahl-i hadith* movement. Hira Amin and Azhar Majothi (2021) provide an in-depth theological and institutional history of the movement in Britain. They correctly argue that the *ahl-i hadith* have been subsumed under wider Middle Eastern Salafism in academic studies, and the unique contribution of the movement to British Islam has been overlooked. The key *ahl-i hadith* organization, Markaz Jamiat Ahl-e-Hadith, operates from Green Lane Masjid and has fifty mosques affiliated with it (Amin and Majothi 2021: 10). Understanding this diversity within Salafism is important to understand contemporary British Muslims.

Green Lane Mosque, already discussed, is a key landmark for many Salafi preachers, hosting international scholars of repute. Its Salafi orientation has attracted criticism, both from political and academic circles (Shavit and Spengler 2021), yet it has also attracted commendation. 'Their projects include social campaigns such as dealing with knife crime, homelessness and plastic waste. This led to them winning the prestigious title of "Mosque of the Year" at the British Muslim Awards in January 2020' (Amin and Majothi 2021: 26). They previously won the Victorian Society's 2017 Birmingham & West Midlands Conservation Award (Victorian Society 2017) for their efforts in preserving the original architecture and design of Green Lane Mosque (originally a Victorian public library and baths). Green Lane occupies a unique role. In Chapter 3 I discussed how the mosque manager, Kamran Hussein, recognized Green Lane as an authority amongst Salafis in Britain, but even then, Kamran and the mosque leadership are careful not to exclude members of their congregation. In practical terms, this is achieved through their careful rhetoric:

> So we are conscious of what we say, and you know, how we say it, so that we don't come across too critical of other groups. Criticism where it's needed, but not criticising just for the sake of criticism or to differentiate yourself from another group. If you look at Green Lane Masjid now, you'll see that we've got an eclectic congregation mashallah, not only racially, but also different schools of thought. Also what you'll find is that you'll find people come here who aren't traditionally Salafi, so you'll have Deobandis, even Barelvis. And that's because if you look at the way that we teach it's very much you know middle of the path, very fact based. We are clear about our teachings and where our teachings are derived from I think people respect that.

The reception of this 'middle of the way' and 'fact based' teaching is another matter, but it's clear that even for a mosque recognized internationally as a Salafi mosque, the management and leadership are keen to remain ecumenically palatable.

Another example of a prominent British Salafi mosque is the Brixton Mosque and Islamic Cultural Centre, also known as Masjid Ibn Taymeeyah, founded in 1990. In 1994, the then 27-year-old Abdul-Haqq Baker was elected as chairman. Baker told me that his first strategy upon taking up leadership of the mosque was to address the internal conflicts that beleaguered it prior to his election. There was 'disillusionment' over 'harshness the abruptness with how the previous leadership was dealing with the whole congregation, who were predominantly not Salafi'. Instead Baker says he immediately began 'unifying the practice within the mosque, but I wanted to do it in a way that was palatable'. This unified practice was based on 'making us British Muslims, Salafi and proud of these identities'. He continues:

> So that's the first thing that I did . . . consolidating what my predecessor had done in trying to unify and have a focused ideology and practice, just like the Hanafi Mosques or the Deobandi mosques. So we then did that, as a convert mosque, and I dare say even if you go back to the first convert, Abdullah Quilliam[7], I don't think any [other] convert mosque has done that in the history of mosques in in the UK.

Even in the case of denominational mosques, there is an ecumenical impulse, a need to accommodate the unavoidable diversity present amongst British Muslims.

Amongst the Shias, the predominant group is the Ithna Asharis, the Twelvers, called such for their recognition of twelve imams who are the divinely-decreed successors after the death of the Prophet Muhammad. There are also the minority Ismaʻilis and the even rarer Zaydis. Though all have a presence in Britain, the British Ithna Asharis are the largest group. Their migration history emerges predominantly from Pakistan and Iran (Spellman 2004) though with notable communities from India, Iraq, Lebanon and Yemen. The structures of authority and hierarchy are more ordered amongst Twelvers than their Sunni counterparts, with international networks of scholarship and authority (Corboz 2015). While much of this authority stems from Iran and other parts of the Middle East, there are alternative networks of authority; for example, those maintained by South Asian Shiʻis who seek to preserve their South Asian history and identity as Shia in Britain in the face of a more organized collective drawing on the Middle East (Dogra 2017).

Shia Mosques are numerous, though a minority in the wider religious landscape. Shia activity has key localities across the UK, with the London borough of Brent being referred to as 'Shia Mile'. Scharbrodt explains that many of the centres of Shia worship are not mosques in a traditional Sunni sense:

> There are at least 20 Shia community centres located in Brent representing different national backgrounds but also different religious and political factions within contemporary Shia Islam. These community centres, referred to as husayniyya in Arabic and Persian or *imambarga* in the South Asian context, are not mosques but congregational halls used for Shia commemoration ceremonies, in particular those associated with 'Ashura', the first ten days of the Islamic month of Muharram when Shiʻis worldwide remember and mourn the death of Prophet Muhammad's grandson and third Imam Husayn on the plains of Karbala, in southern Iraq, in 680 CE. (2019).

As centres of Shia commemorations, they are important sites for Shia identity. Shia themselves may even attend Sunni mosques for the canonical prayers, but the maintenance and sustaining of particular Shia worship (specifically ceremonies around Muharram) against narratives that seek to emphasize shared Shia-Sunni worship is integral to many British Muslim Shiʻis (Dogra 2019) and part of the continued importance of exclusively Shiʻi sites of worship.

So in a sentence, the denominational diversity of British Islam can be described as Sunnis, Shiʻis, Ibadis and Ahmadis; further divided into the Deobandis, the Tablighi Jamaʻat, the Barelvis, Fultoli Islam, the Jamaʻat-i Islami, the Muslim Brothers, the Salafis, the Ithna Asharis, the Ismailis and the Zaydis. It is a long sentence, but naturally, such a sentence conceals more than it could ever reveal. They are nonetheless the salient terms in understanding the collectives and movements active on the ground of contemporary British Islam.

What next for British mosques?

This chapter has sought to introduce British mosques and their diversity today, but as a necessary consequence of doing so, it has largely been taxonomical by looking backwards to reformers, scholars and debates from the Middle East and South Asia. It has explored the globalized and also historical networks Muslims are part of. There is an important question – how long will these links hold? Will the debates that began in British colonial India or Egypt continue to have relevance to British Muslims today? What might the future look like for British Muslims and mosques in terms of the development of a 'British Islam'?

As this chapter began with a reservation about the utility of denominational analysis, so too it ends. There may, in a generation or two, be a more settled landscape of religious diversity amongst Muslims in Britain. For now, it is an environment of debate, contestation and change. Historically, such times have often been fertile grounds for new religious movements, and so too we must be prepared for radical changes in what it means to be a Muslim in Britain in coming decades.

6

The civil society mosque

In any mosque in the UK, on any given afternoon, you would expect to find the 'mosque uncles' sitting, chatting and conversing. They might be elderly Pakistani men, elderly Somali men, elderly Arab men, but always elderly and always men. In a small mosque outside London, one I was visiting primarily in order to pray before travelling home (rather than with any strict intention of fieldwork), I noticed something that caught my attention. The 'mosque uncles' sat in the corner, conversing as you would expect, but with them was a white British man with plastic bags on his shoes. The plastic bags caught my attention and curiosity. I listened to their casual conversation for a moment or two before approaching, offering a greeting of *salam* to the group. The gentleman with the plastic bags on his shoes said, reasonably fluently, 'wa-ʿalaykum al-salam', but clarified, 'I'm not Muslim, *beta*'. He used the Urdu term *'beta'* or 'son', a term of endearment, something which greatly amused his friends sitting with him. 'No?' I query. 'I'm a Christian', he responds, pulling out a small crucifix around his neck. 'Ah, you look like a regular here, except for the shoes.' He laughs. 'Oh, I am', he says, 'see the chairs here are a lot comfier than the pews'. Tim, I came to learn, was a semi-retired taxi driver. He spent decades speaking to the Pakistani drivers who worked the trade alongside him; they became his friends, and after he retired, he sought out their company still. He discovered that many of them still spent their days idly talking with each other, but sat in the mosque rather than on the bonnet of their cars waiting for the next fare. He saw no reason not to join them, so a few times a week he would come and catch up with his old friends. 'I still prefer the pub though, but these guys don't join me there', he jokes; the others present laugh at what is clearly an old joke they have shared before. This dimension of the mosque (that of a shared community space, a place to discuss and organize, to meet friends and strangers, part public and part intimate) is something not unique to mosques at all, but one which arguably is more difficult to find in contemporary Britain. The comparison to the pub made by Tim is not unreasonable. Both spaces serve similar functions in society by nurturing civil society. Civil society is the frame I wish to use to illustrate an important and overlooked component of mosques – their contribution to wider society. 'Civil society' as a framework is in my view a powerful theoretical disposition by which to analyse mosques and their activities, one that puts away misleading binaries such as religious/secular or organized religion/everyday religion and more appropriately weaves the mosque as an institution into the fabric of the wider society. This argument builds on the contention in Chapter 2 of mosques operating interspatially to provide services and of Chapter 3 that mosques are congregational. If we understand British mosques as having shifting and dynamic functions (Chapter 2) and of achieving this through the congregation which establishes and maintains the mosque through human and financial resources (Chapter 3), then this chapter places the mosque in a broader social sphere. It will show how mosques are sites of civil society organizing in Britain.

In Linda Woodhead and Rebecca Cato's authoritative edited collection, *Religion and Change in Modern Britain* (2012), Woodhead discusses 'regulation' of religion. She writes that

> a de facto deregulation [in the UK] of religion led to a growth in many new forms of religion – from holistic spirituality to Muslim 'radicalism' – which, when they eventually came to secular attention, called forth a panicked reregulation as state bodies struggle to take control of something which had become much harder for them to get a grip on – either intellectually or legislatively. (Woodhead 2012: 24)

Stepping away from an emphasis on the state and its influence, into the area of 'deregulated' religion, brings into focus an important element of mosque activity – the civil society sphere. It has been used in the study of mosques in Amsterdam (Bartels and Jong 2007), Australia (Peucker 2018) and Indonesia (Lussier 2019), but as of yet, has not been applied to the British context. In part, perhaps due to the very sudden growth of mosques that has not yet come to the attention of scholars of civil society.

Civil society itself is a debated and contested term, one with several different definitions. Michael Edwards argues that 'the concept is enduring because it offers a malleable framework' for exploring 'the patterns of collective action and interaction that provide societies with at least partial answers to questions of structure and authority, meaning and belonging, citizenship, and self-direction' (Edwards 2013a: 3). Edwards, and others, refer to what has become a classic definition of civil society by Michael Walzer, that 'civil society is the sphere of uncoerced human association between the individual and the state, in which people undertake collective action for normative and substantive purposes, relatively independent of government and the market' (Edwards 2013: 4; Walzer 1998: 123–4). It is this definition which can provide a rich and insightful perspective on the organizing and activities of Muslims through mosques. In the Islamic historical context, and in some limited places even today, a distinction is made between state-run mosques (*masjid sultani*) and the people-led mosques (*masjid 'ammi*) (Calder 1986: 44). From this perspective, every mosque in Britain is people-led, or *masjid 'ammi*, in other words, they are civil society mosques. While funding might be received for capital costs (as discussed briefly in Chapter 3), the loci of authority remains within the mosque's congregation. The civil society mosques of Britain stand in direct contrast to Kishwar Rizvi's 'transnational mosque' (2015). The civil society mosque is a community-led mosque in diaspora, emerging out of the internal networks of rank-and-file Muslims. In this chapter I argue that civil society, perhaps more than other concepts, provides an important means to understand the underlying functions of mosques and the concerns of those involved in them.

Civil society and religion

Adam Ferguson is credited with the first consideration of civil society in *Essay on the History of Civil Society* (1996 – first published 1767), but its more commonly cited proponents are Alexis de Tocqueville (Tocqueville, Mansfield and Winthrop 2002 – first published 1835) and more recently, Robert Putnam in *Bowling Alone* (2001).[1] Contemporary scholarship on civil society anchors itself: directly or indirectly, in agreement or contradiction with Tocqueville. Tocqueville wrote on the importance of preserving and developing 'civil society' as necessary for a functioning democracy. Religion has regularly featured as a dimension of civil society, and in the view of Tocqueville, a sustaining part of it.

> Religion in America takes no direct part in the government of society, but it must nevertheless be regarded as the foremost of the political institutions of that country; for if it does not impart a taste for freedom, it facilitates the use of free institutions. Indeed, it is in this same point of view that the inhabitants of the United States themselves look upon religious belief. I do not know whether all the Americans have a sincere faith in their religion; for who can search the human heart? But I am certain that they hold it to be indispensable to the maintenance of republican institutions. (1851: 200)

Tocqueville's argument about religion providing a moral component to civil society ('taste of freedom') and indirectly supporting the existence of other civil society institutions ('facilitates the use of free institutions') was taken considerably further by Robert Putnam in his seminal *Bowling Alone: The Collapse and Revival of American Community* (2001). The thesis of Putnam's book is that American society is losing its once vibrant civil society groups and that this threatens the vitality and strength of its democracy. Social capital, Putnam argues, is the key component of civil society, and it is at an all-time low (2001: 60) – thus the phenomenon of individuals bowling alone when at one time it would have been more common to bowl collectively with others in teams and leagues. Putnam argues religion is central to civil society:

> Churches provide an important incubator for civic skills, civic norms, community interest, and civic recruitment. Religiously active men and women learn to give speeches, run meetings, manage disagreements, and bear administrative responsibility. They also befriend others who are in turn likely to recruit them into other forms of community activity. In part for these reasons, churchgoers are substantially more likely to be involved in secular organizations, to vote and participate politically in other ways, and to have deeper informal social connections. (Putnam 2001: 66)

Putnam also maintains that religious institutions hold a high amount of both bonding and bridging capital (2001: 23) and that they provided the philosophical basis for political movements such as the Civil Rights Movement (2001: 68). Summarizing the role of religion in public life, he writes religious institutions support civic society 'directly, by providing social support to their members and social services to the wider community', referring to the institutions themselves, the religious rites but also the social services offered, but also 'indirectly, by nurturing civic skills, inculcating moral values, encouraging altruism, and fostering civic recruitment among church people' (Putnam 2001: 73).

Both Tocqueville and Putnam view religion as a positive force contributing to civil society and view religion in largely Christian, Protestant, Western terms. Putnam writes that 'for simplicity's sake I use the term church here to refer to all religious institutions of whatever faith, including mosques, temples, and synagogues' (2001: 65). This is largely a symbolic nod to religious diversity, since Putnam still deals primarily with a concept of religion that best describes American Christian congregationalism. While both Tocqueville and Putnam only nominally consider religion, and neither consider non-Christian traditions, their significance in the history of the idea of civil society makes their observations important, especially as Putnam's framing of the role of religion within civil society has remained influential. Putnam described religion as offering both 'bonding' and 'bridging' capital (two different forms of social capital), something that has continued to be central in the study of religion in society (see Furbey and Joseph Rowntree Foundation 2006; Lewis 2006a; Clarke, Jennings, and Carey 2008; Dinham and Lowndes 2009; Gale 2011). A more nuanced consideration has been offered by other scholars such as Miller (2013: 259) who argues the following:

> First, [religion] provides a place where moral conversation is encouraged, where people can debate ideas and policies and hone their arguments about what is right and wrong. Second, vibrant religious institutions inspire their members to act out their convictions – through voting, public demonstrations, and other political acts that embody their moral values. Third, religious institutions have a long history of establishing schools, social service agencies, and responding to crisis situations related to natural disasters such as earthquakes, floods, and drought. Fourth, religious institutions provide opportunities for human community through music, the arts, and various means for caring for one another. And fifth, religious institutions have time-honoured means of dealing with rites of passage: birth, puberty, marriage, child rearing, and death, the final passage.

Miller's argument is that religion intersects with civil society in five ways (spaces for moral conversation, collective action, provision of services, mutual care and rites of passage). There is a tendency to consider religion as a subset or minor component of 'real civil society', articulated well by Mario Peucker who writes that 'volunteering within a minority community context, however, does not receive the same appreciation and support as volunteering in "mainstream" civil society groups' (2018: 1). This attitude is present in both Tocqueville and Putnam's framing too, as they consider religion a preparatory ground for wider civil society, rather than an important dimension of civil society in its own right. This devaluing of religion in civil society is perhaps one of the reasons why mosques have been overlooked in the study of contemporary British civil society. In a single lifetime, the number of mosques in Britain has burgeoned from a mere handful to over 2,000. Each is congregationally run, receiving the bulk of their financial support from other Muslims. Each is run to meet the needs and services of Muslims, and sometimes a wider community. All rely significantly on volunteer contributions in terms of time, finances and expertise. They are testaments to the health and vitality of civil society, yet no scholarship on civil society has interrogated the emergence of the British mosque.

The three dimensions of civil society operation in mosques can be thought of as 'Us', 'You' and 'We'. 'Us' refers to the activities of mosques designed to meet the social and civic needs of Muslims themselves, providing services, organizing and responding to the challenges faced by Muslims directly. 'You' refers to a space of engagement and interaction where the attention of the mosques turns away from the immediate needs of their congregation or Muslims more generally and towards the locality and community in which they are based. 'We' refers to the coalitions, alliances and partnerships that Muslims forge with others in civil society to address collective needs, perhaps best illustrated through their participation in community organizing. As with any generalization, these divisions are not strict. Nor are they chronological (moving from 'Me', 'You' and 'We' in an ordered fashion). There are also clearly ways in which providing services to others ('You') can address important internal goals ('Us'). They do, however, indicate the orientation of activities and the networks and relationships in action.

Us

As discussed in Chapter 2, the impetus for mosque building is directly related to the settlement of Muslim families (following the first waves of migration consisting largely of single working men). There were religious, cultural and social needs that Muslim families had that might have been supported by families, communities and even the state in their countries of origin, but absent in Britain. The primary civil society focus of mosques, from their inception till today, is the internal needs of the Muslim community and a desire to preserve and further their interests. More specifically, the education and socialization of children.

The creation of a space, both physical and symbolic, for Muslims, helped the Muslim community express their agency in a range of other arenas in public life. This would fall, in terms of Miller's division, of the mosque as a space for moral conversation, service and mutual support (2013: 259). It is also useful to think of this dimension of the mosque in terms of Nancy Fraser's 'subaltern counterpublics'. Fraser noted that access to the public sphere was not universal. She argues that 'where there is only a single, comprehensive public sphere ... members of subordinated groups would have no arenas for deliberation among themselves about their needs, objectives, and strategies' (Fraser 1992: 123). Muslims, excluded from the mainstream public sphere by virtue of their race, language and religion, created alternative spaces via mosques. In such counterpublics, the subaltern (anyone excluded in the hegemonic culture) 'formulate oppositional interpretations of their identities, interests and needs' (1992: 123). This dimension of the mosque, as a 'semi-public sphere' for Muslims, was referred to in a sermon at one mosque with the imam encouraging the congregants to think of the mosque as a 'coffee-shop', he drew on his own Middle Eastern heritage and the coffee shop as not just a place for socializing but also for intellectual debate, networking and organizing (see Mostafa and Elbendary 2021 for a study of the Egyptian coffee house). This dimension of the coffee shop was noted as an important component, alongside social media, of the Arab Spring (Lim 2012). The idea of a 'coffee-shop mosque' is comparable to a subaltern counterpublic, and throughout my continued research, it emerged as something invariably present in British mosques in the contemporary period. This seems equally true of mosques in their earlier stages of British Muslim development; Werbner in her studies of a Pakistani community in England described the mosque thusly:

> Urban mosques in Britain are centers of communal affairs. . . . The mosque is the base for teaching collective discipline, organization, and internal fund raising, the springboard for regional and national political alliances, and a training ground in polemics and adversary politics. Mosques link town and country and constitute public arenas for political debate. (Werbner 1996: 115)

Additionally, Sophie Gilliat-Ray's description of British mosques as 'places for the production of Islamic discourse and for the sustaining of Muslim identity in the context of wider British society' (2010a: 182) resembles the discursive nature of Fraser's subaltern counterpublics; mosques in Britain are spaces where subalterns 'invent and circulate counter discourses to formulate oppositional interpretations of their identities, interests and needs' (1992: 123). Rhys Dafydd Jones (2010) explicitly applies the framework of the subaltern counterpublic to mosques in rural Wales. His focus, however, is on 'storefront' mosques, arguing that rural mosques seek to be hidden from view and the public landscape. 'These inconspicuous spaces, private in the sense that admission is regulated by knowledge of its purpose, are home to public actions, although not those that are necessarily the concern of society-at-large' (Dafydd Jones 2010: 764). Not all mosques in Britain are inconspicuous, however, with many established as landmarks and symbols of Muslim settlement; London

Central Mosque (also known as Regent's Park Mosque) is one such example of a mosque which both architecturally and in terms of its organizing seeks to be a recognized landmark.

Why is it useful to think of mosques as 'subaltern counterpublics'? The answer is in the way it sheds light on the relationship between Muslims and the wider society, the internal dynamics of Muslim heterogeneity, and attempts at Muslims to develop power and resources to meet their own needs. Fraser summarizes Habermas's public sphere as 'the space in which citizens deliberate about their common affairs' (1992: 57). Yet, as Fraser argues, this is not something all citizens have access to equally. There is a hierarchy of acceptance of what issues matter, what identities belong, and an implicit rationalization of some concerns being more valid (universal) than others (particular or personal). Instead of trying to describe the world as it should be, the failure of Habermas, Fraser attempts to describe the world, or rather the public sphere, as it is. She writes that 'subordinate social groups – women, workers, peoples of color, and gays and lesbians – have repeatedly found it advantageous to constitute alternative publics' (1992: 67). What is the function of subaltern counterpublics? Fraser is broad in her conceptualization, considering them to hold 'emancipatory potential' writing they are both 'spaces of withdrawal and regroupment' as well as 'bases and training grounds for agitational activities' (1992: 68). Mosques acting and operating as subaltern counterpublics stress the agency of British Muslims. Having found themselves in a new country and facing the challenges of exclusion, mosques became a means to organize and exert their influence. They are not just places where doctrinal adherence is manifested, but as seen in examples later in this chapter, also mediums through which Muslims can shape their new contexts.

There are two features that support mosques acting as subaltern counterpublics. The first is its accessibility. Any Muslim can attend any mosque, meet and discuss with friends or co-religionists, enjoy the privacy of the mosque or seek out company. There are no strict reasons why a non-Muslim could not do the same (and indeed, like Tim, many do), though just as the public sphere at large is designed to be comfortable and familiar to certain people and not for others, so too is the mosque. Second, and most importantly, is the mosque as an intellectual space of discussion and debate. From the regular Friday sermon, to specifically hosted lectures, mosques are places of discourse. During my fieldwork, I often captured mosque activity with a sound recorder. These audio snippets would often capture hundreds, if not thousands, of words in a short period of time. These could be as routine as announcements, but more often reminders, *halaqa*s, *wa'z*, the *khutba* and so on. They might be commentary on Quranic verses and *hadith*s, expositions of hagiographic stories, reflections on current affairs. And while the speaker was often male and given the privilege of a pulpit, it was rarely a one-way affair. Congregants would discuss the sermons afterwards, or if they strongly agree or disagree, approach the speaker after they completed their talk. These discussions were not siloed either. Many Muslim scholars maintain some form of itinerant preaching, travelling from mosque to mosque by invitation or design, creating a discursive national space for Muslims.

Bonding capital

Robert Putnam argues religion supported civil society through the creation of 'bonding' and 'bridging' capital. He explains:

> Examples of bonding social capital include ethnic fraternal organizations, church-based women's reading groups, and fashionable country clubs. Their networks are outward looking and encompass people across diverse social cleavages. Examples of bridging capital include the civil rights movement, many youth service groups, and ecumenical religious organisations. (2001: 22)

Like Putnam, I am keen to stress 'bonding and bridging are not "either-or" categories into which social networks can be neatly divided, but "more or less" dimensions along which we can compare different forms of social capital' (2001: 23). Mosques offer the capacity for 'bonding' in various, functional ways. In 2017, I had the opportunity to meet local authorities participating in the Syrian Vulnerable Persons Relocation Scheme. The scheme was funded by the Home Office and open to any local authority in Britain. It provided an attractive option for local authorities who had not traditionally housed migrants prior nor participated in asylum dispersal systems, but had available housing stock, places in schools and budgets in need of bolstering with available funding. One local authority Community Cohesion Officer from a small rural village told me how surprised he was at the resourcefulness of some of the new settlers from Syria. 'They had only been here a few weeks, but already knew a doctor, knew a dentist, where to find halal food, some of the stuff we had been trying to set up for them. One had already found a job.' When I queried how they managed to achieve this, he responded, 'well one of the first things they did when they arrived was ask about a mosque, and we have a small one that we put them in touch with. It seems they managed to connect with people there'. The ability to meet, connect and network with new people is one of the key benefits of mosques to the congregants.

'Social capital', as it is described by Pierre Bourdieu (1986), is the 'aggregate of the actual or potential resources which are linked to possession of a durable network of more or less institutionalized relationships of mutual acquaintance and recognition – or in other words, to membership in a group' (1986: 21). Every mosque brings together Muslims, and very often, across lines of class, age, ethnicity and, less commonly but still present, gender. This process is a natural by-product of the congregational and rhythmic attendance of mosques. The sacred rhythm discussed in Chapter 4, which brings congregants to the mosque regularly throughout the day, and even more so on key festivals and days, becomes a mechanism to build the social capital amongst mosque attendees. By being a physical place of coming together, it not only contributes to the forming of community but also establishes relationships that can be utilized in more tangible and concrete ways. Bourdieu writes that 'the volume of the social capital possessed by a given agent thus depends on the size of the network he can effectively mobilize and on the volume of the capital (economic, cultural or symbolic) possessed in his own right by each of those to whom he is connected' (1986: 24). In any given mosque, a congregant can establish relationships with professors, doctors and politicians, as well as mechanics, plumbers and business owners. These are consciously facilitated through Islamic etiquette, or *adab*, echoing Bourdieu's contention that a 'network of relationships is the product of investment strategies, individual or collective, consciously or unconsciously aimed at establishing or reproducing social relationship that are directly usable in the short or long term'. Thus in any mosque, strangers will exchange *salam* as they enter and leave. Life cycle events, such as births celebrated through *aqiqas*, funerals and weddings are also encouraged in the Islamic tradition to be marked with food shared widely, events mosques often host. These further consolidate familiarity and congeniality. Some mosques facilitate this further with coffee mornings, quiz nights, board game nights and social outings. The regular prayers, bolstered by the specific events, hosting talks or charity fundraisers, all bring people into regular contact. These create both formal and informal moments of interaction, the exchange of names, eventually contact details and subsequently the building of a network easily accessed. The informality by which these networks develop is easily overlooked, and certainly from the perspective of mosques, something rarely considered as their primary function. But it allows, as in the example earlier, for a relative newcomer to an area to quickly get in touch with a wide range of individuals from varying backgrounds.

Building capital

Werbner, in her previously cited description of the mosque, describes it as 'the springboard for regional and national political alliances' (1996: 115). This sentence in passing points to an important capability and capacity created through the network of mosques in Britain, namely its ability to support the establishment of other civil society groups.

An illustration of this relationship is demonstrated clearly if one attend's the *tarawih* prayers held during Ramadan in almost any British Sunni mosque. The specifics of the *tarawih* may differ between mosques – for example, the precise timing, whether it is eight or twenty *raka'at*, the amount of Quran recited – but something which invariably remains the same is the fundraising. The ubiquity of fundraising during Ramadan has become a point of humour amongst Muslims who bemoan its predictability. Nonetheless, this has not stopped their generosity. The Muslim Charities Forum estimated that during Ramadan 2018, £130 million was donated to British charities by Muslims. This is a sizable and significant figure for British Muslims who are largely still on the lower end of socio-economic scales. It is common that during a break in the *tarawih* prayers, fundraisers will pass around buckets in the mosque, or appeal for direct debit subscriptions, and sometimes even ask for more substantial pledges of support (ranging from the tens of thousands to the hundreds). Charities themselves begin booking fundraising slots in mosques months in advance, with volunteers or paid employees sometimes travelling across the country to pitch and collect the donations on the night. The most in-demand nights are the last ten nights, when Muslims are encouraged to seek *laylat al-Qadr* (or the Night of Power) through acts of worship and charity. If one were to attend the *tarawih* prayers at any sizable British mosque, then they could expect to see fundraising appeals from Muslim schools, both supplementary and full-time, international relief charities such as Muslim Aid and Islamic Relief, single issue campaign groups such as Muslim Engagement and Development (MEND),[2] broader alliances such as the United Kingdom Islamic Mission (UKIM), local youth groups including Muslim Scouts and local causes and campaigns. The diversity speaks to the interconnected relationship between mosques and other civil society groups.

Returning to the idea of a subaltern counterpublic, the mosque is an institution to tap into both financial resources and human resources. The ability for a charity in northern England, for example, to access funds and support across the breath of the UK is a sizable advantage for any civil society start-up, until such a time that they can maintain those networks independently. It is not uncommon for hyperlocal projects to receive funding and resources from across the UK, appealing to a Muslim sense of solidarity. The UK networks of mosques, and the networks each mosque can access more locally, act to reinforce and grow Muslim civil society, nurturing and sustaining other parts of it. The mosque is not just a site of civil society, but also a nursery – wider civil society groups and networks emerge out of it.

You

The previous section shows how mosques can function to serve the needs of Muslim communities themselves, reinforcing social bonds, creating networks, providing a space for discursive resistance and safety, as well as providing a springboard for other projects and activities. It underlined a continuing argument that mosques act as subaltern counterpublics. One important dimension of such spaces, as argued by Nancy Fraser, is that they allow for minorities to engage with the mainstream, but from a position of strength, organizing and confidence. Despite being spaces of withdrawal, they maintain 'an orientation that is publicist' (1992: 67) and its purpose is to engage 'into ever widening areas' (1992: 67). This section turns to address that engagement. In particular, it will examine interfaith and welfare provision as two key activities mosques have engaged in. While the framework of 'Us', 'You' and 'We' is continued, these divisions are simply to emphasize the forms of civil society operation mosques engage in. Interfaith, for example, also meets the needs of Muslim communities in addressing misconceptions, creating alliances and fostering positive relationships as much as it is about creating 'bridging capital' or fostering community cohesion.

Interfaith

In 2016, Amazon Prime launched their Christmas advert. A Christian priest, identifiable from his clerical collar, is visited by a friend, a visibly Muslim imam bearing a beard and topi (a round skull-cap with a flat top). Both are elderly, and share a cup of tea while talking jovially. As they stand to depart, both laugh as they struggle to get up. The next scene shows them order gifts for each other independently, and then their mutual amusement as they open the gifts once they arrive; both purchasing knee braces for the other. The final scene shows the priest, in long black flowing robes, kneel on one knee for prayer in a church, and the imam, in a white thobe, prostrate for prayer in a mosque. The advert closes with the Amazon logo, and the backing music (*I Giorni* by contemporary classical musician Ludovico Einaudi) helps convey the tone of optimism and warmth. The advert emphasizes the shared faith of the priest and imam, their similarities, and friendship, as well as the potential for next day delivery offered by the website.

It was a well-received advert, getting positive news stories in multiple outlets (Kuruvilla 2016; Sweney 2016; Westbrook 2016). Part of its success was that it did not describe a completely fictional aspirational story. The idea of a meaningful friendship between an imam and priest was recognizable and celebrated because it was in-part true to life. Mosques across Britain have been part of interfaith activities, ranging from the local to the international, for over a decade. In Chapter 2, the interspatial mosque model was utilized to describe how some mosques have added new functions in addition to the daily prayers, education and communal rituals that form the bulk of mosque activities. These new functions are often categorized as fulfilling the *sunna*, a vision of what a mosque should be inspired by the Prophet's Mosque during the Prophet Muhammad's lifetime. Interfaith is often included in these activities. Chapter 3 argued that mosques are increasingly congregational; this too has been important in the development of interfaith activities. It has provided an institutional model familiar to other faith groups as a platform for engagement. On a national level, Christian, Jewish and other faith leaders (as well as politicians) have struggled to identify Muslim counterparts equivalent to the Jewish Chief Rabbi or Christian Archbishops; however, this problem is absent at the local level. An individual church is able to easily identify and engage with a mosque, recognizing some parity between the size, parish model and authority of the imam and that of a local priest (despite such comparisons in religious leadership often being unhelpful).

Interfaith activity itself has been common in the UK but the involvement of mosques and Muslims is something that had its impetus in the last two decades. One of the first recorded examples of interfaith activity in Britain dates to May 1901. London hosted a congress that brought together twenty-one religions under the banner of the 'International Council of Unitarian and Other Liberal Religious Thinkers and Workers'. It is one of the first recorded examples of an interfaith organization on British shores, and the organization still operates today as the International Association of Religious Freedom (IARF British Chapter). A small number of less grand examples of interfaith can also be found in the same era. Abdullah Quilliam, the Victorian lawyer and convert to Islam who founded and ran the Liverpool Institute (see Chapter 1), travelled across the country sharing a platform with priests and rabbis and speaking on topics of religion. His title (declaring himself 'Shaykh al-Islam of the British Isles'), education, and British heritage all helped to shape him as an ideal counterpart to other religious leaders from Christian and Jewish backgrounds. While there are the exceptional cases of interfaith activity involving Muslims in the early part of the twentieth century, it was only after the Second World War that Muslims settled in numbers meaningful enough to provide opportunities for interfaith activity more broadly. These early interfaith groups were pioneers, and often incredibly local in their focus, with an aim of building relationships across churches, mosques, temples and synagogues in a given town or city.

In the late 1980s, Brian Pearce, a civil servant and himself an advocate of interfaith understanding, took a sabbatical to explore the possible need for a new interfaith linking mechanism which could enable faith communities, interfaith groups and other relevant types of body to come together and make common cause. After a two-year period of consultation, the Inter Faith Network for the UK was brought into being by its then sixty founding bodies in 1987. Its director in 2023 is Harriet Crabtree who started working there in 1990 after studying and teaching in the United States where she was based at the Centre for the Study of World Religions and Harvard Divinity School.

For a variety of reasons, the 2000s was a decade that saw an acceleration on local inter faith group formation and also the formation of some of the largest and most significant interfaith organizations in Britain. 'The growth in local interfaith activity in recent years has been very rapid' writes Brian Pearce, 'from around 30 in 1987, the number of local inter faith bodies rose to just under 100 in 2000, and in 2010 reached around 240' (Pearce 2012: 152). It is also the era in which Muslims became active players in interfaith, driven by a series of crises bringing Muslims into the public eye. The first of these was the 'race riots' in the north of England during the summer of 2001, followed shortly by the terror attacks of 9/11. 'Local Inter Faith Activity in the UK: A Survey by the Inter Faith Network', published in 2003, gives insight into the rapid acceleration of local activity after 2001. The July bombings of 2005 in London which saw fifty-two people killed was a watershed moment in Britain. Amongst other things, the political establishment viewed the attack as underlining the importance of community cohesion and further interfaith work. The findings and recommendations of the 'Commission on Integration and Cohesion', a commission set up in the wake of 7/7, recommended interfaith work as a remedy to 'Islamic terrorism' (CLG 2007). In the years since, the logic of community cohesion and radicalization has become further entrenched. It is something Bilal Hassam is particularly concerned about. Bilal is a medical doctor by training but a Muslim activist by vocation; his father also starred in the Amazon advert as the imam.

While studying medicine at university, he became involved in Muslim community groups, both local and national. His passion for organizing and interfaith work led to him enrolling for a Masters in Theology and Interreligious Relations at De Montfort University during his final year of medical studies. After spending several years working as a doctor, he decided to leave the profession to take up a leading role in British Muslim TV, a television channel aimed at Muslims. Reflecting on his involvement in interfaith work over the years, he shared his views that 'interfaith, or inter-religious encounter, happens everywhere. It's a big spectrum'. He is critical of the direction taken by the national interfaith scene, however: 'the conversation on faith and interfaith have become politicised, councils, governments and political parties have become involved in interfaith on a big national level, but they introduce counter-productive rules of engagement, there are certain conversations you can't have, certain views you can't hold'. It is why the local mosque interfaith engagement is so important in his view. 'The mosque is the only place with potential, it's unadulterated, they're coming to it new, raw, and it tends to be more genuine and longer lasting, and it is cut off from the wider agenda. The engagement is just so much more richer.'

In terms of the national scene, interfaith activity flourished during the 2000s. Archbishop Rowan Williams convened the Christian Muslim Forum in 2006, led by Julian Bond as Director, born out of work started by the previous Archbishop, George Carey. It sought to 'develop strong and committed relationships' between Muslims and Christians, while also hoping to draw on both traditions for peace and conflict resolution. 'Our faith encourages us to work together and we are committed to pluralism; our outlook on our society is pluralistic', explains Bond. The Forum has had a number of achievements, including a significant set of guidelines to help couples in Christian–Muslim marriages. However, Bond considers one of the Forum's most significant achievements is responding to national narratives about religion.

> The biggest effect of our work had been the positive response to and media interest in our 'Religious Festivals' statement (first issued in 2006). This arose out of secular concerns in the UK that celebrating, or even referring to, Christmas could be offensive to people of other faiths. Our statement responded to these concerns and generated a huge media interest, including outside the UK. The statement's impact continues each year at Christmas-time and it has begun to change attitudes.

Julian, however, is confident in what the Forum has meant for interfaith in Britain: 'In recent years we have seen increasing cooperation between churches and mosques encouraged by the Forum but also by our partners at the Islamic Society of Britain, Muslim Council of Britain and the Mosques and Imams National Advisory Board.'

Inter-community

Another type of encounter organized by mosques is the 'Visit My Mosque' campaign, run by the MCB. It moves beyond the interfaith category, opening up even further to the general public as a whole. The project launched in 2015 with an intention of providing a unified platform for mosque visits. While 'mosque open-days' were not uncommon activities, 'Visit My Mosque' was a national project that helped fuse together disparate mosque outreach events into a single national event. The first year it ran, twenty mosques took part; in 2016 this number increased to over eighty. In 2019, the last year it ran physically before coronavirus restrictions forced a digitalshift, 250 mosques took part across the UK. The event drew interest from journalists, politicians, celebrities and even large businesses, with Ben and Jerry's Ice Cream publishing a post about the event and encouraging people to 'try a different flavour' (Ben and Jerry's 2019). The campaign encapsulates the way in which mosques can be places for building bridges across community groups. 'Visit My Mosque' was a national project, but the local activity is what made it possible, and local relationships were built as a result. Dr Kumail Versi from Mahfil Ali (a small house mosque in London, also known as the Shia Ithna'ashari Community of Middlesex) issued a statement in 2019 describing the event intending to 'reach out and build bridges, encourage deeper religious understanding and above all, to provide the opportunity for more people to get to know one another'. The same idea was conveyed in the MCB's 2016 press release, stating that they wished the project to 'provide a platform for Muslims to reach out to fellow Britons and explain their faith and community beyond the hostile headlines' (Muslim Council of Britain 2016). The Visit My Mosque campaign illustrates well the desire mosques have to engage and build links beyond the Muslim community alone.

Mosques in Britain are sites of interreligious and inter-community encounter, by fomenting and strengthening internal networks, they develop the capacity to meaningfully reach out to other communities. This dual capacity, to withdraw as well as to reach out, is a dimension of the mosque's function as a subaltern counterpublic (Fraser 1992: 68). It also helps illustrate how civil society itself operates. For people to create networks, engage in communal activities, and foster relationships, there need to be institutions, organizations and groups by which to achieve this. The mosque is one such institution of this type. A poor reading would view this capacity as being in addition to the mosques' religious function but a more accurate reading would recognize that this is in fact part of its religious character.

Service

The inclusion of a broader welfare-focused services in mosques has been a slow process. There are early examples noted in the literature from the mid-2000s (Ghouri 2005; McLoughlin 2005; Muslim Council of Britain 2006). Their emergence can be tied to the increasing involvement of younger Muslims in the mosques, and growth in the mosque resources, financial security and outlook. It is also part of a wider shift in the British welfare provision. Evers et al. (2005) describe the historic roots of the contemporary 'welfare mix' of the UK. Religion, namely the Church, was the first provider of social welfare. It was a responsibility increasingly undertaken by the state with various legal reforms in the twentieth century, reaching its cultural zenith following the Second World War. In recent years, they argue, welfare provision has been delegated to the 'third sector', charities part or wholly funded by the state monies, and now, by 'Faith Based Organisations' (Evers, Laville and Taylor 2005). The mosque, like many other faith groups, provides these charitable services as part of their social mission, but in contrast to faith-based organizations and the contemporary welfare mix, does so without funding from the government, local authority or grant-making bodies.

Today, the provision of services by mosques is so expansive that it is difficult to either quantify or calculate. There is a regular stream of 'good news' stories from local outlets highlighting foodbanks, litter picks, homeless shelters, and so on. There are also those crisis moments in which mosques provide services. After flooding in the north of England in 2015, 2019 and 2020 ('Mosques Mobilise to Help Those Affected by Floods in Northern England' 2015; BBC News 2019), local mosques responded with on-the-ground support by providing a base for relief operations, food and shelter and teams of volunteers, many of whom had an intimate knowledge of the local area. During and after the Grenfell Tower fire, the nearby Al-Manaar Mosque provided support both materially and pastorally to the victims of the tragedy, including professional counselling (Kellaway 2018).

However, the most recent critical moment emerged during the Covid-19 pandemic, when many mosques either started or expanded the services and provision they offered to the wider community. The pandemic thus serves as a useful case study to understand how mosques have moved into welfare provision more widely. Understanding this community service as emerging from the mosque as a site of civil society is revealing for numerous reasons. The first is that it underlines the resources the mosque has available that allow it to undertake this function in the first place. Mosques have access to 'organised people' and 'organised money', what may also be described as both social and financial capital. They can mobilize volunteers in significant numbers for a common goal, as well as access networks to raise funds needed either to carry out a project or to support another endeavour. They have the physical space available too. More than that, through their networks and volunteers, they are able to draw on a range of experience and knowledge.

One of the most significant services offered by mosques during the pandemic was related to food. The provision of food is a key charitable action within the Islamic ethos, but there are other reasons for its ubiquity amongst mosque services. Churches, in partnership with Trussell Trust, have long been providing 'foodbanks' (Caplan 2016; Denning 2019; Dowler 2014). It provided a model for mosques keen on supporting the local community to follow. The involvement of many South Asian Muslims in the food or catering industry (whether restaurants, takeaways, cash and carries or corner stores) meant that there were also well-established supply chains and a confidence in large scale food provision.

The Unity Centre in Oldham is one mosque which, through its charitable arm the Greengate Trust, offered cooked food as well as food parcels during the pandemic, especially to the elderly and homeless. Similar food parcel services were offered by the Rabbaniah Islamic Cultural Centre in Cardiff, Belfast Islamic Centre, and Kirkcaldy Central Mosque. Foodbanks were set up in dozens of mosques across Britain, as well as open kitchens with hot and tinned foods such as the one at the Qadria Jilania Islamic centre in Manchester, serving around 300 people daily during the spring of 2020.

Other mosques sought to support the British National Health Service (NHS) through fundraising, especially during the first peak of the pandemic in 2020. Fundraising was arranged by several mosques to provide 'Personal Protective Equipment' or PPE (an urgent need during the early days of the pandemic) to healthcare workers. Canterbury Mosque, Green Lane Mosque in Birmingham, Dar ul-Isra in Cardiff, and Al Adab Institute in Oldham were amongst many mosques who raised substantial amounts of money for PPE for healthcare workers, as well as organizing their purchase and delivery. The acts usually garnered media attention. These acts of charity echoed a similar weekly public 'clap' that took place between March and May in 2020, with people across Britain standing on doorsteps to thank the NHS and other 'key workers' for their service. Charity aimed at NHS carers can be seen from the framework of civil religion (Bellah and Hammond 1980), the values, rituals and public displays of piety woven into a nation-state. Steven Kettell and Peter Kerr have argued that in post-Brexit Britain, the NHS was a site of mythological and sacred significance (2021), and Spencer has argued that 'clapping for the NHS' is a religious rite binding the nation, comparable to saint days of the past (Spencer 2021). Gratitude to the NHS is a key component of the values and virtues expected of contemporary Brits in the public sphere, and mosque participation in similar activities emphasized a shared moral framework. That is not to say the acts were cynical or duplicitous but rather indicates that what is considered virtuous by British Muslims is as much influenced by the British context as it is Islamic sources.

Several mosques also organized volunteers in response to the pandemic, providing a broad range of services from doing food shopping and delivery, picking up prescriptions, distributing sanitary items, nappies and other such items. The 'Muhafiz Covid-19 Rotherham Response Unit' is one example, as is the 'Muslim Volunteers Cardiff' group and 'Cambridge Central Mosques volunteer response team'. These volunteer collectives, usually based out of or closely affiliated with mosques, mobilized ready and willing networks of mosque members.

The Al-Abbas Islamic centre in Birmingham became the first mosque to run as a vaccination centre, joined shortly thereafter by several more across the country (at least fifty-four others, though the devolved and localized nature of vaccine delivery through the NHS means a comprehensive list does not yet exist anywhere publicly accessible). The vaccination delivery in mosques was open to any local individuals, either through pre-booking or simply dropping-in. Mosques, along with other places of worship, became strategically important sites for accessible vaccinations to communities. Mosques are often located in highly urbanized parts of towns and cities with high ethnic minority populations – a key target of vaccination schemes. They often had copious open space, which facilitated transforming them into clinical spaces that met strict health regulations.

All these examples of services run by mosques rely on the mosque's strength as sites of civil society. The strong social networks, the capacity to organize money and people, the ability to draw on expertise and knowledge, and the willingness to deliver them voluntarily provide the framework for such acts of service, which have been explored in Chapter 2. This chapter highlights and draws attention to the means and methods by which these services are delivered and achieved.

We

Civil society has been a broad and vibrant field of research within social sciences, as discussed earlier in the chapter. I have argued too that religion, especially more recently established religions in Britain, has been overlooked in these studies. In Britain, the last fifty years have seen a dramatic decline in Christian congregations, accompanied by a significant growth of Muslim ones. What this means for civil society is a question that has not been reckoned with, despite the consequences for British society at large. One of the driving interests in civil society has been its potential as a space of collective action, a counterweight to the influence of the state and market (Edwards 2013: 5). It is this angle we turn to now, to examine how mosques in Britain have participated in a broader political arena, seeking alliances with others. To explore this, the case of community organizing will be introduced, which provides an insight into how mosques have not only been participants, but active leaders, in a wider civil society movement.

Community organizing

In 2009, work started on the Maryam Centre, an extension of the East London Mosque that sought to provide services specifically targeted at young Muslim women. At first glance a mosque expansion project in Tower Hamlets, one of the most populous Muslim boroughs in London, seems entirely ordinary, but the story of how the community arrived at a point to lay the foundations is worth retelling. When the land for the Maryam Centre was first identified by the East London Mosque, they soon discovered it was owned by a private developer who intended to build high-rise flats on the property. The East London Mosque was dismayed and sought the help of The East London Citizens Organisation (TELCO) of which they were a member. TELCO was founded by Neil Jameson, and it sought to bring the American model of 'community organising' to Britain. With the help of TELCO, the mosque pressured the private property developer to sell the land to the East London Mosque, and subsequently, pressured the local authority to grant planning permission for the ambitious mosque and community centre to be built.

TELCO's methodology for change is based on the approach of the Industrial Areas Foundation, which in turn was associated with Saul Alinksy (Alinsky 1989) and subsequently Edwards Chambers (Chambers 2003). The methodology is relatively simple: bring people together around a common concern, identify and meet with the relevant decision makers to enact the change they want to see, and organize 'actions' when needed to pressure the decision makers to bring that change into reality. Actions can take the forms of civil disobedience, protest, boycott and headline grabbing demonstrations – all designed to apply pressure on the individuals with authority until they concede to the wishes of the group. It was 'people power' in Alinsky's view, but it needed civil society organizations to functions. People with ties and connections to each other that facilitated coordinated action. Religious congregations almost always figured strongly in community organizing projects, both during Alinsky's time and afterwards. Richard Wood, tracking the history of community organizing in America, observes that religious congregations have remained central (2002), although schools, trade unions, universities, guilds and other voluntary associations remain active participants.

This was the model of change the East London Mosque utilized when working with TELCO to secure the land and rights to build the Maryam Centre. Christian priests and nuns, along with Muslims and those from other faiths, linked their arms in a circle around the property in question for one 'action', bringing the campaign to the media's attention. Soon the issue was taken to the council, who not only buckled under pressure and sold the land to the East London Mosque but also provided the planning permission necessary. In each step of the process, as the mosque faced hesitancy, bureaucracy or denial from the local authority, they drew TELCO and undertook an 'action' that kept the plans moving forward. Dilowar Hussain recounts that the project was defended by Christian leaders: 'we could not have done this as effectively alone' (Ali, Jamoul and Vali 2012: 40). When I spoke to Neil Jameson, founder of Citizens UK and TELCO, he went even further, recollecting that two Christians in particular took a leading role, an Anglican priest and a Catholic nun. The priest put forward the argument that the council would never allow developers to build a high-rise flat next to Westminster Abbey. This argument, about the equivocal status of Christianity and Islam in Britain, became a linchpin of the campaign. There was also perhaps the most symbolically powerful gesture, a Catholic nun speaking at a council meeting, advocating for the development. The key action took place on a summer evening, a memory fondly recounted by Neil:

The thing that mosque could do well was turn people out. So East London Mosque took four or more buses down to the council house. The Muslims prayed outside the council chamber, on a magnificent summer evening, and inside, Sister Mary and a delegation were arguing strongly in favour of the mosque to the Council. So people outside were there, announcing 'God is Great', 'Allahu Akbar', and everyone could hear it inside. It wasn't threatening at all, but it was very powerful.

This story though it is far from the only example. When I asked Jonathan Cox, Deputy Director of Citizens UK, whether he considered the Citizens movement to be an interfaith one, he responded confidently 'no, we're a broad-based organisation', stressing it was open to organizations with a faith background as well as those with no religious affiliations at all. He noted how this was in contrast to community organizing in America, which is much more vocal about its religious identity but considered it a reflection of British society in general: 'faith is much more dominant as an actor in civil society in the States than it is here.' Neil Jameson, the founder of Citizens, takes a more faith-focused view: 'civil society itself doesn't exist without its faith institutions. People playing golf is not civil society. Watching football is not civil society.' He continues, 'When it comes to organising, you just can't beat faith institutions, frankly.'

Citizens bring together a large range of religious groups, as Jonathan describes, during an interview, a 2015 campaign: 'we did an event to celebrate the cap on payday loans in London where we had Christian, Muslim and Jewish leaders go to Wonga, all wearing caps – that was the joke – and asking Wonga and other payday lenders to respect the cap'. This success, however, came from prior work these faith leaders had done together, explains Jonathan, 'because those participants had come to a better understanding of each other's faith, through crafting a position on payday loans which was respectful of each other's religious teachings but also had a clear political stance'.

> Citizens provides a space and a mechanism by which people can do interfaith work together but within the context of a broad-based organisation, our primary purpose isn't to do interfaith work, it just happens to be quite a good vehicle for doing interfaith work.

The Citizens UK motto is 'reweaving the fabric of society'. This is an appropriate description for the activity of British mosques as well. Mosques are agents of changing, and in their alliance building, campaigning and co-ordination with other civil society groups, they have been part of a wider movement attempting to reshape the landscape of Britain.

Conclusion

The mosques becoming agents within civil society strengthens British civil society as a whole. Edwards warns against 'an over-reliance on any particular form [of community organisations] – such as NGOs with weak roots in society' (2013: 8), considering it dangerous to the health of civil society as a whole. The mosque and Muslims more generally present a case of a new dynamic in British civil society. They are new actors, with different forms of operation (emerging out of the congregational mosque), their own sources of networks (derived from those attending the mosque), and bringing their own priorities (shaped by the concerns of the Muslim community). It is a development in British society worthy of note. In creating links with other institutions and faith groups, they also wield considerable influence and power. If mosques continue to develop their civil society presence and relationships, then this power will only increase, and mosques may soon be shaping the course of British politics and business.

7

The unwelcome mosque

Across the UK, mosques face opposition. This can occur during inception or well afterwards. It can be subversive resistance articulated through bureaucracy, low-level vandalism, arson and even, at times, acts of fatal violence. This chapter explores this resistance, conflict and controversy. It argues that British mosques become a suitable proxy onto which opponents can project wider anxieties about Islam, Muslims and British identity. This chapter provides a handful of examples of mosque conflict and controversy and the theoretical frames used to analyse them, before concluding with my own approach – one that considers mosque conflicts as a product of a renegotiation in society, in which British Muslims are emerging as active agents in civil society, capable of exercising power. British mosques are, I argue, credible evidence of Muslim organizing, financial capital and the capacity for civil society influence.

The mosque in conflict

On the afternoon of 22 May 2013, Fusilier Lee Rigby was murdered in broad daylight. The attackers, Michael Adebolajo and Michael Adebowale, were Muslim converts. From the trial following the murder, it became clear that the two individuals were looking for members of the British Armed Forces, patrolling the area near the Royal Artillery Barracks in London. The murder was brutal, and in the mobile phone footage recorded moments after the attack, Michael Adebolajo stands with hands covered in blood justifying his attack. He states with a chilling calmness that 'the only reason we have killed this man today is because Muslims are dying daily by British soldiers', going on to cite a biblio-quranic[1] verse, 'an eye for an eye' (McEnery, McGlashan and Love 2015). The days that followed would have a dramatic impact on British public discourse, including protests led by the English Defence League and Stephen Yaxley-Lennon (more commonly known as Tommy Robinson), protests that would in coming years become a familiar scene in British towns and cities.

In the same year, there was another series of attacks and murder on the streets of Britain, however, one that did not shape British public consciousness in the same way. On the night of 29 April 2013, Mohammed Saleem, an 82-year-old, was walking home from Green Lane Mosque in Birmingham after finishing his prayers. He was stabbed to death by Pavlo Lapshyn, a Ukrainian PhD student currently on placement in Britain. Lapshyn was convinced that Muslims and Islam posed an existential threat to Western civilization, and he admitted that he targeted Saleem simply because he 'was a Muslim and there were no witnesses' (*The Express and Star* 2013). Before he was caught, Lapshyn prepared and conducted a series of attacks. He targeted three mosques with explosives in June and July. In each case, the device failed to injure or kill its intended targets: Muslims observing the Friday prayers. The final bomb, placed at Jamia Masjid al-Aqsa in Wolverhampton, detonated. However, Lapshyn had miscalculated prayer times, so the mosque was largely empty at that point. Lapshyn was finally apprehended and sentenced to forty years for the murder of Mohammed Saleem and his bombing attempts. Lapshyn is not alone in targeting mosques and Muslim worshippers. He can be placed alongside attackers such as Darren Osbourne, who in 2017 drove a van into a crowd of worshippers outside Finsbury Park Mosque, killing one. Internationally, more fatal attacks have taken place. A shooting at the Islamic Cultural Centre of Quebec City in Canada killed six in 2017, and another livestreamed shooting in 2019 at Al Noor Mosque and Linwood Islamic Centre in New Zealand killed fifty-one with a similar number injured. These attacks represent a pervasive Islamophobia of vigilante attacks against Muslims, often by far-right extremists who have followed through a logic that frames Muslims as a potential threat to its extreme conclusion, that all Muslims are a threat and need to be eliminated. These attackers also share in their choice of targets, the mosque.

Islamophobia and the mosque

There are numerous insightful definitions of Islamophobia that have been put forward. In the British context, the All-Party Parliamentary Group (APPG)[2] on British Muslims (All-Party Parliamentary Group on British Muslims 2019) is perhaps the most influential, being adopted by a broad range of Muslim groups, universities, schools, local authorities and political bodies (Muslim Council of Britain 2021). The definition offered by the APPG on British Muslims is as follows:

> Islamophobia is rooted in racism and is a type of racism that targets expressions of Muslimness or perceived Muslimness.

It built on the Runneymede Foundation's 2017 definition of Islamophobia below:

> Islamophobia is any distinction, exclusion, or restriction towards, or preference against, Muslims (or those perceived to be Muslims) that has the purpose or effect of nullifying or impairing the recognition, enjoyment or exercise, on an equal footing, of human rights and fundamental freedoms in the political, economic, social, cultural or any other field of public life.

This definition is summarized in short by the Runnymede Foundation as simply 'Islamophobia is anti-Muslim racism'. A conceptually robust framework for Islamophobia in my view comes from the United States and the University of California's Center for Race and Gender. Their 'Islamophobia Research and Documentation Project' has outlined the below definition of Islamophobia, which while verbose is also comprehensive:

> Islamophobia is a contrived fear or prejudice fomented by the existing Eurocentric and Orientalist global power structure. It is directed at a perceived or real Muslim threat through the maintenance and extension of existing disparities in economic, political, social and cultural relations, while rationalizing the necessity to deploy violence as a tool to achieve 'civilizational rehab' of the target communities (Muslim or otherwise). Islamophobia reintroduces and reaffirms a global racial structure through which resource distribution disparities are maintained and extended. ('Islamophobia Research & Documentation Project | UCB Center for Race & Gender' n.d.)

In addition, they outline five prevailing attitudes about Islam that can be associated with Islamophobia:

- Islam is monolithic and cannot adapt to new realities.
- Islam does not share common values with other major faiths.
- Islam as a religion is inferior to the West. It is archaic, barbaric and irrational.
- Islam is a religion of violence and supports terrorism.
- Islam is a violent political ideology.

These provide a helpful framework in order to consider the way in which opposition to mosques is articulated. For the purposes of this chapter, I will be dividing them into three broad categories. The mosque as a site of radicalization, violence and support of terrorism. Second, the mosque as a site of conquest, tied to the idea of Islam as a 'violent political ideology'. Finally, the mosque as a site of difference, related to the idea of Islam as a religion that shares no common values with other faiths, and which is inferior to the West.

Sites of radicalization

On the evening of 19 June 2017, during the month of Ramadan, reports came in from news outlets of a car being driven into pedestrians in London. The previous months had seen a spate of similar attacks. Only a fortnight prior, three attackers, Muslims, went on violent rampage, attacking late-night revellers with knives, killing eight. In March that same year, Khalid Masood, a Muslim convert, drove his car into passers-by on Westminster Bridge before fatally stabbing a police officer. In May, Salman Abedi detonated a bomb at a concert in Manchester, killing twenty-two, making it the bloodiest terror attack since 7/7. It was, hitherto, a year which had already seen dramatic acts of Muslim political violence and so many fully expected the attack to join the list of 'Islamic State inspired terrorism'. The first indication that this incident might have been different was that the attack was near a mosque, North London Central Mosque, or as it is more commonly known, Finsbury Park Mosque. By the morning, the identity of the attacker was known, Darren Osbourne, as well as the city from which he came: Cardiff, my hometown.

In the court case and media coverage that followed, numerous conflicting narratives emerged around the attacker's motivations. He was a heavy drinker, unemployed and with a history of violence, according to some who knew him. Others, in particular Osbourne's former partner, told detectives investigating the attack that his turn to violence was motivated by a BBC drama, *Three Girls*, which told the story of the Rochdale grooming scandal.[3] By Osbourne's own admission, he had intended to attack the al-Quds Day March. The march is a relatively minor affair, but it dominated the attention of right-wing conspiracists in Britain. The event is promoted by the Iranian Government as a day of solidarity with Palestinians. The Labour leader at the time of the attack, Jeremy Corbyn, was pictured in attendance in 2012, with the Hezbollah flag in view. The image was heavily used in tabloids and right-leaning newspapers as evidence of Corbyn's questionable affiliations and adopted by far-right groups as evidence of how Islamic extremists had infiltrated into the heart of British political power.

Darren Osbourne planned to plough his vehicle into the marchers and hoped he might even injure or kill Jeremy Corbyn himself, or the Mayor of London in 2017, Sadiq Khan. Upon arriving much too late in London to carry out his initial plan, he changed target and instead decided to drive towards Finsbury Park Mosque. There has been little analysis of why he chose this new target. He was, however, successful in executing his second plan against the mosque. His attack killed Makram Ali, an elderly man, and injured several more. It is possible that the association of Finsbury Park Mosque in previous years as a 'radicalised mosque' figured into Osbourne's choice of new target. From 1997 until 2003, the mosque was led by Abu Hamza al-Masri, an Egyptian-born ideologue with links to numerous violent groups. Abu Hamza's preaching was fiery and often on the borderline of legality; he thus garnered attention of media outlets. Abu Hamza's appearance conveniently facilitated the image of the 'fanatic in the attic' (Allen 2010). Aside from being bearded and dressing in the traditional Middle-Eastern flowing thobe and so suitably 'Muslim' and 'foreign' looking, he had a glass eye and a prosthetic hook attached to his right hand. The latter resulted in the nickname 'Hook' being used in tabloid coverage of Finsbury Park Mosque. In 2003, the mosque was reclaimed by the trustees and Abu Hamza was ousted from his position as imam, but this did not stop him from preaching outside the mosque to his followers. He was arrested on terrorism charges in 2004, finally ending his association with the mosque, allowing an opportunity for the trustees and congregation to dispel its reputation as 'the radical mosque' from the national discourse.

Often, following a terror attack involving a Muslim perpetrator, media and security forces will trace where the individual regularly prayed. The logic of radicalization underlying this presumption is that Muslim terrorism is an issue of theology and Quranic interpretation, and as such, it has at its root someone teaching that theology or interpretation. Mosques are identified as being the providers of this theology. In cases such as the Manchester Arena bombing, the attacker, Salman Abedi, was noted to worship at Didsbury Mosque, where his father was an occasional muezzin. The mosque faced accusations of radicalization from newspapers, especially after it was revealed that a *khatib* had delivered a sermon praising the 'mujahideen', though an investigation by Counter Terrorism Policing North West determined 'no offences had been committed' (*BBC News* 2019). A similar case involved the 'Muthanna Brothers', two individuals from Cardiff who left Wales to join the Islamic State in 2014. Aseel and Nasser Muthanna's departure captured national headlines. The media identified al-Manar Mosque on Senghennydd Road as one of their regular mosques, placing defamatory attention on the mosque's imams, the mosque's management committee and preachers who visited it (Marsden 2014). Again, the accusations were vague and circumstantial. As one former leader of the mosque told me, 'it is hard to defend yourself when you're not really sure what you're being accused of'. No criminal cases were opened in relation to the mosque and the radicalization of the Muthanna Brothers.

There is usually a correlation between being identified as a site of radicalization by the media and hate crimes. Didsbury Mosque, for example, received threatening letters (Webb 2017) and Al-Manar faced a 'mosque invasion' from the far-right group Britain First (Colley 2016). The accusation of extremism, radicalization and terrorism being fostered in mosques is not uncommon, and the examples mentioned above are only some of many mosques accused of radicalization. It is an accusation rarely substantiated. 'Radicals and radical groups are in general not welcome in mosques', writes Mina al-Lami, but instead 'networks of radicalisation' exist in 'multiple private spaces' (2009: 7). Douglas Weeks, examining a mosque-led counter-extremism programme in London, contends that while various government bodies argue '[m]osques are not doing enough to stem the tide of radicalization, in actuality faith-based organizations are decidedly engaged and have been for quite some time' (2019). The rationalization of attacks against mosques in response to perceived support for terrorism is one that rests on the assumption of the purely religious motives of Muslim terrorists. This fallacy has been criticized by many academics and experts on the topic, including academic Matthew Francis. Francis runs 'radicalisationresearch.org', which seeks to make academic research accessible to journalists, politicians and others. He argues that a poor concept of religion, too loose to offer any meaningful insight, is often used to explain the violence of terrorists, and such instead a need to de-emphasize the role of 'radical ideology' in the motivations of those who commit violent acts (Francis 2014). Others have gone even further, criticizing the very concept of 'radicalisation' as misleading and a proxy by which to securitize Muslims (Kundnani 2012). Pavlo Lapshyn's campaign of terror against mosques in the Midlands, Darren Osbourne's decision to drive into a group of worshippers outside Finsbury Park Mosque, and much of the phenomenon of threats, vandalism and abuse faced by mosques can be understood as driven by a view of terrorism that sees religion, specifically Islam, as the prime cause. The mosque is perceived as the site of radicalization and thus the source of terrorism, and of a religion which in the view of some can convince its adherents to commit acts of extreme violence.

Sites of conquest

Britain First is a far-right political organization founded in 2012, one that, according to Chris Allen, combines the party-political organizing of the British National Party with the on-street activism of the English Defence League (Allen 2014). In 2016, members of Britain First were banned from all mosques in England and Wales (Samuels 2016). The reason for the ban was a series of 'mosque invasions' orchestrated by Britain First from 2014 through 2016. The invasions would typically follow the same pattern. Members of Britain First would arrive in uniform (flat caps and branded jackets), usually headed by Paul Golding, the organization's former leader. They would enter the mosque, usually facing no physical prevention. They would seek out an imam, or simply begin addressing whichever Muslims were present. A barrage of questions would follow, asking the individual: to condemn extremism and grooming gangs, their views on Christianity and Jesus Christ, their thoughts on the role of women or Muslims in Britain. Occasionally demands would be made: to remove signs for gender segregation, to publicly denounce terrorism and so on. The entire thing would be recorded by one of the members of Britain First and uploaded onto YouTube (though the videos have now been removed).

The 'mosque invasions' followed various 'Christian patrols' Britain First undertook in cities across England. The first was in East London in 2014, purportedly in response to a 'Muslim patrol' undertaken by young Muslims associated with the now proscribed al-Muhajirun network. During the 'Christian patrols', the members of Britain First recorded their activities that culminated with holding a banner stating 'Resistance' in front of the East London Mosque. Britain First's 'invasions' and activism around mosques, their paramilitary outfits and the physical threat posed by members are a response to a perceived role that mosques play in the imagination of Britain First members. Mosques are seen as expressions of power and force that needed to be met by a similarly militant display.

Mosques, as imagined symbols of conquest and imperialism, are a recurring theme not just in Britain but also in other parts of the world. Minarets in particular have been the focus of debate, often being interpreted as a sign of dominance due to their height (Emmett 2009: 457). Minarets are not found in all mosques, but they have become the most distinguishing aspect of many mosques. They have been a key feature of European imaginings of Islam and often interpreted as a sign of 'Islamicisation' (Ehrkamp in Ward, Silberman and Till 2012).

While the interpretation of the mosque as a symbol of an imperial conquering force is rooted in Islamophobic conceptions of Islam, the argument that minarets (and mosques) themselves are symbols of Islamic power is not inaccurate. They demonstrate the organizing power and financial agency of Muslim communities. The imagined imperial intentions behind the founding of mosques is however tied to older ideas of Islam as a militant political ideology mentioned prior.

Sites of difference

The Trocadero is a Victorian building in the heart of London, a brief walk away from Leicester Square, Trafalgar Square and Piccadilly Circus. The area is full of pubs, nightclubs, high-end restaurants, boutique stores, and of course, dozens of other national landmarks. The building began life as a restaurant in 1896 but through the last century has closed and reopened numerous times, morphing and shifting to serve the various tastes and interests of those visiting London through the years. In February 2020, the Aziz Foundation announced plans to convert the ground floor and basement of the London Trocadero into a mosque. The Aziz Foundation is a sizeable educational charity founded by Asif Aziz, a billionaire and property developer who has, through his foundation, invested substantially in educational opportunities for Muslims. The plans were modest, seeking to accommodate 100 worshippers for daily prayers and 1,000 for the Friday prayers. A predictable pattern of resistance to the mosque emerged soon thereafter.

Aftab Ahmed is the programme manager for the Aziz Foundation and has been involved in its work to convert the two floors of the Trocadero into a prayer room and community centre. He explained to me that after the plans were first published on the Westminster City Council website, as is expected for new planning proposals, there was a small response. 'And then Breitbart published a story on it.' Breitbart, an American-based far-right news organization, put international attention on the issue. It described the plans as a 'mega-mosque' and quoted a former Westminster City councillor, JP Floru, saying 'setting up a 1,000 capacity flagship mosque right next to the long-standing gay district of Soho will damage local cohesion' (Lane 2020).

'After that,' Aftab continues, 'it got picked up by white supremacists':

> So a YouTuber with 100,000 followers, [named] Iconoclast, he made a video on it. It was all scaremongering, saying that the entire Trocadero is going to become

a mosque, there would be *adhān* broadcast five times a day, that there will be thousands of people walking to the Trocadero praying, that there would be an entire obliteration of English identity of London. He was simply playing to white supremacist fears and tropes.

Aftab and the Aziz Foundation reported the video to YouTube, which removed it eventually, but by then it had already agitated large swathes of far-right sympathizers.

The 'Iconoclast' is a YouTube channel run by Daniel Atkinson, initially anonymously until the *Guardian* discovered his identity (Townsend 2020). Atkinson represents a shift in far-right organizing, away from organized movements such as the British National Party, the English Defence League, Britain First, and indeed proscribed neo-Nazi groups and towards a looser association maintained through key online figures such as Atkinson himself, the former English Defence League leader Tommy Robinson and the commentator Katie Hopkins. All three organized against the Trocadero mosque plans and indeed many other mosques.

One result of the attention put on the plans by Breitbart and Atkinson was a significant increase in complaints lodged with Westminster City Council about the potential mosque. Some 2,800 objections to the plans were received by Westminster City Council. Matthew Green, councillor for Westminster, described many of the objections as 'racist, hateful comments' and 'utterly repellent'. A petition was also organized by 'Democracy Counts' on the website change.org, gaining sizeable traction online and being shared on Twitter, Facebook and the social media platform 'gab', popular with far-right groups. A total of 11,585 individuals signed the petition. The petition argued that the mosque should be opposed on the basis of increased traffic in central London: that it is 'not in keeping with local non-Muslim communities', that it does not reflect the local tourism trade and even had improper fire and emergency exits. It highlighted most strongly concerns that the worshippers at the mosque would not mix with bar users nearby, pose a danger to the LGBT community nearby, and that the mosque fails to be a space for gender equality. The mix-bag of reasons, articulated in a language of bureaucracy and equality and diversity, is accompanied by comments made by those who signed the petition:

'Don't want this we are a Christian country'

'Too many mosques in this country now without adding more'

'WARNING : LABOUR PARTY – FOR THE ISLAMIC TAKEOVER OF BRITAIN!!!'

'Islam has proven to be unstable as we have seen by the deaths of lee [*sic*] Rigby and many more of our lovley [*sic*] innocent people in radical terrorist attacks'

'Because they have taken over this country destroying the British way of life'

The resistance to the mosque did not just come from the far-right, however; it also emerged from more mainstream quarters. Karen Harradine of The Conservative Woman blog wrote a piece opposing the plans with the headline 'A mosque in Piccadilly Circus? Wrong, wrong, wrong!' (2020). Harradine argued that the mosque was inappropriate as 'The West End is not a place of religious observance but of secular fun'. She continues, 'No matter how peaceful, the mosque will still be out of character with the rest of the area,' and she concludes, 'A mosque in Piccadilly Circus feels as wrong, though for different reasons, as the proposal to build one near Ground Zero'.

Aftab Ahmed believes the agitation against the mosque was largely from those outside the area. 'Locally, we had plenty of support. One of the reasons put forward for objecting to the mosque was what it would mean for the LGBT community, but there are some prominent LGBT voices in support of the proposals.' The Westminster LGBT Forum was one such organization (Milton 2020). 'You had these people from outside, who weren't involved in any way, what gave them the right to speak for the LGBT community?' Ahmed asks.

The plans were eventually withdrawn by the Aziz Foundation, as Ahmed explains: 'We went back to the pre-application stage, just working through all the local partners, to make sure we have their support and any issues resolved, before resubmitting.' 'But that didn't stop the white supremacists from claiming this as a victory, one campaigner against the mosque was a lawyer, Gavin Boby, who calls himself the "mosque buster", he has painted himself the winner in this issue.' Gavin Boby is a planning permission lawyer, who proudly boasts of forty-five wins out of sixty-eight battles in getting mosque plans withdrawn or rejected ('Mosquebusters | Gavin Boby.Com' n.d.). He is part of a more organized dimension of mosque oppositional politics, actively becoming involved in high-profile cases himself, and sometimes called in for support by anti-mosque campaigners. With considerable experience in the bureaucracy of planning applications, he seeks to frustrate planning permissions in a legal language.

Ahmed is optimistic about the opposition faced by mosques as a whole, arguing that some resistance is 'not based in racism' but simply a fear of change and the unknown. 'You can sit down and talk to them, reason with them, and they listen.' Others, however, are driven by an Islamophobic and ideological hatred of Islam. 'They're not really willing to talk, and if you do, they're not open to changing their mind.' 'It's a culture war', Ahmed concludes.

Opposing mosques

The mobilization against mosques is varied, and as I spoke to mosque leaders to understand the types of opposition they faced, one name that was recommended to me repeatedly was Umair Waheed. Umair is an architect who has specialized in designing mosques, both conversions and purpose-built ones. We had crossed paths in the past, speaking on the same panel at a conference, but it took some time to finally find a time we could meet in person. Despite planning to visit London to see him, in the end he came to Cardiff. Our conversation was had over a platter of grilled meats, chips and rice. We discussed the question of anonymity; Umair told me either to anonymize him or the examples he mentioned. 'There's a lot of relationship management involved in opening a mosque', he tells me, 'even when you sense council is being unfair, you still need them'. This attitude, of grudging recognition of the realpolitik of mosque building, was common amongst my research participants. Before he begins, Umair tells me of one case involving a mosque that built an extension without permission. 'There was a court ruling, and the judge ruled against. But the council weren't enforcing, they were really trying to work with the masjid community to find a solution.' He mentions several opportunities the council gave to address the issue and repeated failures by the mosque management to engage, and identifies the mosque management as being the stumbling block to a successful application. 'I say this for perspective, sometimes it is our own people who are the problem'. From this, however, Umair begins telling me examples of the ways in which councils and organized resistance to mosques utilize a bureaucratic system to their advantage, to frustrate or otherwise hinder mosque projects. 'To be an architect involved in mosque projects, you really need to know your politics. It's not just planning applications and policies, but it's the games people play.' Most of the examples are drawn from London and surrounding areas, where Umair is based. In one case, councillors who opposed the opening of a new mosque in a small borough told their Muslim colleagues they needed to excuse themselves from voting on the planning application of a mosque due to a 'conflict of interest'. The Muslim councillors, younger and less experienced, did as they were instructed, Umair telling me in an exasperated tone that there were no grounds for such an exclusion: 'Stuff like that, it's dirty politics'. In this case, it was opposition to the mosque from within the council, but Umair explains that even if the council is generally supportive, the controversy and conflict surrounding a project can have consequences in the planning procedure.

> I've had clients where the council ask for every document, every survey, every report possible, costing clients thousands and thousands of extra pounds. Sometimes it doesn't really stall the project, sometimes it just costs more, sometimes it means the masjid committee misses the opportunity to buy this property or secure it long term and the whole thing unravels.

The increased scrutiny of a council's actions due to campaigners against a mosque prompts them in having 'a higher bar' for the evidence for their decisions, he tells me, 'even if the same criteria isn't applied to other proposals'. Another common theme in his experiences is the 'concerned local residents'.

> The council and others will say 'local residents oppose this', or 'local residents' are worried about car parking' or 'noise' or whatever. I come across this very often. But you look around, the people coming to the mosque aren't being shipped in via buses. They are local residents too!

I ask how much opposition to mosques emerges out of local networks, and how much of it is dictated from elsewhere. 'It's a mix, there is definitely local people who are concerned, and sometimes it's a fair concern you know, but if you get the combination of local and national resistance, it can get very messy', although he laughs, 'but it doesn't always work out like they plan'.

> I remember one case, in the South East, and the BNP[4] were active back when they were active interrupted the meeting. Shouting about how this mosque was this and that and had to be rejected. And it was the day of voting, and it was so counter-productive for them, because there were quite a few councillors before hand who were very unsure about the mosque, or even opposed. But after the BNP storm in demanding this and shouting that, well anyone who voted against the mosque looked like they were agreeing with the BNP, so the policy passed.

The identity and background of mosque opposition also varies in Umair's experience:

> There was one meeting I remember, small town outside London, and the case got caught in the whirlwind of local media. And so the initial public meetings. You had the EDL crowd, with leaflets saying this and that about the Muslims. You had some LGBT campaigners worried about the impact on sexual freedoms and everything. You had these old people concerned about the local environment

and whether it would still be maintained. They don't agree with each other, except that the mosque is wrong.

The way in which resistance to mosques can come from all quarters of society and expressed in a variety of terms is a surprising facet of the opposition.

Great Baddow is a village located in the borough of Chelmsford in Essex, roughly northeast of London. Hamptons Sports and Leisure Centre, a large complex in the village, was put up for sale in 2018 and purchased by the Chelmsford Muslim Society in 2019. The Chelsmford Muslim Society planned to continue operating the centre in much the same way as previously, with sports facilities and a gym, but with the addition of prayer facilities for the locality's small but growing Muslim population. The purchase of the leisure centre by Muslims was perceived as a loss of a community facility by some, and the 'Save The Hamptons' group was formed in January 2020, very soon after Chelmsford Muslim Society purchased the property. The group hosts a website, www.savethehamptons.co.uk, on which videos and regular posts are uploaded detailing their concerns and dissatisfaction with existing plans and the leisure centre's new owners. The opposition to the plans falls into a category of mosque resistance that is different from the more overtly Islamophobic campaigns mentioned elsewhere in the chapter. The website of the group is keen to insist: 'It's not about race or religion, the group is called Save The Hamptons, not stop the Great Baddow Megamosque', and in fact much of the group's messaging seeks to distance itself from the far-right. Nonetheless, Ayman Syed tells me, 'You know, you can imagine during COVID how difficult it was to run a leisure centre, and then during that time there were protests during Friday prayers with Britain First getting involved'. A charitable reading of the opposition of Save The Hamptons would be a misunderstanding of the functions of contemporary British mosques. Ayman's vision of the mosque certainly reflects the *sunna* mosques of the categorization introduced in Chapter 2.

> My fear was that this becomes a mosque of the 1950s. We wanted to ensure that this is a centre where we pray and play. That's the ethos. There's a café. Come, sit, eat, play badminton, come namaz time, pray. We wanted a centre that does everything. The concept is kind of new. Very few people do that kind of thing. People have lost sight of the Prophetic Model of the mosque. It wasn't just place of prayer. Lots of things in one centre.

The Save The Hamptons core argument is not that they oppose a mosque or mosques in general, but that the leisure centre in question is '*The Wrong Place For A Mosque*'.[5] The dispute is ongoing. Another example is the case of the

Chipping Norton mosque. Chipping Norton is largely unremarkable as a small market town in Oxford, except for being home to several celebrities and public figures, including former Prime Minister David Cameron. In 2012 and 2013 plans were underway by the small Muslim community to purchase a property and open it as a mosque. Hitherto, the community of an estimated 30–50 Muslims had been renting the Town Hall for Friday prayers, but had decided to invest in a more permanent solution. A vacant property was identified and the necessary planning permissions sought. In response, a far-right activist group, the Nationalist Alliance, delivered leaflets titled 'Mosque Alert' warning of the dangers of the incoming mosque to homes in Chipping Norton. Despite this, the mosque plans went ahead until, in February 2013, the landlord pulled out of the sale. He explained he had received an arson threat if the mosque went ahead, and as such, considered it too dangerous to continue. Similar arson attacks against mosques are not uncommon. The Norwich Central Mosque and Islamic Community Trust in 2020 (Johnson 2020), the Nasfat Islamic Centre in Newton Heath in Manchester in 2017 (Halliday 2017), and a proposed mosque in Ipswich in 2011 (*BBC News* 2011) were subject to arson attacks, leading to various degrees of damage. The opposition to the mosque in these cases manifested in violent action.

The strategies utilized in opposing mosques can range from the bureaucratic, the organized resistance and violence. The constant remains the opposition itself; the opening of a mosque, whether a small property or a large leisure centre, a conversion of a church or a prayer room in a larger facility, acts as a lightning rod for broader social concerns. How to analyse and make sense of these conflicts will be considered next.

Making sense of mosque conflicts

Three types of mosque conflicts have been presented thus far, focusing on the mosque as a site of radicalization, a site of conquest or a site of difference. The academic literature documenting and exploring the underlying causes of these conflicts and controversies is broad and constitutes a substantial proportion of all the scholarship authored on British mosques.[6] Collectively they underscore the ubiquity of conflicts around mosques and the salience of the topic.

To understand why it is that mosques have become targets of such hostility, from vandalism to murder, it is helpful to turn to the nature of the space of the mosque. It is sacred, valued, cherished and celebrated by Muslims. It is maintained through worship and invested with a sense of history, community and the divine, as presented in Chapter 4. But 'sacred space is contested space' as Lily Kong (2001: 213) writes. Chidester and Linenthal outline why sacred spaces are prone to conflict. They first note that space is by its nature limited. If space is 'claimed – owned – operated' (Luz 2008: 1037), then it can only be done so by a limited number as 'no two objects can occupy the same point in space' (Chidester and Linenthal 1995: 18). Building on this necessary limitation, however, is the possibility for infinite divergent meanings attributed to the same space. It is this relationship between the finite and infinite that leads to spatial contestation, according to Chidester and Linenthal (1995: 18). These divergent meanings can themselves relate to a variety of cultural, religious and ethnic markers. Collins-Kreiner, Shmueli and Ben Gal argue that 'conflicts in holy places often cause nationalistic and ethnic sensitivities to rise to the surface and to assume the form of violence that extends far beyond the boundaries of the site' (2013: 104).

Chad Emmett provides a thorough discussion about how the location of churches and mosques can provide an insight into Christian–Muslim relationships historically and geographically. He examines historic and contemporary examples and provides ten typologies for the relationship embodied by the location of churches and mosques. These can stem from 'destruction of a church or mosque as an indicator of conflict, conquest, change in power, or demonstration of power' to 'sharing religious structures as a sign of compromise' (Emmett 2009). Ultimately, many of Emmett's typologies rely on how motivation is interpreted by the reader of the article, but they recognize the symbolic value of buildings as well as their link with power. Symbols can act as bridges between a physical context and a spiritual world (Beyer 2013: 2); this theory outlines how religious symbols operate between a duality of worlds (the visible, physical world and an unseen spiritual world) and connect a material world with one of values, transcendental truths and convictions. Combining both Emmett's theorization with the notion of mosques as sacred, we can see how the symbolic nature of religious sites can lead to contest about the nature of communities and the values they hold to be important. Mosques can act as symbols of the 'spiritual identities' of space (Collins-Kreiner, Shmueli and Ben Gal 2013: 103). The frames of mosques as sites of radicalization, conquest and difference demonstrate how the differing interpretations of the mosque come into tension.

Historically, mosques were no doubt used as symbols of imperial power. In Oleg Grabar's 2006 study on the Dome of the Rock, he notes that the unique octagonal structure of the mosque, its 'semicircular arches' and even the arrangement of calligraphy (rather than the calligraphy itself) are reminiscent of the architectural 'language of the Mediterranean world, particularly the Roman Empire' (Grabar 1996: 103–5). His thesis is that the Dome of the Rock was the result of the expanding Umayyad Empire's attempts to convey themselves as the new superpower. They did this by borrowing from the Romans and recreating their architectural techniques but within an Islamic paradigm. Thus the Dome of the Rock conveyed to both the locals and visitors that the Umayyad Empire was the new Roman Empire. It is a sacred site with religious significance in the worldview of Muslims, located as it is in proximity to Masjid al-Aqsa, but it also has clear worldly objectives. The argument is developed by a number of other scholars of architecture, such as Cristina Paredes who contends that

> power, closely linked to religion, has used religious architecture for its own benefit. Governors and other powerful figures over the centuries financed the construction of religious buildings to disseminate beliefs but also to legitimise their power or atone for sins. (2009: 7)

The Dome of the Rock's continuity with pre-existing Roman architectural styles is thus a way of establishing a new identity for the region. In Britain, however, the role and function of mosques is markedly different. British Muslims are not an imperial power and mosques have generally been established through the efforts of usually poor first-generation migrants. Yet they are statements of power. They indicate the capacity of Muslims, their values and just as the Dome of Rock combined Roman imperialism with Islamic aesthetics, contemporary mosques convey a claim about the role of Islam in Britain. The mosque communicates a permanence; Muslims are now part of Britain, not just migrants passing through. This is all to say that a single place, in this case, the mosque, means different things to different people, and that the very act of inscribing meaning and significance to a place invites conflict. Places are 'claimed – owned – operated' (Luz 2008: 1037), which are all expressions of power and authority.

Noga Collins-Kreiner, Deborah Shmueli and Michal Ben Gal (2013) use the theory of spatial transgression to analyse the ways in which religious sites can stimulate conflict. Collins-Kreiner et al. look at three new religious sites in Israel using a framework of spatial transgression. The theory of spatial transgression emerges out of the work of Tim Cresswell (1996) who argued about the importance of being in and out of place and the significance of this belonging or lack of belonging to geographers. Spatial transgression refers to 'particular spatial actions that make people feel as if their identities and senses of place are being challenged' (Collins-Kreiner, Shmueli and Ben Gal 2013: 103). The transgression, via a spatial action, oversteps the appropriate place where something is perceived to belong. The transgression, by challenging the 'existing socio-political orders', results in 'boundary maintenance' to assert the appropriate use of space and location of others (Collins-Kreiner, Shmueli and Ben Gal 2013: 104).

Boundary maintenance can be acts of violence or asserted in a more palatable language about planning permission and aesthetics. Three 'frames' are presented as the ways in which a mosque can transgress spatial boundaries. The first is 'issues', specifically that a mosque does not fit into the aesthetic of an area, or would cause unacceptable disturbance. This can be described as 'NIMBY' or 'not in my backyard'; there is no objection articulated to a mosque per se but rather its location is contested (Landman and Wessels 2005: 1128). The second is the 'process' frame, which is when a mosque is objected to due to perceived flaws in the planning process and decision making. The third and final frame is 'values', which is an overt discussion about the place of Islam within that particular society (Collins-Kreiner, Shmueli and Ben Gal 2013: 106).

All three frames can be viewed in the conflicts over mosques presented prior, often all at the same time (the Trocadero Mosque, for example, was argued to be in the wrong location, failed to adhere to existing bureaucratic norms, and represented a value system foreign to that of contemporary central London).

Landman and Wessel argue that most instances of mosque controversies they studied took place in rural towns rather than urban locations (2005: 1138), a pattern not uncommon in Britain, but by no means comprehensively accurate. In fact, Seán McLoughlin examines the absence of conflict or controversy in establishing a mosque in Bradford (2005). Bradford presents a case study of a location in which, in various ways, the Muslim presence has already been normalized. In other words, the acceptance of Muslim power demonstrated in the mosque was already accepted as part of the varied landscape of contesting authorities in Bradford. A 'dominant group's approval or rejection of the other depends on the degree to which the stereotype of other groups fits in the place in which it is located' (Collins-Kreiner, Shmueli and Ben Gal 2013: 105). It can be argued that Muslims are seen to belong at the margins of society by hegemonic discourses. By establishing prominent mosques in urban locations, there is an important symbolic declaration about where Islam belongs. Nasser's examination of expressions of Muslim architecture in Birmingham notes that the presence of a dome or minaret can cause debate more than the mosque itself or its use (2005: 74). There are examples of Muslim communities who are conscious of this and operate so as not to transgress boundaries. Dafydd Jones theorizes that the mosques in his study of rural West Wales are 'subaltern counter-publics'. This refers to 'store-front' mosques which do not indicate a Muslim presence in the urban landscape. The drawback of such space is that it can fail to foster a sense of belonging to the local environment but can be perceived to benefit local Muslims by not openly contesting the hegemony of local space (2010: 764). They can also act to justify discourses about Islam and reinforce narratives of 'absence' about where Islam is. One can relate Dafydd Jones's subaltern counterpublics with Ural Manço and Meryem Kanmaz's observation that first-generation Muslim migrants intentionally sought to avoid conflict by worshipping in unassuming mosques – thereby respecting what they saw as the 'law of the guest' (2005: 1117).

In the case of overtly identifiable mosques, they are sometimes objected to on the basis of failing to 'blend in' with the local environment (Nasser 2005: 74). This echoes the comments of former cabinet minister Baroness Sayeeda Warsi, who argued:

> There is no need for a minaret. There is no need for a mosque to look like it doesn't fit into its environment. It doesn't need to be like that. I would love for there to be English-designed mosques. (Dodd 2015)

Yet some mosques are intentionally built to be landmarks – which by their very nature indicate a level of discontinuity with the local environment. The size, dimensions and architecture are all markedly different from the local landscape so as to attract attention and impress upon the community the symbolic significance of the building (Serageldin 1996: 8). The question and debate over the design and aesthetic of mosques is ultimately a debate about authority over landscapes. A prominent, identifiable mosque is asserting a claim and ownership over the immediate space as well as the visual landscape.

The theory of spatial transgression and being 'out of place' can be taken further in considering time. Richard Gale discusses planning policy in Birmingham which set 'limitations on the numbers of people that could attend religious gatherings and the hours during which gatherings could take place, each of which was designed to restrict the impact of "new" religious establishments upon surrounding residential areas' (2008: 30). The policy is a clear example of boundary maintenance by the local planning council. Yet these limits effectively stopped the mosque from being used as a mosque, as they prevented the early morning *fajr* (dawn) prayers. The hegemonic notion of what worship should look like, when it should take place, and where it should be placed, according to the councillors resulted in a deeply discriminatory planning policy.

Conclusion

Jocelyne Cesari's summary of the literature on mosque conflicts, despite being written in the early 2000s, remains true today:

> The arguments put forward on the local level to justify refusal [of mosques] are the same throughout Europe: noise and traffic nuisance, incompatibility with existing urban planning, non-conformity with existing security norms. But beyond these technical obstacles, the resistance to new mosques is always linked to a meta-narrative about Islam. This narrative, prevalent on the international level, also exists on the national level, and in many European countries; Islam is systematically conflated with threats to international or domestic order. (2005: 1019)

Mosque conflicts can be seen as examples of the latent Islamophobia in British society, manifested in actions of 'boundary maintenance' when Muslims seek to establish themselves physically in the landscape. Resistance to mosques is both organized, by far-right groups, and also organic, emerging from the nearby residents to the proposed plans. The resistance can take the form of bureaucratic issues of policy, to more aggressive protests and 'mosque invasions' and acts of vandalism and arson. Yet the negotiation of these challenges underscores an important dimension of mosque building in Britain, namely the capacity of British Muslims to negotiate this terrain, to organize around and through the mosque, and to act in relation to it. A repeated theme of this book is to emphasis the contemporary British mosque as emerging as a sizable and organized agent in society. Such an emergence will naturally create contest, controversy and conflict.

8

The women's mosque

In 2015, Cardiff University launched its first 'Massive Online Open Access Course', titled 'Muslims in Britain: Changes and Challenges'. It ran annually for four years, attracting nearly ten thousand students. I was a tutor for the course for each delivery, providing online support and guidance to the digital learners and presenting (in the form of pre-recorded videos) some of the content on British mosques. By a very strong margin, the most common question and query from the learners every year related to women and mosques. The questions could be expressed in different ways, such as 'do women attend the mosque?', to more aggressive questions such as 'why aren't women allowed in the mosque?' In one video, I provided a tour of a local mosque, describing the features, architecture and general activities. The mosque in question was open to both men and women and notable for being very vocally and practically committed to this equality of access. The video did not demonstrate this, however, on account of the mosque being empty during the tour. Nonetheless, every single year, the same question was asked: 'why can't we see any women in the mosque?' The mosque being empty of both men and women at the time was the answer. Nonetheless, the question highlights the assumptions of a secondary or diminished role for women in Islam that some people can bring to their engagements with Muslims. It is an assumption that Hafiza (a pseudonym), an *'alima*[1] in Birmingham speaking to me anonymously, is very conscious of.

> I would love to shout from the rooftops 'let me in to the mosques!', or knock down the door and make a scene, but that does more harm than good. People are just waiting for something like this to point and say 'oh look, it's the backward Muslims at it again!'

Hafiza could be described as a campaigner for women's access to mosques, but she hates that term. 'I'm an *'alima*, that is what I studied to become, that's who I am, my duty is to the teachings of Islam, I'm not a campaigner.' She nonetheless dedicates herself to convincing mosques to provide space for women. 'You have to speak their language, literally sometimes, and you have to be patient, but it is possible.' She hesitates to answer when I ask her how many mosques she convinced to provide space for women: 'I don't count it like that, and it's not just me, but others, the women in the congregation, the daughters of the mosque chairman, it's always a collective effort', but finally she relents, 'about thirty now'. Hafiza's success could easily make her a well-known figure, but she dislikes attention, in part because of Hafiza's own introverted personality, but also since she considers it an anathema to her goals. 'Convincing some of these guys', referring to the mosque committees, 'it's like talking to a toddler', she explains while laughing.

> If you fight with a toddler, insisting he or she do something, they dig their heels in and refuse, and boy, you don't want to have a battle of wills with a kid. But if you're gentle, willing to suggest something a few times, and let them have space to figure it out, and then take ownership of the idea, so it's not them losing a battle but their great new initiative, well then, it's a lot easier.

I visit some of the mosques she has convinced to provide space to women in Birmingham. Sometimes the space allocated is just small backrooms, in other instances, it is allowing women to join at the back of the main prayer hall behind some form of temporary physical divider. They may be small wins, but they are incredibly valuable to the Muslim women who use them. 'I know it shouldn't have to be [like] this, but Muslim women are stuck between *shaytan* [i.e. satan] and the deep blue sea, between Islamophobic non-Muslims, and misogynistic Muslim men.' Hafiza, like many Muslim women, must navigate between disadvantages Muslim women face in accessing mosques, without conceding to a wider collection of presumptions, and prejudices held by wider society about Muslims.

This tension is a recurring theme in studying women and the mosque. On the one hand, a great deal of public interest in the role of women in Islam and on the other hand, the importance of the issue of access of mosques to Muslim women, and the very awkward relationship between the two. Interest in the role of women in British mosques expressed by politicians and the media is sometimes driven by uncharitable or hostile assumptions about Islam. They can draw on Islamophobic ideas about the oppression and suppression of women. It would be overstating things to consider all external interest in mosques and women as a result of Islamophobia or orientalized notions of Muslims, but it is nonetheless an identifiable theme. For example, a government review into integration conducted by Louise Casey (2016: 107) found '[m]osques and

Islamic organisations offering regressive advice about the behaviours expected of Muslim women and girls' and called for government policies '[e]mancipating marginalised groups of women', which previously read 'Muslim women' in an earlier draft. The framing and focus on Muslim women in particular and their need to be saved was criticized by several Muslim groups and activists (Taylor 2016), including Bana Gora of the Muslim Women's Council (MWC) who will feature later in the chapter. In 2020, Zara Mohammed was elected the Secretary General of the Muslim Council of Britain, the largest umbrella body of mosques in the UK. She stated several times in media interviews, including to me directly, that 'my age was a stumbling block amongst the affiliates much more than my gender'. Zara's win against her opponent, Ajmal Masroor, a well-known imam and preacher, was decisive (nearly double the votes). In an interview on BBC Radio 4's *Woman's Hour*, Emma Barnett quizzed Zara Mohammed on the number of female imams, a question that was criticized as inappropriately hostile. An open letter from the MCB to the BBC after the interview, co-signed by Labour MPs Diane Abbot and Naz Shah, Conservative Baroness Sayeeda Warsi, and a range of other prominent figures, accused the presenter of repeating stereotypes about Islam and making a 'false equivalence between imams with rabbis and priests in a religion that has no clergy reflected a basic lack of religious literacy needed for authentic engagement with British Muslim communities' (*BBC News* 2021). The narrative of needing to save Muslim women from Islam has been explored by scholars such as Lila Abu-Lughod as a 'moral crusade' that has justified a range of domestic and international policies (2013). The same underlying logic and assumptions have driven counter-terror policy in the UK; Katherine Brown documented how inclusion of Muslim women in mosques has been seen as a solution to issues of radicalization and extremism, something she terms the 'just-add-women' approach (Brown 2008, 2014).

Whether these are examples of Islamophobia or not is a subject to debate, but they provide a sense of the climate in which Muslim women feel conscious that campaigning for greater access to mosques can be misconstrued or subsumed into broader narratives about Islam and women. Nonetheless there is a significant movement amongst British Muslims that seeks to renegotiate the terms by which women access, use and participate in mosques. The following chapter will explore the contours of this 'debate', though the term 'debate' is used cautiously. It is mistaken to consider the challenge of women's inclusion in mosques to be an argument between two sides, one calling for inclusion and one calling for exclusion. The reality is a generational shift in how British Muslims engage in communal religion, which is underway currently, and the renegotiation of the role of the mosque in society more broadly.

Drawing on the past

The history and historicity of the events of the Prophet Muhammad's life as recorded in collections of *hadith* and *sira* remain a debate that has preoccupied scholars through the centuries (not just Muslims). The Prophet's Mosque provides the superlative religious mandate for religious practice in mosques. Thus a historical discussion of what took place in the Prophet's Mosque is one which has legal weight in Islam; it establishes boundaries for what is considered the norm, the limits of acceptable conducts, and the actions which are forbidden. Legal scholars of Islam may wrestle with the historical practice of the Prophet Muhammad and excuse or exceptionalize it in different ways, but the significance of the reports of early practice of Muslims as a textual basis for ascertaining correct behaviour is rarely lessened. The Prophetic example is also something that is used and referred to by the general populace who will regularly draw upon it and utilize it in their own ways, much to the frustration of legal scholars who insist on a stricter methodological application. For an insight into this tradition of Islamic legal thought, Jonathan Brown's *Misquoting Muhammad* (2014) provides a view into the traditions of interpretation within Islamic history. Additionally, scholar Marion Katz's *Women in the Mosque: A History of Legal Thought and Social Practice* (2014) presents a comprehensive exploration of the legal texts of Islam in relation to women in the mosque, and contextualizes it alongside historical practice. I draw on Katz significantly in assessing historical practice as she provides a robust historical account. There are numerous *ahadith* recording women's attendance, presence and worship in mosques collected by the *muhaddithun*. There are two *hadiths* however that are the most important in legal rulings on women in the mosque. They are recorded with different wordings, but the key content remains the same.

The first establishes a right for women to attend the mosque:

> One of the wives of 'Umar (bin Al-Khattab) used to offer the Fajr and the 'Isha' prayer in congregation in the Mosque. She was asked why she had come out for the prayer as she knew that 'Umar disliked it, and he has great *ghaira* (self-respect). She replied, 'What prevents him from stopping me from this act?' The

other replied, 'The statement of Allah's Messenger (ﷺ): 'Do not stop Allah's women-slaves from going to Allah's Mosques' prevents him.'[2] (Sahih al-Bukhari, Book of Friday Prayer)

The second, however, undermines this right:

Had Allah's Messenger (ﷺ) known what the women were doing, he would have forbidden them from going to the mosque as the women of Bani Israel had been forbidden. Yahya ibn Sa'id (a sub-narrator) asked 'Amra (another sub-narrator), 'Were the women of Bani Israel forbidden?' She replied 'Yes.'[3] (Sahih al-Bukhari, Chapter on Call to Prayers)

These two *ahadith*, along with numerous others describing the activity of women in the Prophet's Mosque, constitute the sacred sources upon which later Muslim scholarship would rest their case as to the permissibility of the presence of women in the mosque. They're introduced only to highlight that both a legal right to attend the mosque for Muslim women, as well as a legal prohibition, are found in the earliest sources of the Islamic authority (in this case, through a close companion of the Prophet Muhammad and through the wife of the Prophet Muhammad).

Alongside the legal tradition, it is worth remembering the social history of Muslims. First is the diversity of practice, both historically and today. Legal prescriptions aside, what takes place on the ground varies tremendously through time and place. Second, the category of 'women' itself should not be taken for granted, since this varies just as much across time and place. As Katz writes, 'jurists universally presumed that women of different ages or statuses were subject to significantly different standards of behaviour', and 'might also be divided in terms of physical allure, religious learning, or personal propriety' (Katz 2014: 3). Thus in considering the forthcoming key sources, one must not only keep in mind the various scholarly interpretations of them, but also that they are also not necessarily read as generic statements about all women as a whole. A further consideration of the legal discussions, relevant especially to the varying roles of mosques in contemporary Britain, is that as people 'used (and continue to use) mosques for many purposes . . . the question of women's presence or absence in mosques should not be conflated with their participation in specific activities' (Katz 2014: 5). Legal discussions in the Islamic tradition tend to focus on the legally prescribed matters of the Friday prayer and the canonical *salah*, and as such, tend to omit references to a broad range of practices in the mosque outside of this.

Women in the mosques historically and geographically

The diversification of mosque functions globally means there is a broad range of 'norms' geographically and temporally that defy easy categorization. What is the 'norm' in relation to gender and segregation varies not only from time to time, country to country, but mosque to mosque, inflected by local customs, legal schools, denominational identity, and of course, the agency of women themselves. A full survey of Muslim mosque usage historically, other than being a gargantuan task, is also made impossible due to the paucity of sources. The most thorough reconstruction available is via Marion Katz's survey of social practice of mosques in the pre-modern era in the Middle East. Her work is both the most comprehensive and authoritative available in English and so forms a key source in the subsequent analysis. She approaches the scant historical sources creatively, inferring and deducing mosque usage cautiously and reliably. The picture she finds is an active congregational life amongst women. The mosque was often home to these activities, though rarely in the same way or on equal footing with men. The rhythmic use of mosques is something that emerges clearly as an important factor in British Muslim mosque usage (Chapter 4) and is present too in Katz's study. Women attended congregational prayers less often than men, but for key sacred days in the week or the year, they may take over the mosque, such as Thursday evenings or the middle of the month of Shaʿban (Katz 2014: 196).

Overall, one thing that emerges repeatedly and clearly is that women did attend the mosque historically. The strictest prohibitions for women's mosque attendance focused on congregational prayers; women could and did attend in between prayer times. Furthermore, there emerges a clear disparity in Katz's work between legal texts and social practice. Katz herself undertakes effort to disturb the notion that Islamic legal writ is determinative of Muslim behaviour (Katz 2014: 10) and demonstrates well how fatwas issued about women in the mosque were polemical and exhortative, responding to a reality in which women were present. So while the canonical Sunni law schools might have agreed on the undesirability of young women attending the mosque, in practice, this seemed to operate in tandem with other forms of orthodoxy.

Shahab Ahmed presents a way to understand and locate legal works. In *What is Islam? The Importance of Being Islamic* (2015), Ahmed articulates the peripheral role legal scholars occupied in the 'Balkans to Bengal Complex' (a historical and geographic arena covering most of Eurasia from 1250 to 1850, intersecting with some of the historical periods Katz explores). There were numerous forms of religious authority, the *fuqaha* was only one form amongst many. There was what he terms the 'para-nomian' approach of the Sufis, an approach that places itself as '*beside*, beyond, and above law [emphasis in original]' (Ahmed 2015: 454). These various approaches to understanding and practising Islam existed side by side, stressing once again the diversity historically. Katz offers her own analysis too; she sees the social reality as existing in tandem with legal teachings. She concludes that women had access to mosques by and large, but that 'to say that women had access to mosques, however, does not imply that they frequented mosques to the same degree, at the same times, or for the same reasons as men' (2014: 195). She highlights the importance of women's 'own distinctive goals and priorities, which sometimes favoured other religious venues and activities' (Katz 2014: 196). She concludes that 'if the evidence suggests that legal doctrine influenced or constrained women's mosque-going behaviour, it also suggests women's behaviour had an impact on the thinking of legal scholars' (Katz 2014: 197).

So many mosques historically were male-dominated and male-run spaces, but they were not exclusively so. There existed numerous spatial and temporal accommodations for women, though with a degree of segregation between the genders. The least segregated, historically and now, have always been the two sacred mosques in Mecca and Medina. The necessities of pilgrimage, a pillar of Islam for both men and women, have meant that it has largely been open to both genders, and due to the sheer influx of numbers as well as the way in which men and women travelled together as families, it has generally kept segregation in both mosques to a minimum.

There are also historic and contemporary examples of what can be termed 'women's mosques'. Of these, those in China received increased attention following the publication of Maria Jaschok and Shui Jingjun's *The History of Women's Mosque in Chinese Islam* (2000). The book, though now produced over two decades ago, has occasionally been the basis for journalists covering the mosques, with a subtext that the presence of the Chinese mosque is an exception and in contrast to Islam's otherwise patriarchal norms.[4] The distinctiveness of a women's mosque is that it not only subverts the presumed masculinity of mosques but also in the leadership role women play in management of the space, teaching, instruction and sometimes leading prayer. A more recent publication by Jacqueline Fewkes, *Locating Maldivian Women's Mosques in Global Discourses* (2019), presents a further example of women's mosques, the *nisha miskii*. Though now all closed, until recently the *nisha miskii* were women-only and women-run spaces, part of the religious life on the Maldivian Islands. Fewkes is keen throughout the work to de-exceptionalize the notion of a women's mosques. Rather than being a unique phenomenon in China, she lists examples both historic and contemporary, in places such as Senegal, Somalia and Malaysia, as well as recently founded women-only mosques in Europe and the United States (Fewkes 2019: 111–33). There has also been historical work examining the broad provision for Muslim women in mosques in the Balkans (Dişli 2015).

If one broadens the perspective to consider all regular places of prayer and to entertain a broad range of institutional models, then the women's mosque, rather than being a unique phenomenon, begins to look more commonplace. There are examples of women's mosques, in the sense of dedicated spaces of prayer for women, managed, run and attended exclusively by women, in places across the globe. Katz lists several historic examples from her research: an arcade for women in the Prophet's Mosque during the eighth century, an approach emulated in the Great Mosque of Cordoba, designated prayer rooms in mosques in North Africa and Spain (Katz 2014: 120–4). There is also a historic building attached to al-Aqsa identified as *jami' al-nisa'*, which could quite accurately be translated as the 'women's congregational mosque' (Katz 2014: 167–8). Today, the prayer halls and spaces dedicated for women in mosques in various parts of the globe can operate with a degree of separation and autonomy from the mosque to which it is attached that it can be more accurate to think of them as women's mosques. The historical practice is thus diverse, and this is met with an equally diverse strategy in contemporary times; in Britain, the strategies for dividing space in mosques are considered next.

British mosques and women

Hind Makki, an interfaith campaigner and Muslim activist, launched a website called 'Side Entrance' (side entrance n.d.). It documented pictures of women's entrances in mosques in North America and Europe, which are invariably the side entrances to buildings, often smaller, less accessible, and both symbolically and physically peripheral. The side entrances would lead to smaller and poorly maintained spaces. The website is still occasionally updated today and documents the experiences of Muslim women in seeking to find places to pray. Makki represents a campaigner who is both critical of the status quo amongst Muslims in diaspora but sympathetic to the financial and social pressures facing mosque leaders. She writes that she often does not name mosques posted on the blog, but rather seeks to highlight the reality for many Muslim women when it comes to accessing mosques. Similar projects with a UK focus include the 'My Mosque Story' ('My Mosque Story' n.d.) social media campaign, which aims to capture the experiences of Muslim women in British mosques, and 'Open My Mosque' ('Open My Mosque | Facebook' n.d.), a project set up by campaigner Julie Siddiqi. Both projects hope to stimulate change amongst mosques in Britain. The diminution of women in British mosques is a historical constant. Sariya Cheruvallil-Contractor, for example, explores the forgotten histories of Muslim women in one of Britain's earliest mosques, the Liverpool Muslim Institute in Liverpool. She documents their agency, inclusion and exclusion, and observes it is 'not dissimilar to the debates around gender in contemporary British societies' (2020).[5]

The challenge of capturing the practice and provision for Muslim women in British mosques is difficult. There is no unified or singularly reliable database of mosques. The statistics which are available are of varying degrees of reliability. The website 'Muslims in Britain', maintained by Mehmood Naqshbandi (discussed previously), provides a reliable database which indicates that around 28 per cent of British mosques do not have space for women (Naqshbandi 2017). Of the 72 per cent of identified mosques that do have women's spaces, it is difficult to identify how meaningful this provision is. Some may be regularly accessible and well-maintained spaces, whereas others are likely to be spaces only operating at certain times. There is also the constantly changing nature of mosque provision for women, with spaces being both opened up to women and restricted depending on circumstances. A BBC News article by journalist Sophia Smith Galer (2021) documented how mosques re-opening following the pandemic restricted access to women, even if there was space provided prior. Mosques opening spaces for women, and then ceasing this provision for other reasons, is also not uncommon.

Models of mosque use

For mosques which in some way accommodate women in the mosque, there are four models of gender segregation in operation. The first model is architectural. It allocates different rooms or halls for the men and women. This usually takes the form of a 'women's section' or 'women's room' and is commonly found in converted properties. The majority of British mosques that have space for women follow this approach. Architectural segregation in purpose-built mosques can also have specifically designed platforms, arcades or floors for women. Oxford

Central Mosque, a purpose-built mosque, is a typical example of the strategy with separate designated entrances for men and women. In smaller 'house mosques', the same strategy is visible on a smaller scale. The al-Manar Mosque in Cardiff, for example, provides space for women on the second floor while the ground floor (renovated to remove walls) is used by the men.

The second model is spatial segregation, where men and women use the same space (hall or room) but separate physically within it, as it is believed to have been done in the Prophet's Mosque during the lifetime of the Prophet. There may be a makeshift divider, or some other way of distinguishing the sections. This is rare in Britain, and while there are cases where it is adopted by preference, it is more commonly a result of a congregation only having a single room or hall available (in the case of an institutional prayer room for example). Markfield Institute's mosque maintains this practice, with a physical divider of moveable screens used to distinguish between where men congregate and where women congregate.

The third approach is temporal segregation. Here the space is occupied entirely by men or entirely by women, but at different times. The ways in which this is distributed can vary. For example, in some mosques, prayer times are staggered. There is a time allocated for men and subsequently for women. This is common where congregational demand is greater than the space available. This strategy, in varying degrees of formality, can be seen in institutional or commercial prayer rooms or multifaith rooms in locations such as airports or shopping centres. In a central airport outside London, for example, the prayer times for men and women are listed on a scribbled piece of paper attached to the door. In other similar locations, such as a shopping centre, the men might wait outside until the women are finished praying. The strategy is much less common in mosques.

The final approach is having no segregation, found exclusively amongst a small number of progressive mosques where there is no boundary or segregation between men and women at all, who not only pray in the same space but side by side. The Muslim Educational Centre of Oxford (MECO) is one such group which maintains no separation of genders in their regular activities. The small group, currently operating out of Chester House in George Street, not only holds classes and seminars but also Friday congregational prayers.

There is, in all of these cases, a degree of fluidity. Segregation in mosques is rhythmic, breaking down and being reasserted at various points in the day. Erving Goffman argues that all societies operate a form of gender segregation, which has a 'sort of with-then-apart rhythm, with a period of the sexes being immersed together followed by a short period of separation, and so on' (1977: 316). In many mosques, the prayer times are the moments when separation is most keenly observed. In between these times, the boundaries become more porous, and can break down entirely. Like wider society there is a 'with-then-apart rhythm' in the mosque but with a rhythm that is distinct and unique to the mosque itself. Here the typology discussed in Chapter 2 does not overlap with the typologies used. Interspatial mosques at all levels can be either open to women or restrict their access.

Factors against inclusion

There are several factors that push against the inclusion of women into mosques, or even the provision of space. The first key factor is that in Britain, the majority of first-generation migrants who settled and then established mosques are from South Asia, where Muslim women's presence in mosques is limited (both emerging from Islamic teachings and custom). Collectively, Bangladeshis and Pakistanis make up 53 per cent of the British Muslim population according to the 2011 census (though the census is now nearly a decade out of date, it still provides the most robust figures on Muslim demographics available). Furthermore, South Asians are over-represented in establishing mosques in Britain. The Hanafi school is the most common amongst South Asians, whether Deobandi, Barelvi or Fultoli in terms of denomination. The Hanafi school is the most restrictive in terms of women's presence in mosques (Katz 2014, 71–87). First-generation migrants from this background then recreated the Islam they were familiar with. In the context of the Indian subcontinent, women observed communal worship in a variety of spaces and places, from the shrine to the *zawiya*, and the mosque was seldom part of this. This is true not only of South Asia; Lois Beck observes the pattern in her study of Muslim women's religious lives in the Middle East (1980), as does Katz in her reflections of mosque usage historically (Katz 2014: 141, 154), and Cleo Cantone explicitly writes about Senegal and the shift from Sufi forms of communal worship towards a 'reformist Islam' in which activities are more intentionally focused in the mosque (2002: 29). In establishing Islam in Britain, however, few of these additional spaces carried across. The *zawiya* is absent and there are only a small number of shrines in Britain (see Chapter 4 for details of one such shrine). As surveyed in Chapter 3, in Britain, Muslim communal religion became congregational, with greater emphasis on the mosque as a site of communal worship. This shapes the contemporary challenge.

Women do not have access to a diverse religious landscape in which they could engage in communal religion as they did in South Asia, but they also do not have the access to mosques in Britain. The fidelity to the Islam of 'back home' is important to many first-generation migrants who established British mosques and presents one of the most challenging stumbling blocks to changing practice.

A second factor is the priorities of mosques. As covered in Chapter 2 and the model of the interspatial mosque, there are several distinct motivations for opening a mosque. These include: a place for the men to pray regularly, to undertake key rites such as weddings and funerals, and perhaps most importantly, the education and socialization of Muslim children. Amongst these motivations, providing a space for communal religious practice of Muslim women was low amongst their priorities. The picture today has shifted, and a survey conducted by the MCB in 2019 with 1,024 women found that amongst the respondents, the wish to access mosques was very high. A total of 78.3 per cent of respondents considered it important for women to go to the mosque. The majority of respondents were under the age of forty-four, and so from a younger generation. The results, when taken alongside the previously mentioned campaigns and initiatives by Muslim women to access mosques, make it clear that Muslim women in Britain today seek a place in mosques. Mosque leaders and management have only recently begun to recognize the sea-change that means that the context of the mosque-building era of the 1960s to 1990s is very different from the context of the new millennium.

These two factors collectively mean that the majority of the mosques founded during the post-war period did not account for women in their design and provision at all, and their inclusion is a retroactive change that often includes more financial cost and resources than if provision was included from the inception of the mosque. This is especially true if the mosque management or congregation seek to maintain a stricter boundary between the genders than would be afforded by strategies that utilize shared space. This leads to a third factor. The British Muslim population, both historically and in the contemporary period, is on the lower end of the socio-economic scale (Stevenson et al. 2017); mosques reflect this. Many mosques are converted terraced homes, or converted churches, both of which are more affordable than a purpose-built mosque. Providing meaningful and adequate provision for Muslim women is costly, and this cost provides an additional significant barrier even when there is willingness in principle to accommodate women in mosques.

This combination of factors creates, more than anything, an inertia against change. First, there is a theological-cum-legal challenge to establish that Muslim women have a need and right to access mosques (even if, as some traditions in Islam teach, a women's prayer is better at home). Second, the practical considerations for allocating space for women must be made in the face of resistance, and finally, when space has been allocated, it must be preserved in order to make the case that such a change was valuable in the first place.

The campaigners

In the beginning of this chapter, I outlined the fallacy of considering the issue of women in mosques a debate with clear sides, for and against. In terms of advocates and campaigners for women in mosques, here too we find complexity and variety, and despite sharing some of the same goals, they address the challenges from different starting points and with different solutions. Rather than being a united front, they can often be critics of one another. They can be described as the legal scholars, the bureaucrats, the reformists and the pioneers.

The legal scholars

The legal scholars make a legal case for the inclusion of women in the mosque drawn out of the Quran and the Sunna and within a concern for upholding a historic legal tradition within Islam. Ultimate truth, for the legal scholars, is found in the tradition and the text, and as such, providing scriptural evidence is indispensable for them, echoing the epistemological framework Ahmed (2015: 113–29) ascribes to the 'jurists', for whom scriptural evidence is the source of ultimate authority. The underlying logic is that Muslims must adhere to Islamic teachings and Islamic teachings are derived from the sacred sources, and so by excavating the text and historical practice of early Muslims, a clear moral imperative is established that should change social practice on the ground.

Jasser Auda's 2017 work *Reclaiming the Mosque: The Role of Women in Islam's House of Worship*, published by Claritas Books in Wales, is an example of a contemporary (male) scholar advocating for the inclusion of women in mosques. Auda is an academic and theologian, and part of the European Council for Fatwas. His book is the product of a series of short articles written over several years that document and articulate the practice in the Prophet's Mosque, as well as arguing against the fatwas of other scholars who include provisions or restrictions on women. He compiled these articles into a book due to their popularity online. The work is rooted in a modernist trend amongst contemporary Muslim scholars, willing to break ranks with historical opinion and work outside the established schools of law, but who nonetheless utilize the same epistemological framework (i.e. that of the supremacy of law) to do so. A similar approach can be found in the figure of Shaykh Akram Nadwi. Nadwi is a graduate of Darul Uloom Nadwatul Ulama, Lucknow, India, which establishes him as a scholar in the South Asian Hanafi tradition. In Britain, Nadwatul Ulama are often seen as compatriots of the Deobandi seminaries, following a similar syllabus and tradition but with a different lineage. His further studies brought him to Britain where, alongside pursuing academic studies at the universities of Oxford and Cambridge, he also undertook teaching in various Islamic institutions including Markfield Institute of Higher Education. Nadwi is an interesting figure; unlike modernists such as Auda, he locates himself fully within what is usually considered the more conservative traditionalism of the *madhhab*. In 2013, Nadwi published *Al-Muḥaddithāt: The Women Scholars in Islam*, a compilation of biographies of Muslim women who are transmitters of *hadith*. The book, and Nadwi himself, argued for a recentring of women in Islamic scholarship, something which Nadwi believes was the norm in Islamic society historically, but has been lost due to a combination of social and political factors. Nadwi also authored a translation and commentary titled *Ibn Hazm on the Lawfulness of Women Attending Prayers in the Mosque* (2018). Unlike Auda, whose theological arguments are rooted in a revision of scholarly tradition in favour of returning to the sources and by-passing the classical tradition, Nadwi locates his argument through a classical and celebrated historical Muslim jurist. Ibn Hazm is often associated with the now extinct Zahiri *madhhab*, rather than Nadwi's own Hanafi *madhhab*, but in drawing upon Ibn Hazm, Nadwi speaks to other like-minded Muslims. Ibn Hazm is a historical figure, and thus cannot be accused of bowing to pressure from modernity. The Zahiri *madhhab* is also known for being strict textualists, and indeed Ibn Hazm's scholarship on the issue quotes copiously from the sacred sources of Islamic scholarship (the Quran and the Sunna), and a detractor cannot argue his rulings are based on convoluted legal precepts. Finally, Ibn Hazm's scholarship in this area addresses, sometimes directly and sometimes indirectly, the four canonical schools of Sunni law. In doing so, his own work had a lasting legacy in being 'assimilated into those of the major schools' (Katz 2014: 9) and remains relevant as a piece of scholarship aimed at other's who identify the schools as important methodological disciplines to maintain. By way of example, Ibn Hazm discusses at length whether the Prophet's permission to attend the mosque only applied to older women, a distinction made by the four schools of law. Auda's work, by contrast, does not address this point at all.

Another example of the legal approach can be found in a fatwa issued by Mufti Muhammad ibn Adam, a British-born and educated Deobandi scholar. In his fatwa (Adam 2005), he cites the classical Hanafi restrictions on the attendance of women (only older women, only with certain key conditions around dress, lack of perfume, permission from the women's husband, only for the night-time prayers and so on) and the rationalizations made by classic Hanafi scholars for these injunctions, defending them from any accusation of being based in cultural or misogynistic bias. Adam argues that just as Hanafi scholars imposed restrictions on women's mosque attendance based on Aisha's statement that the times have changed, the times have changed again. Whereas it was appropriate to prohibit women's attendance in the past, today, Adam contends, women are in the workforce, the marketplaces and public life in general, and so it is fitting to provide a space for them in mosques. This argument then backtracks on the classical Hanafi view that women should not attend the mosque, but without abandoning previous scholarship by the school. The three scholars cited, Auda, Nadwi and Adam, represent different trends within British Muslim scholarship. They are relevant both in that their scholarship holds weight with British Muslims, but also in that their scholarship is a response to the increasing demand for women's spaces in mosques. They do not agree with each other on methodology or interpretation of Prophetic practice, yet they all reach the same conclusion, that women should be included within mosques, and on the same framework, that *fiqh* or Islamic law is the final arbitrator of truth. Despite their efforts, legal texts are unlikely to change social practice in Britain alone, but they provide others the leverage and weight to campaign and advocate for change, including some of the campaign groups discussed next.

The bureaucrats

For the bureaucrats, gender equality in the mosque is best achieved through the establishment of policies, procedures, regulations and good management. They can differ on their basis for their claims for women's presence in the mosque, but they can be understood collectively for focusing on mosque bureaucracy as an avenue for change. Activist Anna Nayyer runs, with Julie Siddiqi, Open My Mosque, a campaign group focused on lobbying mosques to make space for women and highlighting the experiences of frustration, isolation and rejection felt by Muslim women in Britain. Nayyer called for the Equality Act 2010, legislation designed to regulate government and statutory bodies, to be extended into the private sphere of the mosque. She is quoted in a 2018 *Guardian* article:

> 'My right as a religious minority is protected in the workplace,' says Nayyar, 'but how is my right as a woman protected when mosques are turning me away?' We need bodies like the Charity Commission and the Equality and Human Rights Commission to challenge how these mosques govern their spaces. As British Muslims, the only way for us to move forward is by a commitment to equal rights. (Aly 2018)

Nayyer's argument helps to shed light on the underlying precepts of the bureaucratic approach. Access to mosques is viewed as a right (akin to Human Rights), and this right requires management and regulation. The mechanisms to bring about this change are the state, mosque policies and procedures.

Another example of the bureaucratic approach is the MCB's 'Women in Mosques Development Programme' in 2018 and 2019, 'aiming to develop upcoming female leaders to become the mosque trustees, committee members, volunteers and centre managers of the future' (Muslim Council of Britain 2019). The programme is reminiscent of corporate feminism, which sees boardroom diversity as an avenue to greater grassroots change for women through a theory of 'trickle-down equality'. The emphasis on women leadership as a means to achieve emancipation for women is generally identified as a feature of 'third-wave feminism' (Iannello 2010).

A third example is 'Vibrant Scottish Mosques', which is led by Dr Sahira Dar, a medical doctor by profession. The organization seeks to encourage the inclusion of women in Scottish mosques at all levels, from provision of services and space, inclusion in management and leadership, and provision of female religious leadership. Sahira shared her motivation for establishing the organization in 2017.

> I was actually volunteering quite regularly in a very large mosque in Scotland during *Ramzan*, and I saw the benefits that it brought to the women that were attending, also the connection I was building with a mosque, and the connection my children were building through me. So it was that dichotomy, between how beneficial engagement and involvement with mosques is, and how isolating and challenging it can be when you can't be involved.

Sahira tells me in Scotland the majority of mosques have women's spaces, but for her, the challenge is bigger than that, 'We're not asking for equal space, we want equitable spaces. There's a big difference'. Sahira's reflections on the barriers to inclusion are sympathetic to mosques and their founders:

> The biggest barrier we're facing is that as a community we're really defensive. That's understandable, if you think about our forefathers and what they had to do to establish the first mosques, the climate they were living in of islamophobia and racism, it's very understandable the defensiveness when someone is seeming to attack our mosques or criticising them. But we're keen to stress, we're not outsiders, we're part of your community.

Sahira's campaigning is based on an awareness of the mosque as an institution with a shifting and changing remit of responsibilities.

> And we're not asking for 'reform', we're asking for evolution, the next phase, the natural progression. Because the mosques were fit for purpose when they were established. But the community has changed, it's not what it used to be, it is a younger population, more diverse, more professional. So our mosques need to adapt, to listen and engage.

The relationship between the bureaucratic approach and that of the legal scholars is both explicit and intentional:

> One of the pieces of advice I had from scholars part of our advisory board was 'do not approach this from a *fiqhi* point of view' because that's the beauty of Islam, we have different views and diversity. Come from it from a social aspect, the social need, that's the angle.

In early 2022, Vibrant Mosques for All issued a report based on focus groups and interviews with Muslim women in Scotland (Adam 2022). The report, issued both in full and with an executive summary, included twenty-four recommendations in nine key areas of work they identified, providing suggestions for who should be responsible or could assume ownership over the delivery of the recommendation. The report is rigorous, robust, well-evidenced and instructive. It also adopts the framework of institutional development and professionalization that reflects a bureaucratic model of leadership.

It would be wrong to think that the bureaucrats do not care about legal reasoning through the Islamic texts. In general, they see Muslim women's presence in mosques and equality with men as something enshrined in the Quran but prevented through contemporary practice in British mosques. The question is thus not one of piety but power, and how best to bring the teachings of the Quran into fruition. The success of their model, however, lies in the continuing bureaucratization of mosques as a whole, a process El-Yousfi (2019) considers part of a wider process of state control of religious populations. There is no reason to believe that the process of bureaucratization is inevitable, and if British mosques adopt a different strategy of development in future, the impact of campaigning for women's access through bureaucratic models will be lessened.

The progressives

The progressives are distinct from other groups since their focus is not just the inclusion of women in the mosque, but a much broader range of issues. These can include issues of LGBT inclusion, secularism or terrorism. They seek a foundational change in the epistemological framework and tradition of Islam. Whereas the theologians and bureaucrats seek to work within the existing frameworks and traditions of Islam, the reformers pursue an entirely new relationship to the sacred sources and historical practice.

Perhaps the most well-known campaigner from this category is Amina Wadud. Wadud is an African American convert to Islam, with an extensive academic background both in Western institutions and in the Middle East and South East Asia. She has authored a feminist reading of the Quran (Wadud 1999) as well as more recently *Inside the Gender Jihad* (2018), which more explicitly articulates her case for reform. Wadud has also twice led mixed-gender Friday prayers in Britain, once in Oxford in 2008 (Butt and Nixon 2008), and again in London in 2015 (Gledhill 2015). She has advocated for the permissibility of female imams and mixed prayers and based her case in both legal and more broadly theological terms, but her approach is more direct and practical. In leading prayers as a woman, she is making the case for permissibility vociferously through her actions, which in many ways can be read as a form of protest against established norms.

Seyran Ateş can be classed as a progressive in her approach to the existing Islamic legal traditions and positions. Ateş is a German feminist campaigner who runs the 'liberal' Ibn Ruschd-Goethe Mosque in Berlin, a mosque which seeks to be inclusive to both genders as well as LGBT Muslims, and which bans the face-covering (or *niqab*). Ateş visited the UK in 2017 and announced her intentions to open a similar mosque in Britain (Sherwood 2017). As of now, no further progress has been made on the plans. It is notable that the legal scholars, Auda, Nadwi and others, even if advocating for women's rights, are men. Wadud and Ateş represent a wave of female Muslim leaders challenging the religious status quo, and who source their authority away from the legal reasoning that characterizes the approach of Auda, Nadwi and Ibn Adam. The progressive movement in Britain, however, has remained numerically small, unable to gain traction amongst the broader Muslim demographic.

The pioneers

The pioneers seek to lead by example and so create the types of institutions they wish to see. In Britain, Tamsila Tauquir and Dervla Shannahan founded the Inclusive Mosque Initiative, which hosted Amina Wadud for her 2015 visit. The Inclusive Mosque Initiative seeks to establish a mosque space that is radically inclusive, to Muslims as well as non-Muslims, to LGBT Muslims and disabled Muslims, essentially all those who feel – for whatever reason – excluded by mainstream British Muslim institutions. It currently runs Friday prayers from 'New Unity' in London, an institution that describes itself as a 'non-religious church' (complete with non-religious ministers and non-religious Sunday Assembly) as well as monthly *halaqa*s from St Ethelburga's (a Church of England-run 'Centre for Peace and Reconciliation' in the City of London).

There is also an initiative run by the MWC, a Bradford-based charity led by Bana Gora. I interviewed Bana Gora about her work, and about the plans for a women's mosque. She began with the inception of the MWC itself, telling me that the charity 'wasn't just about masjids, but about a structure Muslim women can affiliate themselves too, instead of looking to Muslim men to advocate on their behalf'. The MWC engaged with women in Bradford and Britain more broadly, and access to mosques emerged as a key challenge Muslim women they spoke to faced. Around the same time, Bana said she was 'trying to secure places for gathering during Ramzan in the masjid for women, and we were really struggling, in a city like Bradford with over 150 mosques, it was clear something had to be done'. In this context, Bana and the leadership of the MWC decided to launch a project aimed at creating a mosque space that was welcoming and accessible to women. The idea was to announce plans in a conference held in 2015 by the Council, and use it as an opportunity to begin a period of consultation with Muslim women and to create a vision for a mosque-institution that could solve the problems Muslim women faced. Bana insists that the conference was an in-house affair, and efforts were made for no journalists to be present as the Muslim women discussed their challenges and solutions.

> But there was some local journalist who had snuck into the back of the hall, so that same evening it was on the front page of the newspapers 'Muslim Women's Council opening a women's only mosque', and it just spiralled out of control.

The coverage that followed was national and international, and Bana recounts how she received a flood of messages, both from supporters and critics. She explains, 'we had to bring in a media company to manage the fall out, and to clarify that it wasn't a women-only mosque, but a woman-governed mosque'. As part of the crisis management following the story, Bana Gora held a meeting with the senior Muslim leadership of Bradford, she made it clear 'this was happening', but also that there were no plans for a femaleimam, or to exclude Muslim men. The response was largely positive in her view, with all endorsing the plans. The website hosts endorsements by Shaykh Akram Nadwi, Dr Musharraf Hussein OBE, Imam Zaid Shakir, and Dr Shuruq Naguib, representing a broad spectrum of influential, respected and – most importantly – mainstream Sunni Muslim scholars. The most radical departure of the 'Women-Led Mosque' is simply that it puts women in the decision-making position, and thus in a position to address the needs and priorities of Muslim women directly, rather than through petitions to the men, who are traditionally found in positions of leadership within mosques. The plans have since developed beyond the title of a 'mosque'. Bana explains:

> We've moved away from women's led mosque title. We held three public consultations, one with men and women, then one with just women, and there was a third one with MPs and councillors. We identified that people want a building that incorporates everything, like social enterprise, a Muslim children's hospice, nuns were speaking about a peace garden, parents wanted social activities for kids. So we are looking at an all-inclusive building.

The move away from the mosque/masjid name was, according to Bana, in part due to expectations from those outside the Muslim community, explaining that it 'takes away the masjid stigma that some people have outside our religion'. While the term mosque has been dropped, Bana remains inspired by the Prophet's Mosque:

> And really going back to the prophetic model of what the masjid was, an all inclusive space for all communities, our Prophet (peace be upon him) never told people to leave. So we wanted to go back to that, and remove the barriers we as Muslims have created.

A final example, mentioned briefly prior, is the Muslim Educational Centre in Oxford (MECO), founded by Taj Hargey, who is also involved in the Oxford Institute for British Islam, which describes itself as a think-tank and research centre 'neither beholden nor subject to medieval interpretations, patriarchal oppression, political authoritarianism, cultural baggage, tribal customs, and bygone practices from distant ancestral homelands' ('Oxford Institute for British Islam – Advancing a Qur'an-Centric Faith in the UK' 2022). MECO has regularly run Friday prayers with no gender segregation (and hosted Aminda Wadud on her visit to the UK in 2008) and is a centre for progressive Muslims discussed prior.

The Inclusive Mosque Initiative, the MWC project, and MECO project reflect an ideal of how things should be done, and a desire to break away from the confines and restrictions of established institutions. They differ in their intellectual grounding and vision of Islam more broadly. The Inclusive Mosque Initiative and Oxford Muslim Educational Centre seek to be an actualization of a progressive Islam, and are associated with the scholarly contributions of figures such as Amina Wadud. The former women-led mosque was born of a desire to bring into reality the vision of the legal scholars discussed prior. Relatively speaking, all three institutions are in their infancy, but point to future directions of creativity and practice in establishing mosques.

The future of mosques and Muslim women in Britain

The greater inclusion of women in British mosques – despite facing numerous challenges – is inevitable. The opposing factors, the legal tradition's ambivalence to mosque-based worship for women, maintaining the status quo of male primacy in mosques, and material and financial constraints, will buckle as the sheer number of Muslim women seeking space in mosques increases which, given the current trends, will only continue. Time is the key factor. The status quo will change as younger Muslims assume leadership in mosques and financial and material restrictions will not only ease as the community, at one level, becomes wealthier but also is given greater capacity to invest into renovation and re-design through fundraising. The creation of new forms of mosques, ones which side-step the existing legacy of authority in British mosques, will also likely yield new and innovative forms of Muslim institutions that may move beyond the category of 'mosque' entirely.

9

Conclusion

This book has attempted to provide a small snapshot of a much broader ecosystem of British mosques. As mentioned in the introduction, the majority of British mosques have been established within a single lifetime, and to be able to understand, sociologically, what they are, what they do, their functions, their achievements, their role in Britain more generally, will require another generation of scholarship.

The snapshot within this book is one that seeks to advance our understanding of the contemporary British mosque now. Chapter 1, amongst other things, looked at the pioneer mosques, the men who founded them and the diversity between them that was present from the inception. Chapter 2 developed this, considering the malleable functions of the mosque through the concept of the interspatial mosque. At its core, the mosque functions as a location for communal religious worship and rites which require a community (both formal, such as the prayer, and informal, such as the education of children). However, once resources expand, the leadership of mosques often seeks to adopt functions beyond this. These functions vary, but they are always tied to the idea of the Prophet's Mosque. Moving to Chapter 3, the congregation was introduced as a key component of the structure of a mosque, arguably the most important. While the specific relationship between the imam, the committee and the congregation will vary from mosque to mosque, there has been an underappreciation of the role of the congregation that this chapter sought to redress. Chapter 4 looked at how mosques are imbued as a site of sacredness, and how this sacredness is managed in light of the diverse functions a mosque can undertake. The chapter explains some of the ways that mosques are sacralized, in the absence of any formal or universally accepted ritual but also to stress the perspective of the British Muslims who worship at the mosque. Chapter 5 tackled the complex and difficult issue of mosque diversity, and the denominational differences that distinguish them from each other. It argued that some British mosques develop an ecumenical approach, reflecting the internal diversity of British Muslims themselves, alongside the emergence of more vocally denominational mosques. Chapter 6 located the mosque as a site of civil society, arguing that viewing mosques as such provides a more powerful insight into the functioning of mosques and the activities they undertake in society. Chapter 7 considered the contestations and conflicts around the establishment of mosques, the negotiation between British Muslims and Islamophobic prejudices held by parts of society, and how mosques are locations of Muslim agency. Chapter 8 turned to look at the debate around the inclusion of women in mosques, those active in trying to achieve this, and the stumbling blocks to its success. Collectively, it is hoped the reader is able to look at the institution of the mosque in a new, and fuller, light. To be able to see its innovations as well as its continuities. The contemporary British mosque is a nexus of human relationships, of the past and present, of internal ambitions and external pressures, of the cosmic and the everyday, all nestled within four walls.

In addition to hoping that this work has provided the reader with a greater insight, both empirically and theoretically, into the activities of British mosques, it is also an ambition that it prompts further research and exploration. Contradicting the arguments of this work, rather than being a source of dismay, would provide me with a great deal of pleasure, since it would underline that the British mosque is being considered, debated and discussed even more so.

In Chapter 3, I introduced briefly the concept of Anglophone Islam. I draw on Shahab Ahmed's 'Balkans to Bengal Complex' (Ahmed 2015), a period of time stretching from 1250 to 1850 in which Persian was the lingua franca of Islam. Ahmed's complex is not just more than a geographic and temporal arena but 'a common paradigm of Islamic life and thought by which Muslims (and others) imagine, conceptualise, valorize, articulate and give mutually-communicable meaning to their lives in terms of Islam', one that manifests in a 'discursive cannon, embedded in which is a conceptual vocabulary, an array of expressive motifs, and other mutually-held and/or mutually-translatable modes of valorization and self-articulation' (Ahmed 2015: 75). Anglophone Islam strikes me as a comparable context, a 'common paradigm of Islamic life' developing amongst English-speaking Muslims, some in diaspora, some in the historic 'Muslim world'. The paradigm consists of the experiences of migration and colonialism, a network of scholarship and educational institutions operating in some part in English, a digital literacy that is intertwined in the everyday, an engagement with the conceptual framework of the English language itself, a discursive canon of English language texts and associated vocabulary, and a rationalist tendency that reflects the concerns of modernity (see Ahmed 2022 for a more in-depth articulation of Anglophone Islam). I am not the first to suggest this either; Sadek Hamid and Philip Lewis suggest the same, writing, 'for a new global generation of Muslims, English is the language for communication and knowledge transmission – or, arguably, the new Persian' (Lewis and Hamid 2018: 216). It can be comprehended through English-language Muslim scholarship, from the academic works published in journals to the vernacular, accessible on YouTube. It can be seen in the establishment of a library of Islamic works, read across Europe, North America, South Africa and South Asia. There is evidence of it too in the funding by Muslim philanthropists into British and American universities – which underscores the pull of Anglophone Islam that to be relevant to the Islamic world today one needs to be relevant in English.

A distinctive part of Anglophone Islam is the mosque. Whether in the way that mosques have situated the congregation as the key mechanism for communal religion, or in the way that they have taken on a broad range of functions significant that actualize Muslim agency in society, the story of the mosque has been developing for the last 1,400 years. It would be mistaken to view the British mosque simply as the manifestation of an existing tradition in a new context, simply transposing without changing a religious site from one country to another. It would be incorrect also to view the British mosque as a parochial and idiosyncratic development, disconnected from what is happening elsewhere. Rather, the British mosque presents both continuity and innovation. The final chapter looked at the inclusion of Muslim women into the mosque. Its place at the end of the book in part due to its importance to the future of the mosque. From the earliest chapters, I stressed the congregation's role in influencing, shaping and creating the mosque (more so the religious authority or the imam). The increasing involvement of women in British mosques will shape and influence the future direction of mosques, and so to the future direction of Islam in Britain. The future, however, for British Muslims is always rooted in the past; the Prophet's Mosque, time and time again, is cited as a model to emulate, to provide a mandate for the work undertaken by a mosque, and so it's importance can rarely be overstated. Rizvi writes in relation to mosques that time is understood by Muslims as 'a continuum on a Mobius strip that circles back into itself, not as linear progression' (2015: 4). The Prophet's Mosque is the clearest example of this, an anchor point in history that is creatively used for inspiration, but so too historic mosques globally. The contemporary British mosque is both a British institution shaped by local particularities but also a dimension of a global form of religious communal organizing. British Muslims are responding to new challenges by using both their historical and theological tradition combined with the resources and context of Britain. The British mosque will be integral to the future of not just Muslims, but Britain as a whole, and the development of Islam globally.

Notes

Chapter 1

1 *Salam* in short, or *al-salam ʿalaykum* in full, is the traditional greeting used by Muslims; *salam* meaning peace, and the full phrase meaning 'peace be upon you'. The reply expresses the same sentiment: *wa ʿalaykum al-salam.*
2 What is meant by the term 'sacred' is outlined in Chapter 4.
3 The database was checked in November 2021, though is regularly updated.
4 The story of Quilliam and his mosque is documented in Ron Geaves's seminal work (2010), but others since have turned their attention to the institute also (Gilham and Greaves 2017; Asmay 2021; Geaves and Birt 2021).
5 See https://www.everydaymuslim.org/projects/woking-mosque-project/muslim-heritage-trail-woking/. Accessed on 26 June 2023.
6 The author does not name the Shaykh in the text, and there is ambiguity about the precise date of the observation; as such, it is not entirely clear whether or not it is in fact Shaykh Abdullah Ali al-Hakimi being described, however I believe it is the most likely possibility.

Chapter 2

1 https://sunnah.com/muslim/5
2 This would be a standard Sunni legal description. Shia Muslims would further specify that prostration take place upon a natural fibre or piece of earth as a result of interpreting the aforementioned *hadith* more literally.
3 A surgery with a Member of Parliament is an open time, usually pre-determined and advertised, for one-to-one meetings between an elected representative and members of the public.
4 The four leaders, immediately following the Prophet's death, were described as the righteous caliphs by Sunni historians.
5 The Deobandi movement can be traced to South Asia and is one of the most important denominations in Britain, especially due to the large number of full-time seminaries which runs in the UK, which produce hundreds of graduates annually. They are discussed in further depth in Chapter 5.
6 https://cambridgecentralmosque.org/faq/ Accessed on 14 March 2022.

7 http://cambridgemosquetrust.org/ Accessed on 1 July 2021.
8 In November 2022, Dar ul-Uloom Dewsbury announced plans to cease under-18 educational provision and re-structure following a critical report from Ofsted, the regulatory body for educational institutes in the UK. Dar ul-Uloom Dewsbury still continues to run its wider services, including education for adults.

Chapter 3

1 Referring to a reformist movement within Islam. See Chapter 5 for more details.
2 https://mcb.org.uk/press-releases/mcb-calls-for-the-suspension-of-congregational-activities-at-uk-mosques-and-islamic-centres/ Accessed on 2 February 2023.
3 https://britishima.org/covid-open-letter-to-muslim-community/ Accessed on 2 February 2023.
4 https://twitter.com/MINAB_UK/status/1240573220430000128 Accessed on 2 February 2023.
5 https://www.wifaqululama.co.uk/covid19/ Accessed on 2 February 2023.
6 https://faithassociates.co.uk/coronavirus-legal-advice-and-opinion-to-mosque-trustees Accessed on 2 February 2023.
7 http://www.bbsi.org.uk/bbsi-statement-on-mosque-re-opening/ Accessed on 2 February 2023.
8 The 2011 census counted 2.6 million Muslims in Britain. The 2021 census (released in early 2023) estimates 3.9 million Muslims in England and Wales (Scottish and Northern Irish census figures have not yet been added to releases, though will likely not significantly alter the total). Given the survey cited was in 2016, the estimate of weekly congregations is based on the 2011 census figures.
9 A solitary article, emerging from computer sciences, proposes algorithmic approaches to counting congregation sizes at the *Masjid al-Haram* in Mecca (Sajid, Hassan, and Khan 2016). While not directly relevant to the topic of this article, it nonetheless raises new possibilities for gathering data on congregation sizes in the future, should such technology become more reliable.
10 While the survey informed the MCB's work, it was never published.

Chapter 4

1 Though the term 'saint' is used within this work, as well as by many Muslims themselves, it is worth noting that the concept being referred to is that of being a *wali*, or close friend, of Allah.
2 In Arabic, *al-Haramayn*.
3 Ahmed here uses truth in the terms of *haqq*, divine transcendental truth.

Chapter 5

1. Taken from the publisher website https://www.hurstpublishers.com/book/medina-in-birmingham-najaf-in-brent/ Accessed on 5 August 2022.
2. A British idiom meaning an informed but informal guess.
3. Driven by curiosity, I once divided the number of mosques in a given area by the number of Muslims within the area. A reasonably consistent figure of 950 Muslims per mosque emerged. While the method is questionable, there is no doubt a numerical threshold at which a new mosque can be sustained by a population (subject, no doubt to other factors ranging from class, local property prices and level of organization).
4. Arabic in origin, though the specific meaning in this context emerges from a South Asian context. A practice maintained by the Tablighi Jamaat movement of visiting mosques for a set period of time, for example three or forty days.
5. The Tablighi Jama'at have been studied in Britain as early as the 1990s with Sikand's (1998) offering one of the first published works; more recently Siddiqi (2018) and Timol (2015, 2017, 2020) have provided in-depth scholarship on the movement's growth, dynamics and reception in the UK.
6. Such confusion occurs between Deobandis and Barelvis too, with the *Oxford Dictionary of Islam* listing Sayyid Ahmed Reza Khan Barelvi as the founder of the Deobandi movement (Esposito 2004) – despite tracing the lineage correctly in another section (Moosa 2004).
7. Referring to Abdullah Quilliam and his mosque covered in Chapter 1.

Chapter 6

1. Ernest Gellner's 1996 *Conditions of Liberty: Civil Society And Its Rivals* can also be mentioned, though Gellner contrasts civil society with an 'Islamic society'.
2. The acronym is stylized without capitalization.

Chapter 7

1. Chapter 5, verse 45 of the Quran makes reference to the Torah ordaining an 'eye for an eye'.
2. An 'All Party Parliamentary Group' is a voluntary association of Members of Parliament from across the political spectrum who meet on a particular area of concern; there is a relatively open interpretation of the remit and work of an APPG.
3. The Rochdale grooming scandal refers to the systematic sexual abuse and trafficking of underage teenage children in Greater Manchester (where Rochdale

is located). An independent report conducted by the local authority estimated 1,400 girls were abused between 1997 and 2013 (Jay 2014). The identity of the men (predominantly, but not exclusively, Pakistani Muslims) and those of the underage girls (predominantly, but not exclusively, white non-Muslims) became a focal point of media and political discussion, including the alleged inaction of local police due to fear of being labelled 'racist'. Ella Cockbain and Waqas Tufail (2020) provide an examination of the way in which religious and racial framing became a central feature of the coverage and subsequent policy response.
4 The British National Party, a far-right nationalist political group in the UK.
5 https://www.savethehamptons.co.uk/the-wrong-place-for-a-mosque
6 These include works by geographers that locate mosques as spaces within a wider urban context and the importance of political influences (Gale and Naylor 2003; Gale and Peach 2003; Gale 2004, 2005, 2008). Other literature included is from a special edition on mosque controversies in the *Journal of Ethnic and Migration Studies* which highlighted many examples of conflicts in, around and about Muslim religious space (or lack of it) and the wider implications of such conflicts. The authors looked at mosques in Brussels (Manço and Kanmaz 2005), Berlin (Jonker 2005), Dutch towns (Landman and Wessels 2005), Bradford (McLoughlin 2005) and France (Cesari 2005a). The theme of mosques as sites of conflict in Europe was continued by Stefano Allievi (2009) and has been highlighted in studies on Islamophobia (Malik 2012; Allen 2010).

Chapter 8

1 Literally a female scholar (the male word being *'alim*), however, it also often refers to a graduate of a seminary programme, especially amongst South Asians.
2 https://sunnah.com/bukhari:900
3 https://sunnah.com/bukhari:869
4 For a brief selection, see BBC https://www.bbc.co.uk/news/magazine-3a5629565, *Global Times* http://www.globaltimes.cn/content/1105312.shtml, and *The National* https://www.thenational.ae/special-report-meet-the-female-imams-of-muslim-china-1.808330.
5 Dimensions of this debate have been explored previously by scholars such as Shannahan (2013) who discussed the gendered privilege of space of the mosque and Nyhagen (2019) who seeks to document the negotiation of both compliance and challenge presented by Muslim women to established norms of British mosques. A case study of women's Muslim religious leadership is presented by Liberatore (2019), which includes women teachers who operate within mosque spaces, but who nonetheless face the disadvantage of restricted access and prioritization compared to men.

References

Abdel Haleem, M. A. 2005. *The Qur'an*. Oxford University Press.
Abu-Lughod, Lila. 2013. *Do Muslim Women Need Saving?* Cambridge, MA: Harvard University Press.
Adam, Maariyah. 2022. 'Hear My Voice - A Report on the Experiences of Muslim Women's Engagement with Mosques in Scotland'. *Vibrant Scottish Mosques*. https://www.vibrantscottishmosques.com/uploads/2/6/8/5/26859197/hear_my_voice_-_full_report.pdf.
Adam, Muhammad ibn. 2005. 'Women Praying at the Mosque'. *Darul Iftaa* (blog). 12 May. https://daruliftaa.com/womens-issue/women-praying-at-the-mosque/.
Adams, Caroline. 1987. *Across Seven Seas and Thirteen Rivers*. London: THAP.
Adams, Charles. 1983. 'Mawdudi and the Islamic State'. In *Voices of Resurgent Islam*, edited by John L. Esposito, UK ed., 99–133. New York: Oxford University Press.
Ahmad, Waqar I. U. and Venetia Evergeti. 2010. 'The Making and Representation of Muslim Identity in Britain: Conversations with British Muslim "Elites"'. *Ethnic and Racial Studies* 33 (10): 1697–717. https://doi.org/10.1080/01419871003768055.
Ahmed, Abdul-Azim. 2017. 'The Other Ethical Approval: The Importance of Being "Islamic"'. *The Journal of Fieldwork in Religion* 12 (2). https://journals.equinoxpub.com/index.php/FIR/article/view/35668.
Ahmed, Abdul-Azim and Mansur Ali. 2019. 'In Search of Sylhet – The Fultoli Tradition in Britain'. *Religions* 10 (10): 572. https://doi.org/10.3390/rel10100572.
Ahmed, Farah. 2012. 'Tarbiyah for Shakhsiyah (Educating for Identity): Seeking out Culturally Coherent Pedagogy for Muslim Children in Britain'. *Compare: A Journal of Comparative and International Education* 42 (5): 725–49. https://doi.org/10.1080/03057925.2012.706452.
Ahmed, Fiaz. 2014. 'Manchester Muslims: The Developing Role of Mosques, Imams and Committees with Particular Reference to Barelwi Sunnis and UKIM'. Doctoral, Durham University. http://etheses.dur.ac.uk/10724/.
Ahmed, Ishtiaq and Waheed Ali. 2021. 'Bradford Council for Mosques - Celebrating 40 Years of Leadership and Unparalleled Service to the Community'. *Bradford Council for Mosques*. www.councilformosques.co.uk.
Ahmed, Mohammed. 2016. 'Sacred Rhythms: An Ethnography of a Cardiff Mosque'. PhD, Cardiff University. http://orca.cf.ac.uk/100628/.
Ahmed, Shahab. 2015. *What Is Islam? The Importance of Being Islamic*. 1st ed. Princeton: Princeton University Press.

Akram, Zubair. 2020. 'Press Release: GLMCC Wins "Mosque of the Year" – Green Lane Masjid'. 2 January. Accessed 8 December 2023. https://www.greenlanemasjid.org/press-release-glmcc-wins-mosque-of-the-year/.

Alexander, Claire E. 2000. *The Asian Gang: Ethnicity, Identity, Masculinity*. Oxford: Berg.

Ali, Mansur. 2014. 'Is the British Weather Anti-Islamic? Prayer Times, the Ulama and Application of the Sharia'. *Contemporary Islam* 9 (2): 171–87. https://doi.org/10.1007/s11562-014-0318-7.

Ali, Ruhena, Lina Jamoul, and Yusufi Vali. 2012. *A New Covenant of Virtue: Islam and Community Organising*. London: Citizens UK and IAF.

Alinsky, Saul D. 1989. *Rules For Radicals: A Pragmatic Primer for Realistic Radicals*. Vintage Books ed. New York: Vintage Books.

All Party Parliamentary Group on British Muslims. 2019. 'Islamophobia Defined - The Inquiry into a Working Definition of Islamophobia'. *All Party Parliamentary Group on British Muslims*. https://static1.squarespace.com/static/599c3d2febbd1a90cffdd8a9/t/5bfd1ea3352f531a6170ceee/1543315109493/Islamophobia+Defined.pdf.

Al-Lami, Mina. 2009. 'Studies of Radicalisation: State of the Field Report'. *Politics and International Relations Working Paper* 11 (7): 9–79.

Allen, Chris. 2014. 'Britain First: The 'Frontline Resistance' to the Islamification of Britain'. *The Political Quarterly* 85 (3): 354–61. https://doi.org/10.1111/1467-923X.12118.

Allen, Christopher. 2010. *Islamophobia*. Farnham, Surrey; Burlington, VT: Ashgate.

Allievi, Stefano. 2009. *Conflicts Over Mosques in Europe*. London: Alliance Pub. Trust.

Allievi, Stefano. 2010. *Mosques in Europe*. London: Alliance Pub. Trust.

Aly, Remona. 2018. 'UK Mosques Must Make Space for Women – Not Turn Us Away'. *The Guardian*. 19 February. Accessed 8 December 2023. https://www.theguardian.com/commentisfree/2018/feb/19/british-muslim-women-open-mosque-initiative.

Amin, Hira, and Azhar Majothi. 2021. 'The Ahl-e-Hadith: From British India to Britain'. *Modern Asian Studies*, 1–31. https://doi.org/10.1017/S0026749X21000093.

Ammerman, Nancy T. 2014. 'Finding Religion in Everyday Life'. *Sociology of Religion* 75 (2): 189–207. https://doi.org/10.1093/socrel/sru013.

Ammerman, Nancy T., Jackson W. Carrol, Carl S. Dudley, and William McKinney, eds. 1998. *Studying Congregations: A New Handbook*. Nashville: Abingdon Press.

Ammerman, Nancy Tatom, ed. 2007. *Everyday Religion: Observing Modern Religious Lives*. Oxford; New York: Oxford University Press.

Ammerman, N.T. 2009. 'Congregations: Local, Social, and Religious'. In *The Oxford Handbook of the Sociology of Religion*. https://doi.org/10.1093/oxfordhb/9780199588961.013.0032.

Ammerman, T. Nancy. 2016. *Lived Religion as an Emerging Field: An Assessment of Its Contours and Frontiers*. OpenBU. https://open.bu.edu/handle/2144/19161.

Amoateng, Geoffrey B. 2019. 'The Role of Culture and Beliefs in Healing: An Ethnography within an Inner-City Pentecostal Church'. Ph.D., Anglia Ruskin University. http://arro.anglia.ac.uk/704243/.

Anani, Khalil. 2016. *Inside the Muslim Brotherhood: Religion, Identity, and Politics*. New York: Oxford University Press.

Ansari, K. Humayun. 2002. *Muslims in Britain*. London: Minority Rights Group International.

Ansari, K. Humayun. 2002. 'The Woking Mosque: A Case Study of Muslim Engagement with British Society since 1889'. *Immigrants & Minorities* 21 (3): 1–24. https://doi.org/10.1080/02619288.2002.9975044.

Ansari, K. Humayun. 2004. *The Infidel Within*. London: Hurst and Co.

Ansari, K. Humayun. 2011. *The Making of the East London Mosque, 1910–1951: Minutes of the London Mosque Fund and East London Mosque Trust Ltd: 38*. Cambridge: Cambridge University Press.

Anwar, Muhammad. 1979. *The Myth of Return*. London: Heinemann.

Anwar, Muhammad. 1985. *Pakistanis in Britain*. Dublin: New Century Publishers.

Anwar, Muhammad. 1993. 'Muslims in Britain Demographic and Social Characteristics'. *Institute of Muslim Minority Affairs. Journal* 14 (1–2): 124–34. https://doi.org/10.1080/13602009308716286.

Armstrong, Karen. 2007. *Muhammad: Prophet for Our Time*. Reprint ed. New York: Harper Perennial.

Armstrong, Karen. 2010. *The Case for God What Religion Really Means*. London: Vintage. http://www.vlebooks.com/vleweb/product/openreader?id=none&isbn=9781409058335.

Asad, Talal. 1993. *Genealogies of Religion*. Baltimore: Johns Hopkins University Press.

Astor, A., M. Burchardt, and M. Griera. 2019. 'Polarization and the Limits of Politicization: Cordoba's Mosque-Cathedral and the Politics of Cultural Heritage'. *Qualitative Sociology*. https://doi.org/10.1007/s11133-019-09419-x.

Auda, Gasir. 2017. *Reclaiming the Mosque: The Role of Women in Islam's House of Worship*. London: Claritas Books.

Balzani, Marzia. 2010. 'Dreaming, Islam and the Ahmadiyya Muslims in the UK'. *History and Anthropology* 21 (3): 293–305. https://doi.org/10.1080/02757206.2010.496783.

Balzani, Marzia. 2020. *Ahmadiyya Islam and the Muslim Diaspora: Living at the End of Days*. 1st ed. Routledge/ASAA South Asian Studies. New York: Routledge.

Bartels, Edien and Inge De Jong. 2007. 'Civil Society on the Move in Amsterdam: Mosque Organizations in the Slotervaart District'. *Journal of Muslim Minority Affairs* 27 (3): 455–71. https://doi.org/10.1080/13602000701737277.

Barton, Stephen William. 1986. *The Bengali Muslims of Bradford*. Dept. of Theology and Religious Studies, University of Leeds.

Bauer, Thomas, Hinrich Biesterfeldt, and Tricia Tunstall. 2021. *A Culture of Ambiguity: An Alternative History of Islam*. New York: Columbia University Press.

BBC News. 2009. 'Swiss Voters Back Ban on Minarets', 29 November. http://news.bbc.co.uk/1/hi/8385069.stm.

BBCNews. 2011.'Ipswich Church Fire Costs Jimas £200k', 15 March, sec. Suffolk. https://www.bbc.com/news/uk-england-suffolk-12750572.

BBC News. 2018. 'Western Isles' First Mosque Built Ahead of Ramadan'. 10 May, sec. Highlands & Islands. https://www.bbc.com/news/uk-scotland-highlands-islands-44067475.

BBC News. 2019. 'South Yorkshire Flooding: Clean-up Starts in Bentley', 16 November, sec. Sheffield & South Yorkshire. https://www.bbc.com/news/uk-england-south-yorkshire-50445149.

BBC News. 2020. 'Coronavirus: Places of Worship to Reopen for Private Prayer', 7 June, sec. UK. https://www.bbc.com/news/uk-52951853.

BBC News. 2021. 'BBC Woman's Hour Accused of "hostile" Interview with Muslim Leader'. 18 February, sec. Entertainment & Arts. https://www.bbc.com/news/entertainment-arts-56109939.

Beck, Lois. 1980. 'The Religious Lives of Muslim Women'. In *Women in Contemporary Muslim Society*, edited by Jane Smith, 28–60. Lewisburg, PA: Bucknell University Press.

Beckford, James A. 2003. *Social Theory and Religion*. Cambridge; New York: Cambridge University Press.

Bectovic, Safet. 2011. 'Studying Muslims and Constructing Islamic Identity'. *Ethnic and Racial Studies* 34 (7): 1120–33. https://doi.org/10.1080/01419870.2010.528782.

Bellah, Robert N. and Phillip E. Hammond. 1980. *Varieties of Civil Religion*. New York: Harper & Row.

Ben & Jerry's. 2019. 'Visit My Mosque Day: Why We Should All Try a Different Flavour'. 3 March. https://www.benjerry.co.uk/whats-new/2017/01/visit-my-mosque.

Berger, Peter L. 2005. 'Religion and the West'. *The National Interest* 80: 112–19.

Bhimji, F. 2009. 'Identities and Agency in Religious Spheres: A Study of British Muslim Women's Experience'. *Gender, Place and Culture* 16 (4): 365–80. https://doi.org/10.1080/09663690903003850.

Biondo, Vincent F. 2006. 'The Architecture of Mosques in the US and Britain'. *Journal of Muslim Minority Affairs* 26 (3): 399–420. https://doi.org/10.1080/13602000601141414.

Birt, Jonathan. 2004. 'Wahhabism in the United Kingdom: Manifestations and Reactions'. *Transnational Connections and the Arab Gulf*. 10 November. https://doi.org/10.4324/9780203397930-16.

Birt, Jonathan. 2005. '"Locating the British Imam: The Deobandi" Ulama between Contested Authority and Public Policy Post-9/11'. In *European Muslims and the*

Secular State, edited by Jocelyne Cesari and Sean McLoughlin, 1st ed., 183–96. Aldershot: Ashgate.

Birt, Jonathan. 2006. 'Good Imam, Bad Imam: Civic Religion and National Integration in Britain Post-9/11'. The *Muslim World* 96 (4): 687–705. https://doi.org/10.1111/j.1478-1913.2006.00153.x.

Borell, Klas and Arne Gerdner. 2013. 'Cooperation or Isolation? Muslim Congregations in a Scandinavian Welfare State: A Nationally Representative Survey from Sweden'. *Review of Religious Research* 55 (4): 557–71.

Bourdieu, Pierre. 1986. 'The Forms of Capital'. In *Handbook of Theory and Research for the Sociology of Education*, edited by John G. Richardson. Westport, CT: Greenwood Press.

Bowen, Innes. 2013. 'The Muslim Brotherhood in Britain'. In *The Muslim Brotherhood in Europe*, edited by Edwin Bakker and Roel Meijer, 111–26. Oxford University Press. https://doi.org/10.1093/acprof:oso/9780199327638.003.0005.

Bowen, Innes. 2014. *Medina in Birmingham, Najaf in Brent: Inside British Islam*. London: Hurst & Company.

Brenner, Philip S. 2012. 'Identity as a Determinant of the Overreporting of Church Attendance in Canada'. *Journal for the Scientific Study of Religion* 51 (2): 377–85. https://doi.org/10.1111/j.1468-5906.2012.01640.x.

Brown, Jonathan A. C. 2014. *Misquoting Muhammad: The Challenge and Choices of Interpreting the Prophet's Legacy*. London: Oneworld.

Brown, Judith and Ian Talbot. 2006. 'Making a New Home in the Diaspora: Opportunities and Dilemmas in the British South Asian Experience'. *Contemporary South Asia* 15 (2): 125–31. https://doi.org/10.1080/09584930600955218.

Brown, Katherine. 2006. 'Realising Muslim Women's Rights: The Role of Islamic Identity among British Muslim Women'. *Women's Studies International Forum* 29 (4): 417–30. https://doi.org/10.1016/j.wsif.2006.05.002.

Brown, Katherine. 2008. 'The Promise and Perils of Women's Participation in UK Mosques: The Impact of Securitisation Agendas on Identity, Gender and Community'. *British Journal of Politics & International Relations* 10 (3): 472–91. https://doi.org/10.1111/j.1467-856x.2008.00324.x.

Brown, Katherine. 2014. 'Gender and Counter-Radicalization: Women and Emerging Counter-Terror Measures'. In *Gender, National Security, and Counter-Terrorism Human Rights Perspectives*, edited by Margaret L Satterthwaite and Jayne C. Huckerby. Oxford: Routledge.

Brown, Katherine E. and Tania Saeed. 2015. 'Radicalization and Counter-Radicalization at British Universities: Muslim Encounters and Alternatives'. *Ethnic and Racial Studies* 38 (11): 1952–68. https://doi.org/10.1080/01419870.2014.911343.

Bruinessen, Martin van and Julia Day Howell, eds. 2013. *Sufism and the 'Modern' in Islam*. Rev. paperback ed. London; New York: I.B. Tauris; Distributed by Palgrave Macmillan.

Burrell, Rachel-Rose. 2019. 'The Black Majority Church: Exploring the Impact of Faith and a Faith Community on Mental Health and Well-Being'. Ph.D., Middlesex University/Metanoia Institute. http://eprints.mdx.ac.uk/26479/.

Butler, Chris. 2012. *Henri Lefebvre: Spatial Politics, Everyday Life and the Right to the City*. Nomikoi: Critical Legal Thinkers. Oxfordshire: Routledge-Cavendish.

Butt, Riazat and Niki Nixon. 2008. 'US Academic First Woman to Lead Muslim Prayers in UK'. *The Guardian*, 17 October, sec. World news. https://www.theguardian.com/world/2008/oct/18/amina-wadud-mecca-muslims.

Calder, Norman. 1986. 'Friday Prayer and the Juristic Theory of Government: Sarakhsī, Shīrāzī, Māwardī'. *Bulletin of the School of Oriental and African Studies* 49 (1): 35–47. https://doi.org/10.1017/S0041977X00042476.

Cameron, Helen, Philip Richter, Douglas Davies, and Frances Ward, eds. 2005. *Studying Local Churches: A Handbook*. London: SCM.

Candea, Matei. 2007. 'Arbitrary Locations: In Defence of the Bounded Field-Site'. *Journal of the Royal Anthropological Institute* 13 (1): 167–84. https://doi.org/10.1111/j.1467-9655.2007.00419.x.

Cantone, Cleo. 2002. 'Women Claiming Space in Mosques'. *ISIM Newsletter* 11 (January): 29.

Cantone, Cleo. 2012. *Making and Remaking Mosques in Senegal*. Leiden: Brill. https://doi.org/10.1163/9789004217508.

Caplan, Pat. 2016. 'Big Society or Broken Society?: Food Banks in the UK'. *Anthropology Today* 32 (1): 5–9. https://doi.org/10.1111/1467-8322.12223.

Casey, Louise. 2016. 'The Casey Review: A Review into Opportunity and Integration'. *Ministry of Housing, Communities & Local Government*. https://www.gov.uk/government/publications/the-casey-review-a-review-into-opportunity-and-integration.

Cayton, Horace R. and St. Clair Drake. 1946. *Black Metropolis*. London: Jonathan Cape.

Cesari, Jocelyne. 2005a. 'Mosques in French Cities: Towards the End of a Conflict?'. *Journal of Ethnic and Migration Studies* 31 (6): 1025–43. https://doi.org/10.1080/13691830500282634.

Cesari, Jocelyne. 2005b. 'Mosque Conflicts in European Cities: Introduction'. *Journal of Ethnic and Migration Studies* 31 (6): 1015–24. https://doi.org/10.1080/13691830500282626.

Chambers, Edward T. 2003. *Roots for Radicals: Organizing for Power, Action, and Justice*. New York: Continuum.

Chapman, Rachel. 2009. 'Faith and the Voluntary Sector in Urban Governance: Distinctive yet Similar?'. In *Faith in the Public Realm: Controversies, Policies and Practices*, edited by Adam Dinham, Robert Furbey, and Vivien Lowndes, 203–22. Bristol: Policy.

Chaves, Mark and Laura Stephens. 2003. 'Church Attendance in the United States'. In *Handbook of the Sociology of Religion*, edited by Michele Dillon, 85–95. Cambridge: Cambridge University Press.

Cheruvallil-Contractor, Sariya. 2012. *Muslim Women in Britain: De-Mystifying the Muslimah*. Routledge Islamic Studies. London; New York: Routledge.

Cheruvallil-Contractor, Sariya. 2020. 'Women in Britain's First Muslim Mosques: Hidden from History, but Not Without Influence'. *Religions* 11 (2): 62. https://doi.org/10.3390/rel11020062.

Chidester, David and Edward Linenthal. 1995. *American Sacred Space*. Bloomington: Indiana University.

Christian Today. 2005. *New Study Finds Mosque Goers to Double Church Attendance*. http://www.christiantoday.com/article/new.study.finds.mosque.goers.to.double.church.attendance/3858.htm.

Church of England Research and Statistics. 2019. 'Statistics for Mission 2018'. https://www.churchofengland.org/researchandstats.

Chryssides, George D. and Stephen E. Gregg, eds. 2019. *The Insider/Outsider Debate: New Perspectives in the Study of Religion*. Bristol: Equinox Publishing Ltd.

Clarke, Gerard, Michael Jennings, and Lord Carey. 2008. *Development, Civil Society and Faith-Based Organizations: Bridging the Sacred and the Secular*. 2008 ed. Basingstoke, Hampshire: AIAA.

Clarke, Peter B. and Nancy T. Ammerman. 2009. *Congregations: Local, Social, and Religious*. Oxford: Oxford University Press. http://www.oxfordhandbooks.com/view/10.1093/oxfordhb/9780199588961.001.0001/oxfordhb-9780199588961-e-032.

CLG. 2007. 'Commission on Integration and Cohesion: Our Shared Future'. *Equally Ours*. https://www.equallyours.org.uk/commission-on-integration-and-cohesion-final-report/.

Cockbain, Ella and Waqas Tufail. 2020. 'Failing Victims, Fuelling Hate: Challenging the Harms of the "Muslim Grooming Gangs" Narrative'. *Race & Class* 61 (3): 3–32. https://doi.org/10.1177/0306396819895727.

Cohen, Anthony P. 1993. *The Symbolic Construction of Community*. Oxfordshire: Routledge.

Coleman, Simon and Pauline Von Hellermann. 2011. *Multi-Sited Ethnography*. Oxfordshire: Routledge.

Colley, Jan. 2016. 'Ex-Britain First Leader Jailed after Cardiff "Mosque Invasion" - Wales Online'. *Wales Online*, 15 December. https://www.walesonline.co.uk/news/wales-news/ex-britain-first-leader-jailed-12326200.

Collins-Kreiner, Noga, Deborah F. Shmueli, and Michal Ben Gal. 2013. 'Spatial Transgression of New Religious Sites in Israel'. *Applied Geography* 40 (June): 103–14. https://doi.org/10.1016/j.apgeog.2013.02.002.

Corboz, Elvire. 2015. *Guardians of Shi'ism: Sacred Authority and Transnational Family Networks*. Edinburgh: Edinburgh University Press. https://www.jstor.org/stable/10.3366/j.ctt14brxb0.

Cormack, Margaret, ed. 2013. *Muslims and Others in Sacred Space. Religion, Culture, and History*. Oxford; New York: Oxford University Press.

Cresswell, Tim. 1996. *In Place/out of Place*. University of Minnesota Press.
Dafydd Jones, Rhys. 2010. 'Islam and the Rural Landscape: Discourses of Absence in West Wales'. *Social & Cultural Geography* 11 (8): 751–68. https://doi.org/10.1080/14649365.2010.521853.
Damrel, David. 2013. 'Baraka Besieged'. In *Muslims and Others in Sacred Space*, edited by Magaret Cormack, 1st ed., 15–39. Oxford University Press.
Davie, Grace. 2015. *Religion in Britain: A Persistent Paradox*. 2nd ed. Oxford: Wiley-Blackwell.
Davies, Douglas James and Mathew Guest. 2007. *Bishops, Wives and Children: Spiritual Capital across the Generations*. Aldershot, England; Burlington, VT: Ashgate Pub. Ltd.
Dawood, Iman. 2020. 'Who Is a "Salafi"? Salafism and the Politics of Labelling in the UK'. *Journal of Muslims in Europe* 9 (2): 240–61. https://doi.org/10.1163/22117954-12341416.
Day, Abby. 2017. *The Religious Lives of Older Laywomen: The Last Active Anglican Generation*. 1st ed. Oxford; New York: Oxford University Press.
DeHanas, Daniel Nilsson and Zacharias P. Pieri. 2011. 'Olympic Proportions: The Expanding Scalar Politics of the London "Olympics Mega-Mosque" Controversy'. *Sociology* 45 (5): 798–814. https://doi.org/10.1177/0038038511413415.
Denning, Stephanie. 2014. 'An Exploration Through Affect of Two Faith-Based Foodbanks in Bristol'. https://pureportal.coventry.ac.uk/en/publications/an-exploration-through-affect-of-two-faith-based-foodbanks-in-bri.
Denning, Stephanie. 2019. 'Voluntary Sector Responses to Food Poverty: Responding in the Short-Term and Working for Longer-Term Change'. *Voluntary Sector Review* 10 (3): 361–9. https://doi.org/10.1332/204080519X15698349753281.
Denzin, Norman K. and Yvonna S. Lincoln. 2000. *Handbook of Qualitative Research*. Thousand Oaks, CA: Sage Publications.
DeRogatis, Amy. 2009. '"Born Again Is a Sexual Term": Demons, STDs, and God's Healing Sperm'. *Journal of the American Academy of Religion* 77 (2): 275–302. https://doi.org/10.1093/jaarel/lfp020.
Desplat, Patrick. 2012. 'Introduction – Representations of Space, Place-Making and Urban Life in Muslim Societies'. In *Prayer in the City*, edited by Patrick Desplat and Dorothea Schulz, 1st ed., 9–36. Piscataway, NJ: Transaction Publishers.
Desplat, Patrick A. and Dorothea E. Schulz. 2012. *Prayer in the City*. Berlin: De Gruyter.
Dinham, Adam, Robert Furbey, and Vivien Lowndes. 2009. *Faith in the Public Realm: Controversies, Policies and Practices*. Bristol: Policy.
Disli, Gulsen. 2015. 'Women's Prayer Space in the Case Studies of the Historic Mosques in Three Balkan Countries'. *Prostor* 23 (2): 196–207.
Dobbernack, Jan, Nasar Meer, and Tariq Modood. 2015. 'Misrecognition and Political Agency. The Case of Muslim Organisations in a General Election'. *The British Journal*

of Politics and International Relations 17 (2): 189–206. https://doi.org/10.1111/1467-856X.12033.

Dodd, Liz. 2015. 'Islam Should Have a "quintessentially British" Version with Minoret-Less Mosques and No Burqas, Warsi Says'. *The Tablet*. 11 December. https://www.thetablet.co.uk/news/2898/islam-should-have-a-quintessentially-british-version-with-minoret-less-mosques-and-no-burqas-warsi-says.

Dogra, Sufyan Abid. 2017. 'Karbala in London: Battle of Expressions of Ashura Ritual Commemorations among Twelver Shia Muslims of South Asian Background'. *Journal of Muslims in Europe* 6 (2): 158.

Dogra, Sufyan Abid. 2019. 'Living a Piety-Led Life beyond Muharram: Becoming or Being a South Asian Shia Muslim in the UK'. *Contemporary Islam* 13 (3): 307–24. https://doi.org/10.1007/s11562-019-00437-8.

Dowler, Elizabeth. 2014. 'Food Banks and Food Justice in "Austerity Britain"'. In *First World Hunger Revisited: Food Charity or the Right to Food?*, edited by Graham Riches and Tiina Silvasti, 160–75. London: Palgrave Macmillan UK. https://doi.org/10.1057/9781137298737_12.

Drake, St Clair. 1954. 'Value Systems, Social Structure and Race Relations in the British Isles'. PhD Thesis, University of Chicago.

Durkheim, Emile. 1915. *The Elementary Forms of the Religious Life*. George Allen & Unwin Ltd.

Dwyer, C. 1999. 'Contradictions of Community: Questions of Identity for Young British Muslim Women'. *Environment and Planning A: Economy and Space* 31 (1): 53–68. https://doi.org/10.1068/a310053.

Dyke, Anya Hart. 2009. *Mosques Made in Britain*. Quilliam Foundation.

Eade, John and David Garbin. 2006. 'Competing Visions of Identity and Space: Bangladeshi Muslims in Britain'. *Contemporary South Asia* 15 (2): 181–93. https://doi.org/10.1080/09584930600955291.

Eade, John and Michael J Sallnow. 1991. *Contesting the Sacred*. London: Routledge.

Ebaugh, Helen Rose and Janet Saltzman Chafetz. 2000. 'Dilemmas of Language in Immigrant Congregations: The Tie That Binds or the Tower of Babel?'. *Review of Religious Research* 41 (4): 432–52. https://doi.org/10.2307/3512314.

Ebner, Julia. 2017. *The Rage: The Vicious Circle of Islamist and Far-Right Extremism*. London: I.B. Tauris & Co. Ltd.

Edwards, Michael. 2013a. 'Introduction: Civil Society and the Geometry of Human Relations'. In *The Oxford Handbook of Civil Society*. Oxford: Oxford University Press.

Edwards, Michael, ed. 2013b. *The Oxford Handbook of Civil Society*. Oxford: Oxford University Press.

Ehrenberg, John. 2013. 'The History of Civil Society Ideas'. In *The Oxford Handbook of Civil Society*, edited by Michael Edwards. Oxford: Oxford University Press.

Eliade, Mircea. 1958. *Patterns in Comparative Religion*. Sheed & Ward.

Eliade, Mircea and Willard R. Trask. 1959. *The Sacred and the Profane*. New York: Harcourt, Brace & World.
Elshayyal, Khadijah. 2018. *Muslim Identity Politics: Islam, Activism and Equality in Britain*. Library of European Studies 23. London: I.B. Tauris.
Elshayyal, Khadijah, and Fatima Rajina. 2021. 'United Kingdom'. In *Yearbook of Muslims in Europe, Volume 13*, edited by Stephanie Müssig, Egdūnas Račius, Samim Akgönül, Ahmet Alibašić, Jørgen S. Nielsen, and Oliver Scharbrodt, 690–706. Leiden: Brill. https://brill.com/view/title/61349.
El-Yousfi, Amin. 2019. 'Conflicting Paradigms of Religious and Bureaucratic Authority in a British Mosque'. *Religions* 10 (10): 564. https://doi.org/10.3390/rel10100564.
Emmett, Chad F. 2009. 'The Siting of Churches and Mosques as an Indicator of Christian–Muslim Relations'. *Islam and Christian–Muslim Relations* 20 (4): 451–76. https://doi.org/10.1080/09596410903194902.
Es, Murat. 2012. 'Turkish-Dutch Mosques and the Construction of Transnational Spaces in Europe'. PhD Thesis, University of North Carolina.
Evans-Pritchard, E. E. 1965. *Theories of Primitive Religion*. Oxford: Clarendon Press.
Evers, Adalbert and Jean-Louis Laville, eds. 2005. *The Third Sector in Europe*. Reprinted. Globalization and Welfare. Cheltenham: Elgar.
Evers, Adalbert, Jean-Louis Laville, and M. Taylor. 2005. 'The Welfare Mix in the United Kingdom'. In *The Third Sector in Europe*, 122–43. Globalization and Welfare. Cheltenham: Elgar.
Express and Star. 2013. 'Ukrainian Student in One Man Racist Reign of Terror Targeting Black Country Mosques', 22 October. https://www.expressandstar.com/news/2013/10/22/pavlo-lapshyn-ukrainian-student-in-90-day-race-hate-campaign-targeting-black-country-mosques/.
Falzon, Mark-Anthony. 2009. *Multi-Sited Ethnography*. Aldershot: Ashgate Pub.
Fenton, Allison. 2017. 'Meaning-Making for Mothers in the North East of England: An Ethnography of Baptism'. Ph.D., Durham University. http://etheses.dur.ac.uk/12045/.
Ferguson, Adam. n.d. *An Essay on the History of Civil Society | Online Library of Liberty*. Accessed 4 March 2021. https://oll.libertyfund.org/title/ferguson-an-essay-on-the-history-of-civil-society.
Fewkes, Jacqueline H. 2019. *Locating Maldivian Women's Mosques in Global Discourses*. Cham: Springer International Publishing. https://doi.org/10.1007/978-3-030-13585-0.
Francis, Matthew. 2014. 'How Do We Prevent Radicalisation?'. *Theos Think Tank*. 26 September. Accessed 9 October 2022. https://www.theosthinktank.co.uk/comment/2014/09/26/how-do-we-prevent-radicalisation-by-matthew-francis.
Francis, Matthew. 2014. 'Radical Ideology Isn't What Makes Extremists Turn Violent'. *Radicalisation Research*, 22 May. https://www.radicalisationresearch.org/debate/radical-ideology-isnt-what-makes-extremists-turn-violent/.

Francis, Matthew D. M. 2016. 'Why the "Sacred" Is a Better Resource Than "Religion" for Understanding Terrorism'. *Terrorism and Political Violence* 28 (5): 912–27. https://doi.org/10.1080/09546553.2014.976625.

Francis, Matthew, Amanda van Eck, and Duymaer van Twist. 2015. 'Religious Literacy, Radicalisation, and Extremism'. In *Religious Literacy in Policy and Practice*, edited by Adam Dinham and Matthew Francis, 1st ed., 113–34. Bristol: Policy Press.

Fraser, Nancy. 1992. 'Rethinking the Public Sphere'. In *Habermas and the Public Sphere*, edited by Craig Calhoun, 2nd ed. Cambridge, MA: MIT Press.

'Fundraising Appeal Starts for UK's First Women-Led Mosque'. n.d. Accessed 22 August 2022. https://advance.lexis.com/document/?pdmfid=1519360&crid=47ec2185-f38a-4c3c-bbd5-fdef256730f1&pddocfullpath=%2Fshared%2Fdocument%2Fnews%2Furn%3AcontentItem%3A5NCD-2NX1-F0JC-M2XH-00000-00&pdcontentcomponentid=323689&pdteaserkey=sr8&pditab=allpods&ecomp=rbzyk&earg=sr8&prid=52b467bc-95c7-430a-9499-8cfaf22be5f2.

Furbey, Robert and Joseph Rowntree Foundation, eds. 2006. *Faith as Social Capital: Connecting or Dividing?* Bristol: Policy Press.

Gaddini, Katie Christine. 2018. 'Negotiating Identities: The Case of Evangelical Christian Women in London'. Ph.D., University of Cambridge. https://doi.org/10.17863/CAM.23719.

Gailani, Fatima. 2000. *The Mosques of London*. Henstridge: Elm Grove Books.

Gale, R. and S. Naylor. 2002. 'Religion, Planning and the City: The Spatial Politics of Ethnic Minority Expression in British Cities and Towns'. *Ethnicities* 2 (3): 387–409. https://doi.org/10.1177/14687968020020030601.

Gale, Richard. 2004. 'The Multicultural City and the Politics of Religious Architecture: Urban Planning, Mosques and Meaning-Making in Birmingham, UK'. *Built Environ* 30 (1): 30–44. https://doi.org/10.2148/benv.30.1.30.54320.

Gale, Richard. 2005. 'Representing the City: Mosques and the Planning Process in Birmingham'. *Journal of Ethnic and Migration Studies* 31 (6): 1161–79. https://doi.org/10.1080/13691830500282857.

Gale, Richard. 2008. 'Locating Religion in Urban Planning: Beyond Race and Ethnicity?' *Planning Practice and Research* 23 (1): 19–39. https://doi.org/10.1080/02697450802076415.

Gale, Richard. 2011. 'Muslim Youth, Faith-Based Activism and "Social Capital": A Response to Annette'. *Ethnicities* 11 (3): 398–402. https://doi.org/10.1177/1468796811407857.

Galer, Sophia Smith. 2021. 'Coronavirus: Why Some Mosques Are Closed to Women during Ramadan'. *BBC News*, 3 May, sec. UK. https://www.bbc.com/news/uk-56937289.

Gani, Aisha. 2015. 'Meet Bana Gora, the Woman Planning Britain's First Female-Managed Mosque'. *The Guardian*, 31 July, sec. Life and style. https://www.theguardian.com/lifeandstyle/2015/jul/31/bana-gora-muslim-womens-council-bradford-mosque.

Ganzevoort, Ruard and Johan Roeland. 2014. 'Lived Religion: The Praxis of Practical Theology'. *International Journal of Practical Theology* 18 (1). https://doi.org/10.1515/ijpt-2014-0007.

Garbin, David. 2005. 'Bangladeshi Diaspora in the UK: Some Observations on Socio-Cultural Dynamics, Religious Trends and Transnational Politics'. In *Cancer of Extremism in Bangladesh. Proceedings of the European Human Rights Conference on Bangladesh: Extremism, Intolerance & Violence*, edited by Werner Menski and Biswajit Chanda. SOAS (School of Oriental & African Studies), London: Centre for Ethnic Minority Studies, SOAS and Bangladesh Conference Steering Committee. https://kar.kent.ac.uk/36052/.

Garner, Steve, and Saher Selod. 2015. 'The Racialization of Muslims: Empirical Studies of Islamophobia'. *Critical Sociology* 41 (1): 9–19. https://doi.org/10.1177/0896920514531606.

Geaves, Ron. 1996. *Sectarian Influences within Islam in Britain*. Dept. of Theology and Religious Studies, University of Leeds.

Geaves, Ron. 2000. *The Sufis of Britain: An Exploration of Muslim Identity*. Cardiff: Cardiff Academic Press.

Geaves, Ron. 2008. 'Drawing on the Past to Transform the Present: Contemporary Challenges for Training and Preparing British Imams'. *Journal of Muslim Minority Affairs* 28 (1): 99–112. https://doi.org/10.1080/13602000802011846.

Geaves, Ron. 2010. *Islam in Victorian Britain*. Markfield: Kube Publishing.

Geaves, Ron. 2015. 'An Exploration of the Viability of Partnership between *Dar al-Ulum* and Higher Education Institutions in North West England Focusing upon Pedagogy and Relevance'. *British Journal of Religious Education* 37 (1): 64–82. https://doi.org/10.1080/01416200.2013.830958.

Geaves, Ron and Yahya Birt, eds. 2021. *The Collected Poems of Abdullah Quilliam*. London: Beacon Books.

Geaves, Ron and Theodore P. C. Gabriel, eds. 2014. *Sufism in Britain*. London; New York: Bloomsbury.

Geddes, Andrew. 2003. *The Politics of Migration and Immigration in Europe*. Thousand Oaks, CA: SAGE Publications.

Geertz, Clifford. 1971. *Islam Observed: Religious Development in Morocco and Indonesia*. Chicago; London: University of Chicago Press.

Geertz, Clifford. 1973. *The Interpretation of Cultures*. New York: Basic Books.

Gehman, Joel. 2009. 'Phenomenology and Institutional Theory: Should Institution Be Taken for Granted?'. *SSRN Electronic Journal*, January. https://doi.org/10.2139/ssrn.1327508.

Gellner, Ernest. 1996. *Conditions of Liberty: Civil Society and Its Rivals*. New ed. London: Penguin.

GhaneaBassiri, Kambiz. 1997. *Competing Visions of Islam in the United States: A Study of Los Angeles*. Westport : Praeger.

Ghouri, Nazim. 2005. 'Health Fair in a Mosque: Putting Policy into Practice'. *Public Health* 119 (3): 197–201. https://doi.org/10.1016/j.puhe.2004.05.009.

Gilham, Jamie. 2014. *Loyal Enemies: British Converts to Islam, 1850–1950*. London: Hurst & Company.

Gilliat-Ray, Sophie. 2006. 'Educating the c Ulama: Centres of Islamic Religious Training in Britain'. *Islam and Christian–Muslim Relations* 17 (1): 55–76. https://doi.org/10.1080/09596410500399367.

Gilliat-Ray, Sophie. 2010a. *Muslims in Britain*. Cambridge University Press.

Gilliat-Ray, Sophie. 2010b. 'The First Registered Mosque in the UK, Cardiff, 1860: The Evolution of a Myth'. *Contemporary Islam* 4 (2): 179–93. https://doi.org/10.1007/s11562-010-0116-9.

Gilliat-Ray, Sophie. 2014. 'The United Kingdom'. In *The Oxford Handbook of European Islam*. Oxford: Oxford University Press. https://doi.org/10.1093/oxfordhb/9780199607976.013.4.

Gilliat-Ray, Sophie. 2018. 'From "Closed Worlds" to "Open Doors": (Now) Accessing Deobandi Darul Uloom in Britain'. *Fieldwork in Religion* 13 (2): 127–50. https://doi.org/10.1558/firn.35029.

Gilliat-Ray, Sophie and Jonathan Birt. 2010. 'A Mosque Too Far? Islam and the Limits of British Multiculturalism'. In *Mosques in Europe*, edited by Stefano Allievi, 1st ed. Alliance Publishing Trust. http://www.nef-europe.org/wp-content/uploads/2013/03/mosques-in-Europe-fullpdf.pdf.

Gilliat-Ray, Sophie and Jody Mellor. 2010. 'Bilad Al-Welsh (Land of the Welsh): Muslims in Cardiff, South Wales: Past, Present and Future'. *The Muslim World* 100 (4): 452–75. https://doi.org/10.1111/j.1478-1913.2010.01331.x.

Gledhill, Ruth. 2013. 'Muslims Are Britain's Top Charity Givers'. *The Times*. http://www.thetimes.co.uk/tto/faith/article3820522.ece.

Gledhill, Ruth. 2015. 'Leading Liberal Vicar Defends Right to Hold Muslim Prayer Services'. *Christian Today*, 12 March. https://www.christiantoday.com/article/leading-liberal-vicar-defends-right-to-hold-muslim-prayer-services/49840.htm.

Goffman, Erving. 1959. *The Presentation of Self in Everyday Life*. New York: Doubleday.

Goffman, Erving. 1977. 'The Arrangement between the Sexes'. *Theory and Society* 4 (3). https://doi.org/10.1007/bf00206983.

Gouldner, Alvin Ward. 1970. *The Coming Crisis of Western Sociology*. New York: Basic Books.

Grabar Oleg, Al-Asad M. 1996. *The Shape of the Holy: Early Islamic Jerusalem*. Princeton: Princeton University Press.

Gross, Jo-Ann. 2013. 'Foundational Legends, Shrines and Ismaili Identity in Gorno-Badakshan, Tajikstan'. In *Muslims and Others in Sacred Space*, edited by Margaret Cormack, 1st ed., 164–92. New York: Oxford University Press.

Guardi, Jolanda. 2015. 'Women Leadership in the Mosque'. *HORIZONTE* 13 (39). https://doi.org/10.5752/p.2175-5841.2015v13n39p1427.

Guest, Mathew, Karen Tusting, and Linda Woodhead, eds. 2004. *Congregational Studies in the UK: Christianity in a Post-Christian Context*. Explorations in Practical, Pastoral, and Empirical Theology. Aldershot: Ashgate.

Habermas, Jurgen. 2008. 'Notes on Post-Secular Society'. *New Perspectives Quarterly* 25 (4): 17–29. https://doi.org/10.1111/j.1540-5842.2008.01017.x.

Habermas, Jürgen. 1991. *The Structural Transformation of the Public Sphere: An Inquiry into a Category of Bourgeois Society*. Cambridge, MA: MIT Press.

Hadaway, C. Kirk, Penny Long Marler, and Mark Chaves. 1993. 'What the Polls Don't Show: A Closer Look at U.S. Church Attendance'. *American Sociological Review* 58 (6): 741–52. https://doi.org/10.2307/2095948.

Hadaway, C. Kirk, Penny Long Marler, and Mark Chaves. 1998. 'Overreporting Church Attendance in America: Evidence That Demands the Same Verdict'. *American Sociological Review* 63 (1): 122–30. https://doi.org/10.2307/2657484.

Haddad, Yvonne Yazbeck and Adair T. Lummis. 1987. *Islamic Values in the United States: A Comparative Study*. Revised ed. New York: Oxford University Press.

Hairgrove, Frank and Douglas M. Mcleod. 2008. 'Circles Drawing Toward High Risk Activism: The Use of Usroh and Halaqa in Islamist Radical Movements'. *Studies in Conflict & Terrorism* 31 (5): 399–411. https://doi.org/10.1080/10576100801995201.

Hall, David D., ed. 1997. *Lived Religion in America: Toward a History of Practice*. Princeton: Princeton University Press.

Hall, Donald Eugene. 2006. *Muscular Christianity*. Cambridge: Cambridge University Press.

Halliday, Fred. 2010. *Britain's First Muslims*. London: I.B. Tauris.

Hamid, Sadek. 2016. *Sufis, Salafis and Islamists*. London: I.B. Tauris.

Hanif, Aisal. 2015. 'Muslim Women Break Barriers by Building Their Own Mosque'. 5 May. https://advance.lexis.com/document/?pdmfid=1519360&crid=6aad917b-40e8-4360-ad35-fca104161b66&pddocfullpath=%2Fshared%2Fdocument%2Fnews%2Furn%3AcontentItem%3A5FX9-BK81-F021-61SG-00000-00&pdcontentcomponentid=382503&pdteaserkey=sr19&pditab=allpods&ecomp=rbzyk&earg=sr19&prid=2548a839-4980-4cc3-9390-24ae3cb4427c.

Hanif, Noman. 2012. 'Hizb Ut Tahrir: Islam's Ideological Vanguard'. *British Journal of Middle Eastern Studies* 39 (2): 201–25. https://doi.org/10.1080/13530194.2012.711037.

Harradine, Karen. 2020. 'A Mosque in Piccadilly Circus? Wrong, Wrong, Wrong!' *The Conservative Woman* (blog). 29 May. https://www.conservativewoman.co.uk/a-mosque-in-piccadilly-circus-wrong-wrong-wrong/.

Harris, Margaret, Peter Halfpenny, and Colin Rochester. 2003. 'A Social Policy Role for Faith-Based Organisations? Lessons from the UK Jewish Voluntary Sector'. *Journal of Social Policy* 32 (1): 93–112. https://doi.org/10.1017/S0047279402006906.

Hartung, Jan-Peter. 2014. *A System of Life: Mawdūdī and the Ideologisation of Islam*. New York: Oxford University Press.

Headley, Stephen and David Parkin. 2018. *Islamic Prayer Across the Indian Ocean: Inside and Outside the Mosque*. New York: Routledge.

Helland, Christopher. 2005. 'Online Religion as Lived Religion. Methodological Issues in the Study of Religious Participation on the Internet'. *Online - Heidelberg Journal of Religions on the Internet* 1 (1). https://doi.org/10.11588/rel.2005.1.380.

Hermansen, M. 2009. 'Global Sufism: "Theirs" and "Ours"'. In *Sufis in Western Society: Global Networking and Locality*, edited by Ron Geaves, Markus Dressler, and Gritt Maria Klinkhammer, 26–46. Routledge Sufi Series 9. London; New York: Routledge.

Hiebert, Paul. 1978. 'Conversion, Culture and Cognitive Categories'. *Gospel in Context* 1 (4): 24–9.

Hillenbrand, Robert. 1995. *Islamic Architecture: Form, Function, and Meaning*. Columbia University Press.

Hinnells, John R. and Jamal Malik, eds. 2017. *Sufism in the West*. London; New York: Routledge.

Hoffman, Valerie J. 2012. *The Essentials of Ibadi Islam*. Syracuse University Press.

Hoge, Dean R., ed. 1996. *Money Matters: Personal Giving in American Churches*. 1st ed. Louisville, KY: Westminster John Knox Press.

Holmwood, John and Therese O'Toole. 2017. *Countering Extremism in British Schools?: The Truth about the Birmingham Trojan Horse Affair*. 1st ed. Bristol: Policy Press.

Hopewell, James F. 1987. *Congregation: Stories and Structures*. Philadelphia: Fortress Press.

Hopkins, Nick and Vered Kahani-Hopkins. 2004. 'The Antecedents of Identification: A Rhetorical Analysis of British Muslim Activists' Constructions of Community and Identity'. *British Journal of Social Psychology* 43 (1): 41–57. https://doi.org/10.1348/014466604322915971.

Hopkins, Peter and Richard T. Gale, eds. 2009. *Muslims in Britain: Race, Place and Identities*. Edinburgh: Edinburgh University Press.

Hout, Michael and Andrew Greeley. 1998. 'What Church Officials' Reports Don't Show: Another Look at Church Attendance Data'. *American Sociological Review* 63 (1): 113–19. https://doi.org/10.2307/2657482.

Husain, E. D. 2021. *Among the Mosques: A Journey across Muslim Britain*. London: Bloomsbury Publishing.

Hussain, Serena. 2008. *Muslims on the Map: A National Survey of Social Trends in Britain*. International Library of Human Geography 13. London; New York: Tauris Academic Studies.

Hutnik, Nimmi and Rebecca Coran Street. 2010. 'Profiles of British Muslim Identity: Adolescent Girls in Birmingham'. *Journal of Adolescence* 33 (1): 33–42. https://doi.org/10.1016/j.adolescence.2009.05.016.

Iannello, Kathleen. 2010. 'Women's Leadership and Third-Wave Feminism'. *Political Science Faculty Publications*, January. https://cupola.gettysburg.edu/poliscifac/8.

Ibn Hazm. 2018. *Ibn Hazm on the Lawfulness of Women Attending Prayers in the Mosque by Ibn Hazm Al-Andalusi*. Translated by Akram Nadwi. Oxford: Interface Publications.

ICMUnlimited. 2016. *C4 / Juniper Survey of Muslims 2015*. https://www.icmunlimited.com/wp-content/uploads/2016/04/Mulims-full-suite-data-plus-topline.pdf.

Idriss, M.M. 2017. '"The Mosques Are the Biggest Problem We've Got Right Now": Key Agent and Survivor Accounts of Engaging Mosques with Domestic and Honor-Based Violence in the United Kingdom'. *Scopus* 35 (13–14). https://doi.org/10.1177/0886260517703376.

Inge, Anabel. 2017. *The Making of a Salafi Muslim Woman: Paths to Conversion*. New York: Oxford University Press.

Ingram, Brannon D. 2018. *Revival from below: The Deoband Movement and Global Islam*. Oakland, CA: University of California Press.

Islamic Council of North America. 2015. 'ISNA Statement on the Inclusion of Women in Masjids'. 4 September 2015. https://isna.net/isna-statement/.

'Islamophobia Research & Documentation Project | UCB Center for Race & Gender'. n.d. Accessed 16 August 2022. https://www.crg.berkeley.edu/research/islamophobia-research-documentation-project/.

Ismail, Salwa. 2004. 'Being Muslim: Islam, Islamism and Identity Politics'. *Government and Opposition* 39 (4): 614–31. https://doi.org/10.1111/j.1477-7053.2004.00138.x.

Ivakhiv, Adrian. 2006. 'Toward a Geography of Religion: Mapping the Distribution of an Unstable Signifier'. *Annals of the Association of American Geographers* 96 (1): 169–75. https://doi.org/10.1111/j.1467-8306.2006.00505.x.

Jaschok, Maria and Jingjun Shui. 2000. *The History of Women's Mosques in Chinese Islam: A Mosque of Their Own*. Richmond, Surrey: Curzon.

Jawad, Rana. 2012. 'Religion, Social Welfare and Social Policy in the UK: Historical, Theoretical and Policy Perspectives'. *Social Policy and Society* 11 (4): 553–64. https://doi.org/10.1017/S1474746412000309.

Jay, Alexis. 2014. 'Independent Inquiry into Child Sexual Exploitation in Rotherham (1997–2013)'. *Rotherham: Rotherham Metropolitan Borough Council*. https://www.rotherham.gov.uk/downloads/file/279/independent-inquiry-into-child-sexual-exploitation-in-rotherham.

Jeldtoft, Nadia and Jørgen S. Nielsen. 2011. 'Introduction: Methods in the Study of 'Non-Organized' Muslim Minorities'. *Ethnic and Racial Studies* 34 (7): 1113–19. https://doi.org/10.1080/01419870.2010.528442.

Johansen, Birgitte and Riem Spielhaus. 2012. 'Counting Deviance: Revisiting a Decade's Production of Surveys among Muslims in Western Europe'. *Journal of Muslims in Europe* 1 (1): 81–112. https://doi.org/10.1163/221179512X644060.

Johnson, Patrick Garnett. 2019. 'Health on the Margins: How Can the Seventh-Day Adventist Church, with Its Emphasis on Health, Authentically Proclaim Liberty for People with Disabilities?'. Ph.D., King's College London. https://kclpure.kcl.ac.uk/

portal/en/theses/health-on-the-margins(93770741-cfe6-46b4-80c8-1d447e48c24a).html.
Johnson, Sabrina. 2020. 'Norwich Mosque Thanks Community after Arson on Aylsham Road'. *Norwich Evening News*, 28 July. https://www.eveningnews24.co.uk/news/alysham-road-mosque-arson-community-support-1772996.
Jones, Robert Tudur. 1962. *Congregationalism in England, 1662–1962*. London: Independent Press.
Jones, Stephen H., Therese O'Toole, Daniel Nilsson DeHanas, Tariq Modood, and Nasar Meer. 2014. 'A System of Self-Appointed Leaders? Examining Modes of Muslim Representation in Governance in Britain'. *The British Journal of Politics & International Relations* 17 (2): 207–23. https://doi.org/10.1111/1467-856x.12051.
Jonker, Gerdien. 2005. 'The Mevlana Mosque in Berlin-Kreuzberg: An Unsolved Conflict'. *Journal of Ethnic and Migration Studies* 31 (6): 1067–81. https://doi.org/10.1080/13691830500282683.
Jump, Paul. 2015. 'The Impact of Impact'. *Times Higher Education (THE)*, 19 February. https://www.timeshighereducation.com/features/the-impact-of-impact/2018540.article.
Kabir, Nahid Afrose. 2010. *Young British Muslims*. Edinburgh: Edinburgh University Press. www.jstor.org/stable/10.3366/j.ctt1r1xzn.
Kahera, Akel Ismail. 2002a. *Deconstructing the American Mosque*. Austin: University of Texas Press.
Kahera, Akel Ismail. 2002b. 'Urban Enclaves, Muslim Identity and the Urban Mosque in America'. *Journal of Muslim Minority Affairs* 22 (2): 369–80. https://doi.org/10.1080/1360200022000027320.
Kamran, Bokhari. n.d. 'Jamāʿat-i Islāmī'. Accessed 6 April 2021. http://www.oxfordislamicstudies.com/opr/t236/e0408.
Katz, Marion Holmes. 2007. *The Birth of the Prophet Muhammad: Devotional Piety in Sunni Islam*. Culture and Civilization in the Middle East. London; New York: Routledge.
Katz, Marion Holmes. 2014. *Women in the Mosque: A History of Legal Thought and Social Practice*. New York: Columbia University Press.
Kellaway, Kate. 2018. 'Grenfell One Year on: The Mosque Manager Who Took in Survivors'. *The Guardian*, 10 June. http://www.theguardian.com/uk-news/2018/jun/10/mosque-manager-grenfell-survivors-interview-abdurahman-sayed-al-manaar.
Kettell, Steven and Peter Kerr. 2021. 'The Brexit Religion and the Holy Grail of the NHS'. *Social Policy and Society* 20 (2): 282–95. https://doi.org/10.1017/S1474746420000561.
Khan, Harun, Hassan Joudi, and Zahraa Ahmed. 2020. 'The Muslim Council of Britain: Progressive Interlocutor or Redundant Gatekeeper?' *Religions* 11 (9): 473.
Kibria, Nazli. 2008. 'The "New Islam" and Bangladeshi Youth in Britain and the US'. *Ethnic and Racial Studies* 31 (2): 243–66. https://doi.org/10.1080/01419870701337593.

King, John. 1997. 'Tablighi Jamaat and the Deobandi Mosques in Britain'. In *Islam in Europe: The Politics of Religion and Community*, edited by Steven Vertovec and Ceri Peach, 129–46. Migration, Minorities and Citizenship Series. London: Palgrave Macmillan UK. https://doi.org/10.1007/978-1-349-25697-6_7.

Knott, Kim. 2005. *The Location of Religion*. London: Equinox Pub.

Knysh, Alexander D. 2017. *Sufism: A New History of Islamic Mysticism*. Princeton; Oxford: Princeton University Press.

Kong, L. 2001. 'Mapping New Geographies of Religion: Politics and Poetics in Modernity'. *Prog Hum Geogr* 25 (2): 211–33. https://doi.org/10.1191/030913201678580485.

Körs, A. 2018. 'Congregations in Germany: Mapping of Organizations, Beliefs, Activities, and Relations: The Case Study of Hamburg'. In *Congregations in Europe*, edited by C. Monnot and J. Stolz. 117–37. Cham: Springer. https://doi.org/10.1007/978-3-319-77261-5_7.

Kortt, Michael A., Todd Steen, and Elisabeth Sinnewe. 2017. 'Church Attendance, Faith and the Allocation of Time: Evidence from Australia'. *International Journal of Social Economics* 44 (12): 2112–27. https://doi.org/10.1108/IJSE-05-2016-0140.

Kuiper, Matthew J. 2019. *Da'wa and Other Religions: Indian Muslims and the Modern Resurgence of Global Islamic Activism*. 1st ed. London: Routledge.

Kundnani, Arun. 2012. 'Radicalisation: The Journey of a Concept'. *Race & Class* 54 (2): 3–25. https://doi.org/10.1177/0306396812454984.

Kurd, Nadia. 2018. 'The Mosque as Heritage Site: The Al-Rashid at Fort Edmonton Park and the Politics of Location'. *Journal of Canadian Studies/Revue d'études Canadiennes* 52 (1): 176–92.

Kuruvilla, Carol. 2016. 'Amazon Tackles Islamophobia In Heartwarming Christmas Ad'. *HuffPost UK*, 18 November, sec. Religion. https://www.huffpost.com/entry/amazon-christmas-ad-2016_n_582e0590e4b099512f81919e.

Landman, Nico and Wendy Wessels. 2005. 'The Visibility of Mosques in Dutch Towns'. *Journal of Ethnic and Migration Studies* 31 (6): 1125–40. https://doi.org/10.1080/13691830500282725.

Lane, Edward William and Stanley Lane-Poole. 2003. *An Arabic-English lexicon*. Lahore: Suhail Academy.

Lane, Oliver JJ. 2020. 'Residents Voice Opposition to Proposed Piccadilly Circus "Mega-Mosque"'. *Breitbart*. 18 May. https://www.breitbart.com/europe/2020/05/18/voice-opposition-to-proposed-piccadilly-circus-mega-mosque/.

Lefebvre, Henri. 2004. *Rhythmanalysis*. London/New York: Continuum.

Lefebvre, Henri, and Catherine Regulier. 2004. 'Attempt at the Rhythmanalysis of Mediterranean Cities'. In *Rhythmanalysis*, edited by Henri Lefebvre, 1st ed. London/New York: Continuum.

Lewis, Philip. 1994. *Islamic Britain*. London/New York: I.B. Tauris.

Lewis, Philip. 2006a. 'Imams, Ulema and Sufis: Providers of Bridging Social Capital for British Pakistanis?'. *Contemporary South Asia* 15 (3): 273–87. https://doi.org/10.1080/09584930601098018.

Lewis, Philip. 2006b. 'Only Connect: Can the Ulema Address the Crisis in the Transmission of Islam to a New Generation of South Asians in Britain?'. *Contemporary South Asia* 15 (2): 165–80. https://doi.org/10.1080/09584930600955275.

Lewis, Philip. 2007. *Young, British and Muslim*. London; New York: Continuum.

Liberatore, Giulia. 2019. 'Guidance as "Women's Work": A New Generation of Female Islamic Authorities in Britain'. *Religions* 10 (11): 601. https://doi.org/10.3390/rel10110601.

Lim, Merlyna. 2012. 'Clicks, Cabs, and Coffee Houses: Social Media and Oppositional Movements in Egypt, 2004–2011'. *Journal of Communication* 62 (2): 231–48. https://doi.org/10.1111/j.1460-2466.2012.01628.x.

Lings, Martin. 1983. *Muhammad: His Life Based on the Earliest Sources*. 3rd ed. New York: The Islamic Texts Society.

Lings, Martin. 1993. *A Sufi Saint of the Twentieth Century: Shaikh Aḥmad al-ʿAlawī: His Spiritual Heritage & Legacy*. 3rd ed. Golden Palm Series. Cambridge: Islamic Texts Society.

Little, K. L. 1942a. 'Loudoun Square: A Community Survey-I (An Aspect of Race Relations in English Society)'. *The Sociological Review* a34 (1–2): 12–33. https://doi.org/10.1111/j.1467-954x.1942.tb02744.x.

Little, K. L. 1942b. 'Loudoun Square: A Community Survey-II1'. *The Sociological Review* a34 (3–4): 119–46. https://doi.org/10.1111/j.1467-954x.1942.tb02511.x.

Lotfi, Abdelhamid. 2001. 'Creating Muslim Space in the USA: Masjid and Islamic Centers'. *Islam and Christian–Muslim Relations* 12 (2): 235–54. https://doi.org/10.1080/09596410120051791.

Lowndes, Vivien and Rachael Chapman. 2007. 'Faith, Hope and Clarity: Faith Groups and Civil Renewal'. In *Re-Energizing Citizenship*, edited by Tessa Brannan, Peter John, and Gerry Stoker, 163–84. London: Palgrave Macmillan UK. https://doi.org/10.1057/9780230206915_9.

Lussier, D.N. 2019. 'Mosques, Churches, and Civic Skill Opportunities in Indonesia'. *Journal for the Scientific Study of Religion* 58 (2): 415–38. https://doi.org/10.1111/jssr.12589.

Luz, Nimrod. 2008. 'The Politics of Sacred Places: Palestinian Identity, Collective Memory, and Resistance in the Hassan Bek Mosque Conflict'. *Environment and Planning D: Society and Space* 26 (6): 1036–52. https://doi.org/10.1068/d2508.

Macdonald, Myra. 2011. 'British Muslims, Memory and Identity: Representations in British Film and Television Documentary'. *European Journal of Cultural Studies* 14 (4): 411–27. https://doi.org/10.1177/1367549411404617.

Macguire, Eoghan. 2018. 'The Tiny Mosque on the Outer Hebrides Serving 60 Muslims'. *Al Jazeera*, 15 June. https://www.aljazeera.com/features/2018/6/15/the-tiny-mosque-on-the-outer-hebrides-serving-60-muslims.

Maher, Shiraz. 2016. *Salafi-Jihadism: The History of an Idea*. London: C Hurst & Co Publishers Ltd.

Mahmood, Hamid. 2012. 'The Dars-e-Niẓāmī and the Transnational Traditionalist Madāris in Britain'. *Hamid Mahmood*, September. https://www.academia.edu/2074908/The_Dars_e_Ni%E1%BA%93%C4%81m%C4%AB_and_the_Transnational_Traditionalist_Mad%C4%81ris_in_Britain.

Malik, Maleiha, ed. 2012. *Anti-Muslim Prejudice: Past and Present*. First issued in paperback. London: Routledge.

Manco, Ural and Meryem Kanmaz. 2005. 'From Conflict to Co-Operation Between Muslims and Local Authorities in a Brussels Borough: Schaerbeek'. *Journal of Ethnic and Migration Studies* 31 (6): 1105–23. https://doi.org/10.1080/13691830500282865.

Mandaville, Peter. 2009. 'Muslim Transnational Identity and State Responses in Europe and the UK after 9/11: Political Community, Ideology and Authority'. *Journal of Ethnic and Migration Studies* 35 (3): 491–506. https://doi.org/10.1080/13691830802704681.

Mandaville, Peter. 2010. 'Muslim Networks and Movements in Western Europe - Tablighi Jama'at'. https://www.pewforum.org/2010/09/15/muslim-networks-and-movements-in-western-europe-tablighi-jamaat/.

Mangera, Abdurrahman ibn Yusuf. 2004. 'Masjid or Musalla'. *Albalagh*. https://www.albalagh.net/general/0074.shtml.

Maravia, Usman, Zhazira Bekzhanova, Mansur Ali, and Rakan Alibri. 2021. 'British Muslims Caught Amidst FOGs – A Discourse Analysis of Religious Advice and Authority'. *Religions* 12 (2): 140. https://doi.org/10.3390/rel12020140.

Marcus, G. E. 1995. 'Ethnography In/Of the World System: The Emergence of Multi-Sited Ethnography'. *Annual Review of Anthropology* 24 (1): 95–117. https://doi.org/10.1146/annurev.anthro.24.1.95.

Marsden, Sam. 2014. 'Did This Preacher Groom the Jihadi Britons? Notorious Cleric Visited Mosque Where Terror Brothers Worshipped'. *Mail Online*. 22 June. https://www.dailymail.co.uk/news/article-2665307/Did-Saudi-preacher-groom-jihadi-Britons.html.

Massoumi, Narzanin, Tom Mills, and David Miller, eds. 2017. *What Is Islamophobia? Racism, Social Movements and the State*. London: PlutoPress.

Matar, N. I. 1998. *Islam in Britain, 1558–1685*. Cambridge; New York: Cambridge University Press.

Maussen, Marcel. 2009. 'Constructing Mosques: The Governance of Islam in France and the Netherlands'. PhD Thesis, Amsterdam School for Social Science Research.

Mawani, Rizwan. 2019. *Beyond the Mosque: Diverse Spaces of Muslim Worship*. World of Islam. London; New York; Oxford; New Delhi; Sydney: I.B. Tauris.

Mazumdar, Shampa and Sanjoy Mazumdar. 2004. 'The Articulation of Religion in Domestic Space: Rituals in the Immigrant Muslim Home'. *Journal of Ritual Studies* 18 (2): 74–85.

McCutcheon, Russell T. 1999. *The Insider/Outsider Problem in the Study of Religion: A Reader*. London; New York: Continuum. http://public.eblib.com/choice/publicfullrecord.aspx?p=436720.

McEnery, Tony, Mark McGlashan, and Robbie Love. 2015. 'Press and Social Media Reaction to Ideologically Inspired Murder: The Case of Lee Rigby'. *Discourse & Communication* 9 (2): 237–59. https://doi.org/10.1177/1750481314568545.

McGuire, Meredith B. 2008. *Lived Religion: Faith and Practice in Everyday Life*. Oxford; New York: Oxford University Press.

McLoughlin, Seán. 2005. 'Mosques and the Public Space: Conflict and Cooperation in Bradford'. *Journal of Ethnic and Migration Studies* 31 (6): 1045–66. https://doi.org/10.1080/13691830500282832.

McLoughlin, Seán. 2007. 'Islam(s) in Context: Orientalism and the Anthropology of Muslim Societies and Cultures'. *Journal of Beliefs & Values* 28 (3): 273–96. https://doi.org/10.1080/13617670701712539.

McLoughlin, Seán. 2014. 'The Islamic Foundation in the United Kingdom'. In *Islamic Movements of Europe: Public Religion and Islamophobia in the Modern World*, 212, edited by F. Peter and R. Ortega. London, New York: Bloomsbury Academic. https://books.google.co.uk/books?id=ioqjcQAACAAJ.

Mead, Loren R. 1999. *Financial Meltdown in the Mainline?* http://public.eblib.com/choice/publicfullrecord.aspx?p=1740491.

Meer, Nasar. 2007. 'Muslim Schools in Britain: Challenging Mobilisations or Logical Developments?'. *Asia Pacific Journal of Education* 27 (1): 55–71. https://doi.org/10.1080/02188790601145374.

Metcalf, B. D. 2002. '"Traditionalist" Islamic Activism:Deoband, Tablighis, and Talibs'. Article / Letter to editor. *ISIM Paper*, 1–24. https://openaccess.leidenuniv.nl/handle/1887/10068.

Metcalf, Barbara. 1996. 'New Medinas'. In *Making Muslim Space in North America and Europe*, edited by Barbara Metcalf, 1st ed., 110–27. Berkeley: University of California Press.

Metcalf, Barbara Daly. 1996. *Making Muslim Space in North America and Europe*. Berkeley: University of California Press.

Miller, Donald E. 2013. 'Civil Society and Religion'. In *The Oxford Handbook of Civil Society*, edited by Michael Edwards 1. issued as paperback, 257–69. Oxford: Oxford University Press.

Milton, Josh. 2020. 'Plans for a Mosque in the Heart of London's Gay Village Wins the Backing of LGBT+ Forum – despite Objections from Others'. *PinkNews - Gay News, Reviews and Comment from the World's Most Read Lesbian, Gay, Bisexual, and Trans News Service* (blog). 31 May. https://www.pinknews.co.uk/2020/05/31/london-soho-mosque-westminster-lgbt-forum-sohi-community-campaign-aziz-foundation/.

Mobeen, Noor, Shaan Shahabuddin, Chanda Elbert, and Fred E. Bonner. 2019. 'Failure of Muslim Leadership in America From the Perspective of First-Generation Muslim

Americans: A Phenomenological Study'. *Journal of Muslim Minority Affairs* 39 (1): 93–105. https://doi.org/10.1080/13602004.2019.1589125.
Modood, Tariq. 1992. *Not Easy Being British: Colour, Culture and Citizenship*. Stoke-on-Trent: Runnymede Trust and Trentham.
Modood, Tariq. 2010. 'Multicultural Citizenship and Muslim Identity Politics'. *Interventions* 12 (2): 157–70. https://doi.org/10.1080/1369801X.2010.489688.
Moles, Tarja. 2009. 'The Evolution of the Ahmadiyya Community in the UK'. Ph.D., Royal Holloway, University of London. https://ethos.bl.uk/OrderDetails.do?uin=uk.bl.ethos.536231.
Moore, Leslie C. 2012. 'Muslim Children's Other School'. *Childhood Education* 88 (5): 298–303. https://doi.org/10.1080/00094056.2012.718243.
Moosa, Ebrahim. 2004. 'Deobandi School'. In *The Oxford Dictionary of Islam*, edited by John L Esposito. Oxford; New York: Oxford University Press. http://www.oxfordreference.com/views/BOOK_SEARCH.html?book=t125.
Moosavi, Leon. 2015. 'The Racialization of Muslim Converts in Britain and Their Experiences of Islamophobia'. *Critical Sociology* 41 (1): 41–56. https://doi.org/10.1177/0896920513504601.
Morgahi, Amer. 2015. 'Reliving the "Classical Islam": Emergence and Working of the Minhajul Quran Movement in the UK'. In *Sufism in Britain*, edited by Ron Geaves and Theodore Gabriel. London: Bloomsbury.
'Mosque "Armed Jihad" Sermon Probe Dropped'. 2019. BBC, 29 January, sec. Manchester. https://www.bbc.com/news/uk-england-manchester-47040825.
'Mosquebusters | Gavin Boby.Com'. n.d. Accessed 12 June 2021. https://gavinboby.com/mosquebusters/.
'Mosques Mobilise to Help Those Affected by Floods in Northern England'. 2015. *IlmFeed*. 27 December. https://ilmfeed.com/mosques-mobilise-to-help-those-affected-by-floods-in-northern-england/.
Mostafa, Dalia Said and Amina Elbendary. 2021. *The Egyptian Coffeehouse: Culture, Politics and Urban Space*. London; New York: I.B. Tauris.
Munajjid, Muhammad Saalih. 2011. 'When Does a Place Become a Mosque? - Islam Question & Answer'. *Islam QA*. https://islamqa.info/en/answers/170800/when-does-a-place-become-a-mosque.
Muslim Council of Britain. 2006. *Voices from the Minaret: MCB Study of UK Imams and Mosques*. Stratford; London: Muslim Council of Britain.
Muslim Council of Britain. 2015. *British Muslims in Numbers: A Demographic, Socio-Economic and Health Profile of Muslims in Britain Drawing on the 2011 Census*. Muslim Council of Britain. http://www.mcb.org.uk/wp-content/uploads/2015/02/MCBCensusReport_2015.pdf.
Muslim Council of Britain. 2016. 'Thousands of Britons Take Part in "Visit My Mosque" Initiative'. *Muslim Council of Britain (MCB)* (blog). 8 February. https://mcb.org.uk/press-releases/thousands-of-britons-take-part-in-visit-my-mosque-initiative/.

Muslim Council of Britain. 2019. 'Women in Mosques Development Programme 2019'. *Muslim Council of Britain (MCB)* (blog). 22 July. https://mcb.org.uk/mcb-updates/women-in-mosques-development-programme-2019/.

Muslim Council of Britain. 2021. 'Defining Islamophobia: A Contemporary Understanding of How Expressions of Muslimness Are Targeted'. https://mcb.org.uk/report/defining-islamophobia-a-contemporary-understanding-of-how-expressions-of-muslimness-are-targeted/.

Muslim Council of Britain. 2022. 'Local Muslim Representation Empowering Council of Mosques & Local Umbrella Organisations 2022'. https://mcb.org.uk/report/local-muslim-representation-2022/.

'MyMosqueStory | Twitter, Instagram'. n.d. *Linktree*. Accessed 23 August 2022. https://linktr.ee/MyMosqueStory.

Nadwi, Mohammad Akram. 2013. *Al-Muhaddithat: The Women Scholars in Islam*. 2nd revised ed. Oxford: Interface Publications Ltd.

Nadwi, Mohammad Akram. 2018. 'Some Reflections on 'Aqidah'. *Al-Salam Institute* (blog). 6 November. https://alsalam.ac.uk/aqidah/.

Naqshbandi, Mehmood. 2015. *UK Mosque Statistics / Masjid Statistics*. 1st ed. http://www.muslimsinbritain.org/resources/masjid_report.pdf.

Naqshbandi, Mehmood. 2017. *UK Mosque Statistics / Masjid Statistics*. 1st ed. http://www.muslimsinbritain.org/resources/masjid_report.pdf.

Nasser, Noha. 2005. 'Expressions of Muslim Identity in Architecture and Urbanism in Birmingham, UK'. *Islam and Christian–Muslim Relations* 16 (1): 61–78. https://doi.org/10.1080/09596410520000313246.

Naylor, Simon and James R. Ryan. 2002. 'The Mosque in the Suburbs: Negotiating Religion and Ethnicity in South London'. *Social & Cultural Geography* 3 (1): 39–59. https://doi.org/10.1080/14649360120114134.

Nelson, Carl Ellis. 1971. *Where Faith Begins*. Owensboro, KY: Owensboro Volunteer Recording Unit.

Neumann, Peter R. 2016. *Radicalized: New Jihadists and the Threat to the West*. London; New York: I.B. Tauris.

Nielsen, Jørgen S. and Jonas Otterbeck. 2016. *Muslims in Western Europe*. 4th ed. The New Edinburgh Islamic Surveys. Edinburgh: Edinburgh University Press.

Nyhagen, Line. 2019. 'Mosques as Gendered Spaces: The Complexity of Women's Compliance with, and Resistance to, Dominant Gender Norms, and the Importance of Male Allies'. *Religions* 10 (5): 321. https://doi.org/10.3390/rel10050321.

Office for National Statistics. 2017. 'Population of England, Wales and Selected Local Authorities against Numbers and Percent of Muslims (2015 to 2016)'. https://www.ons.gov.uk/peoplepopulationandcommunity/culturalidentity/religion/adhocs/008332populationofenglandwalesandselectedlocalauthoritiesagainstnumbersandpercentofmuslims2015162017.

Office for National Statistics. 2018. 'Muslim Population in the UK'. 8 February. https://www.ons.gov.uk/aboutus/transparencyandgovernance/freedomofinformationfoi/muslimpopulationintheuk/.

Okely, Judith. 1975. 'The Self and Scientism'. *Journal of the Anthropological Society of Oxford* 6 (3): 171–88.

'Open My Mosque | Facebook'. n.d. Accessed 23 August 2022. https://www.facebook.com/openmymosque/.

Otto, Rudolf and John W. Harvey. 1958. *The Idea of the Holy*. New York: Oxford University Press.

'Oxford Institute for British Islam – Advancing a Qur'an-Centric Faith in the UK'. 2022. Oxford Institute for British Islam. https://oibi.org.uk/.

Packiam, Glenn Previn. 2018. 'Worship and the World to Come: A Theological Ethnography of Hope in Contemporary Worship Songs and Services'. Ph.D., Durham University. http://etheses.dur.ac.uk/12533/.

Paden, Ailliam. 1994. *Religious Worlds: The Comparative Study of Religion by William E. Paden*. Boston: Beacon Press.

Pals, Daniel L. 2006. *Eight Theories of Religion*. New York: Oxford University Press.

Paredes, Cristina, ed. 2009. *Faith: Spiritual Architecture*. Barcelona: Loft Publ.

Peach, Ceri and Richard Gale. 2003. 'Muslims, Hindus, and Sikhs in the New Religious Landscape of England'. *Geographical Review* 93 (4): 469–90. https://doi.org/10.1111/j.1931-0846.2003.tb00043.x.

Pearce, Brian. 2012. 'The Inter Faith Network and the Development of Inter Faith Relations in Britain'. In *Religion and Change in Modern Britain*, edited by Linda Woodhead and Rebecca Catto, 150–5. London; New York: Routledge.

Pedersen, J., R. Hillenbrand, J. Burton-Page, P. A. Andrews, G. F. Pijper, A. H. Christie, A. D. W. Forbes, G. S. P. Freeman-Greenville, and A. Samb. 2012. 'Masdjid'. *Encyclopaedia of Islam*. 2nd ed. April. https://referenceworks.brillonline.com/entries/encyclopaedia-of-islam-2/masdjid-COM_0694?s.num=13&s.rows=20&s.mode=DEFAULT&s.f.s2_parent=encyclopaedia-of-islam-2&s.start=0&s.q=masjid.

Peter, Frank and Rafael Ortega, eds. 2014. *Islamic Movements of Europe: Public Religion and Islamophobia in the Modern World*. Library of European Studies 21. London; New York: I.B. Tauris.

Petersen, Andrew. 2008. 'The Archaeology of Islam in Britain: Recognition and Potential'. *Antiquity* 82 (318): 1080–92. https://doi.org/10.1017/s0003598x00097799.

Petersen, Jesper. 2019. 'Pop-up Mosques, Social Media Adhan, and the Making of Female and LGBTQ-Inclusive Imams'. *Journal of Muslims in Europe* 8 (2): 178–96. https://doi.org/10.1163/22117954-12341392.

Peucker, M. 2018. 'Muslim Community Volunteering: The Civic-Religious 'Culture of Benevolence' and Its Sociopolitical Implications'. *Scopus* 46 (11): 2367–86. https://doi.org/10.1080/1369183X.2018.1543020.

Pieri, Zacharias. 2015. *Tablighi Jamaat and the Quest for the London Mega Mosque: Continuity and Change*. http://site.ebrary.com/id/11061835.

Prickett, P. J. 2014. 'Negotiating Gendered Religious Space: The Particularities of Patriarchy in an African American Mosque'. *Gender & Society* 29 (1): 51–72. https://doi.org/10.1177/0891243214546934.

Putnam, Robert D. 2001. *Bowling Alone: The Collapse and Revival of American Community*. New York: Simon & Schuster.

Quinn, G. J. and J. D. Davidson. 1976. 'Theology: Sociology = Orthodoxy: Orthopraxis'. *Theology Today* 32 (4): 345–52. https://doi.org/10.1177/004057367603200402.

Qureshi, Asim. 2022. 'The Case Against "Islamism"'. *Ummatics Colloquium* (blog). 13 June. https://ummaticscolloquium.org/the-case-against-islamism/.

Qureshi, Regula Burkchardt. 1996. 'Transcending Space'. In *Making Muslim Space in North America and Europe*, edited by Barbara Metcalf, 1st ed., 45–64. Berkeley: University of California Press.

Rabinow, Paul and Robert Neelly Bellah. 1977. *Reflections on Fieldwork in Morocco*. Berkeley: University of California Press.

Rai, Kiran K., Sufyan Abid Dogra, Sally Barber, Peymane Adab, and Carolyn Summerbell. 2019. 'A Scoping Review and Systematic Mapping of Health Promotion Interventions Associated with Obesity in Islamic Religious Settings in the UK'. *Obesity Reviews*. https://doi.org/10.1111/obr.12874.

Rajabi-Ardeshiri, Masoud. 2011. 'Children and Conflict: Exploring Children's Agency at UK Mosque Schools'. *The International Journal of Children's Rights* 19 (4): 691–704. https://doi.org/10.1163/157181810X522306.

Rasdi, Mohamad Tajuddin Haji Mohamad. 2014. *Rethinking the Mosque in the Modern Muslim Society*. Kuala Lumpur: Institut Terjemahan & Buku Malaysia.

Reimer-Kirkham, Sheryl, Sonya Sharma, Barb Pesut, Richard Sawatzky, Heather Meyerhoff, and Marie Cochrane. 2011. 'Sacred Spaces in Public Places: Religious and Spiritual Plurality in Health Care'. *Nursing Inquiry* 19 (3): 202–12. https://doi.org/10.1111/j.1440-1800.2011.00571.x.

Rex, J. 1994. 'The Political Sociology of Multiculturalism and the Place of Muslims in West European Societies'. *Social Compass* 41 (1): 79–92. https://doi.org/10.1177/003776894041001007.

Rex, John. 1991. *Ethnic Identity and Ethnic Mobilisation in Britain*. Centre for Research in Ethnic Relations, University of Warwick.

Rizvi, Kishwar. 2015. *The Transnational Mosque: Architecture and Historical Memory in the Contemporary Middle East*. Islamic Civilization and Muslim Networks. Chapel Hill: The University of North Carolina Press.

Rossi, Maurizio and Ettore Scappini. 2014. 'Church Attendance, Problems of Measurement, and Interpreting Indicators: A Study of Religious Practice in the United States, 1975–2010: CHURCH ATTENDANCE IN THE UNITED STATES'. *Journal for the Scientific Study of Religion* 53 (2): 249–67. https://doi.org/10.1111/jssr.12115.

Ruez, Derek. 2012. 'Partitioning the Sensible at Park 51: Rancire, Islamophobia, and Common Politics'. *Antipode* 45 (5): 1128–47. https://doi.org/10.1111/anti.12004.

Rusli, Farah Nuratiqah and Md Azree Othuman Mydin. 2018. 'Accessible Built Environment for People of Disabilities at Mosque: Universal Design'. *Analele Universității 'Eftimie Murgu' Reșița: Fascicola I, Inginerie* XXV (1): 118–25.

Safi, Omid, ed. 2010. *Progressive Muslims: On Justice, Gender and Pluralism*. Reprinted. Oxford: Oneworld.

Said, Edward W. 2003. *Orientalism*. London: Penguin Classics.

Sajid, Muhamad, Ali Hassan, and Shoab A. Khan. 2016. 'Crowd Counting Using Adaptive Segmentation in a Congregation'. In *2016 IEEE International Conference on Signal and Image Processing (ICSIP)*, 745–9. https://doi.org/10.1109/SIPROCESS.2016.7888363.

Salahi, Adil. 2010. *Muhammad: Man and Prophet*. Rev ed. The Islamic Foundation.

Salamat, Muslim P. 2008. *A Miracle at Woking*. Felphamm: Phillimore.

Saleem, Shahed. 2018. *The British Mosque: An Architectural and Social History*. Swindon: Historic England.

Salkina, M. 2016. 'Institutionalization of Islam in France: A Path from Ethnic to Religious Lobbying'. *Mezhdunarodnye Protsessy* 14 (2): 112–22. https://doi.org/10.17994/IT.2016.14.2.45/8.

Samuel, Geoffrey and Santi Rozario. 2012. 'Sufi Spaces in Urban Bangladesh'. In *Prayer in the City*, edited by Patrick Desplat and Dorothea Schulz, 1st ed., 289–310. London: Transaction Publishers.

Samuels, Gabriel. 2016. 'Britain First Just Got Banned from Every Mosque in England and Wales'. *The Independent*. 18 August. https://www.independent.co.uk/news/uk/home-news/britain-first-banned-all-mosques-england-and-wales-after-police-take-out-injunction-a7196831.html.

Samuri, Mohd Al Adib and Peter Hopkins. 2017. 'Voices of Islamic Authorities: Friday Khutba in Malaysian Mosques'. *Islam and Christian–Muslim Relations* 28 (1): 47–67. https://doi.org/10.1080/09596410.2017.1280916.

Sartawi, Mohammed and Gordon Sammut. 2012. 'Negotiating British Muslim Identity: Everyday Concerns of Practicing Muslims in London'. *Culture & Psychology* 18 (4): 559–76. https://doi.org/10.1177/1354067X12456714.

Sarwar, Ghulam. 1982. *Islam, Beliefs and Teachings*. London: Muslim Educational Trust.

'Sayeeda Warsi on Twitter: "In Response to Popular Demand - Well from @tnewtondunn Here Are the Bad, Confused and Weird Bits of the #Casey Review ...." / Twitter'. n.d. *Twitter*. Accessed 10 February 2020. https://twitter.com/SayeedaWarsi/status/805409248389853188.

'Sayeeda Warsi on Twitter: ". . . This One Made Me Choke on My #Yorkshire Tea. 'The Emancipation of Muslim Women'-Yes Those Words Are in the Report! The Empire Strikes Back!" / Twitter'. n.d. Twitter. Accessed 10 February 2020. https://twitter.com/SayeedaWarsi/status/805413455633203200.

Sayyid, Salman and Abdoolkarim Vakil, eds. 2010. *Thinking through Islamophobia: Global Perspectives*. London: Hurst.

Scharbrodt, Oliver. 2019a. 'Creating a Diasporic Public Sphere in Britain: Twelver Shia Networks in London'. *Islam and Christian–Muslim Relations*, July, 1–18. https://doi.org/10.1080/09596410.2019.1643098.

Scharbrodt, Oliver. 2019b. 'A Minority within a Minority?: The Complexity and Multilocality of Transnational Twelver Shia Networks in Britain'. *Contemporary Islam* 13 (3): 287–305. https://doi.org/10.1007/s11562-018-0431-0.

Scourfield, Jonathan, Sophie Gilliat-Ray, Asma Khan, and Sameh Otri. 2013. *Muslim Childhood*. London; New York: Oxford University Press.

Searcy, Kim. 2010. 'The Khalifa and the Routinization of Charismatic Authority'. *The International Journal of African Historical Studies* 43 (3): 429–42.

Seddon, Mohammed. 2014a. 'Shaykh Abdullah Ali Al-Hakimi, the Alawi Tariqa and British Yemenis'. In *Sufism in Britain*, edited by Ron Geaves and Theodore P. C. Gabriel, 73–92. London; New York: Bloomsbury.

Seddon, Mohammed. 2014b. *The Last of the Lascars*. Markfield: Kube Publishing.

Sedgwick, Mark J. 2017. *Western Sufism: From the Abbasids to the New Age*. New York: Oxford University Press.

Serageldin, Ismail and James Steele. 1996. *Architecture of the Contemporary Mosque*. Academy Editions.

Shannahan, Dervla Sara. 2013. 'Gender, Inclusivity and UK Mosque Experiences'. *Contemporary Islam* 8 (1): 1–16. https://doi.org/10.1007/s11562-013-0286-3.

Shannahan, Dervla Sara. 2014. 'Gender, Inclusivity and UK Mosque Experiences'. *Contemporary Islam* 8 (1): 1–16.

Shavit, Uriya and Fabian Spengler. 2021. 'How Radical Is Birmingham's Salafi Mosque?'. *Democracy and Security* 17 (1): 80–107. https://doi.org/10.1080/17419166.2020.1848557.

Sherwood, Harriet. 2016a. 'Visit My Mosque Day: British Muslims Offer Tours and Tea to Public'. *Guardian*, 5 February. http://www.theguardian.com/world/2016/feb/05/visit-my-mosque-day-muslims-offer-tours-and-tea-to-the-curious.

Sherwood, Harriet. 2016b. 'Women Lead Friday Prayers at Denmark's First Female-Run Mosque'. *The Guardian*, 26 August, sec. World news. https://www.theguardian.com/world/2016/aug/26/women-lead-friday-prayers-denmark-first-female-run-mosque-mariam.

Sherwood, Harriet. 2017. 'Muslim Feminist Plans to Open Liberal Mosque in Britain | World News'. *The Guardian*. 26 June. https://www.theguardian.com/world/2017/jul/26/seyran-ates-muslim-feminist-liberal-mosque-london-britain.

Sherwood, Harriet. 2018a. 'First Mosque Opens on Outer Hebrides in Time for Ramadan'. *The Guardian*, 11 May, sec. UK news. https://www.theguardian.com/uk-news/2018/may/11/first-mosque-opens-on-stornoway-outer-hebrides-in-time-for-ramadan.

Sherwood, Harriet. 2018b. 'Muslim Council of Britain to Train Women to Run Mosques'. *The Guardian*, 4 October, sec. World news. https://www.theguardian.com/world/2018/oct/04/muslim-council-of-britain-women-leadership-training.

Sidat, Haroon. 2018. 'Between Tradition and Transition: An Islamic Seminary, or Dar al-Uloom in Modern Britain'. *Religions* 9 (10): 314. https://doi.org/10.3390/rel9100314.

Sidat, Haroon. 2019. 'Shedding Light on the Modalities of Authority in a Dar Al-Uloom, or Religious Seminary, in Britain'. *Religions* 10 (12): 653. https://doi.org/10.3390/rel10120653.

Siddiqi, Bulbul. 2018. 'Tablighi Jamaat in the UK'. In *Becoming 'Good Muslim': The Tablighi Jamaat in the UK and Bangladesh*, edited by Bulbul Siddiqi, 119–28. Singapore: Springer Singapore. https://doi.org/10.1007/978-981-10-7236-9_8.

'Side Entrance on Twitter: "I Don't Normally Respond to Criticism Given in Bad Faith, but I Do Try to Engage with Sincere Critique Given in Good Faith. I Recently Came across Someone Saying Side Entrance Is Only About Shaming Mosques. That Is Absolutely Not the Intention nor the Impact of This Work." / Twitter'. n.d. *Twitter*. Accessed 17 August 2020. https://twitter.com/SideEntrance/status/1171814093734498306.

Sideentrance. n.d. 'Side Entrance'. *Tumblr*. Photos from Mosques around the World, Showcasing Women's Sacred Spaces, in Relation to Men's Spaces. We Show the Beautiful, the Adequate and the Pathetic. Accessed 23 August 2022. https://sideentrance.tumblr.com/.

Sikand, Yoginder S. 1998. 'The Origins and Growth of the Tablighi Jamaat in Britain'. *Islam and Christian–Muslim Relations* 9 (2): 171–92. https://doi.org/10.1080/09596419808721147.

Silberman, Marc, Karen E. Till, and Janet Ward, eds. 2012. *Walls, Borders, Boundaries: Spatial and Cultural Practices in Europe*, vol. 4. Spektrum: Publications of the German Studies Association. New York: Berghahn Books.

Smith, Jane I. and Harvard University, eds. 1980. *Women in Contemporary Muslim Societies*. Lewisburg, PA: Bucknell University Press.

Smith, Jane Idleman. 1994. *Muslim Communities in North America*. Edited by Yvonne Yazbeck Haddad. Albany, NY: State University of New York Press.

Smith, Jonathan Z. 1987. *To Take Place*. Chicago: University of Chicago Press.

Smith, Tom W. 1998. 'A Review of Church Attendance Measures'. *American Sociological Review* 63 (1): 131–6. https://doi.org/10.2307/2657485.

Spahic, Omer. 2016. 'The Form and Function of the Prophet's Mosque during the Time of the Prophet'. https://www.academia.edu/28193901/The_Form_and_Function_of_the_Prophets_Mosque_during_the_Time_of_the_Prophet_pbuh.

Spellman, Kathryn. 2004. *Religion and Nation: Iranian Local and Transnational Networks in Britain*. Oxford; New York: Berghahn Books.

Spencer, Nick. 2012. 'What Is the Future of English Cathedrals?'. *Theos Think Tank*. https://www.theosthinktank.co.uk/research/2012/10/12/spiritual-capital-the-present-and-future-of-english-cathedrals.

Spencer, Nick. 2020. 'Clapping for the NHS, Our New Religion'. *Theos Think Tank*. Accessed 19 March 2021. https://www.theosthinktank.co.uk/comment/2020/03/27/clapping-for-the-nhs-our-new-religion.

Spickard, James V. 2017. *Alternative Sociologies of Religion: Through Non-Western Eyes*. New York: New York University Press.

Stevenson, Jacqueline, Sean Demack, Bernie Stiell, Muna Abdi, Luna Clarkson, Farhana Ghaffar, and Shaima Hassan. 2017. 'Social Mobility Challenges Faced by Young Muslims'. *Social Mobility Commission*. https://www.gov.uk/government/publications/social-mobility-challenges-faced-by-young-muslims.

Stornoway Gazette. 2018. 'Stornoway's First Mosque Opens in Time for Ramadan'. *Stornoway Gazette*, 14 May. https://www.stornowaygazette.co.uk/news/stornoways-first-mosque-opens-time-ramadan-2053776.

Strothman, Linus. 2012. 'A Shrine Gone Urban'. In *Prayer in the City*, edited by Patrick Desplat and Dorothea Schulz, 1st ed., 265–88. London: Transaction Publishers.

'SuperWEB2(Tm) - Table View'. n.d. Accessed 8 August 2022. https://www.scotlandscensus.gov.uk/webapi/jsf/tableView/tableView.xhtml.

Sweney, Mark. 2016. 'Amazon TV Ad Features Imam and Vicar Exchanging Gifts'. *The Guardian*, 16 November, sec. Media. http://www.theguardian.com/media/2016/nov/16/amazon-tv-ad-imam-vicar-exchanging-gifts.

Swindon, Peter. 2018. 'Muslim Women Launch Equality Campaign amid Claims of "Crisis" at Scottish Mosques | HeraldScotland'. *The Herald*, 8 December. https://www.heraldscotland.com/news/16413492.muslim-women-launch-equality-campaign-amid-claims-of-crisis-at-scottish-mosques/.

Tareen, SherAli K. 2020. *Defending Muḥammad in Modernity*. Notre Dame, IN: University of Notre Dame Press.

Taylor, Matthew. 2016. 'Casey Report Criticised for Focus on UK Muslim Communities'. *The Guardian*, 5 December, sec. Society. https://www.theguardian.com/society/2016/dec/05/casey-report-criticised-for-focus-on-uk-muslim-communities.

The Guardian. 2015. 'Cameron Backing Counter-Extremism Strategy Marks a Fundamental Shift | Counter-Terrorism Policy'. Accessed 9 August 2022. https://www.theguardian.com/politics/2015/jun/29/cameron-backing-theresa-may-counter-extremism-strategy-fundamental-shift.

Timol, Riyaz. 2017. 'Spiritual Wayfarers in a Secular Age: The Tablighi Jama'at in Modern Britain'. Ph.d, Cardiff University. http://orca.cf.ac.uk/104936/.

Timol, Riyaz. 2020. 'Ethno-Religious Socialisation, National Culture and the Social Construction of British Muslim Identity'. *Contemporary Islam* 14 (3): 331–60. https://doi.org/10.1007/s11562-020-00454-y.

Timol, Riyaz. 2015. 'Religious Travel and the Tablighī Jamāʿat: Modalities of Expansion in Britain and Beyond'. In *Muslims in the UK and Europe I*, edited by Yasir Suleiman, 194–206. Cambridge: Centre of Islamic Studies, University of Cambridge.

Tocqueville, Alexis de. 1851. *American Institutions and Their Influence*. New York: A.S. Barnes & Co. http://www.gutenberg.org/files/8690/8690-h/8690-h.htm.

Tocqueville, Alexis de, Harvey C. Mansfield, and Delba Winthrop. 2002. *Democracy in America*. Paperback ed. Chicago, IL: University of Chicago Press.

Townsend, Mark. 2020. 'The Iconoclast Unmasked: The Man behind Far-Right YouTube Channel'. *The Guardian*, 21 June, sec. World news. http://www.theguardian.com/world/2020/jun/21/the-iconoclast-unmasked-the-man-behind-far-right-youtube-channel.

Travis, Alan. 2015. 'Cameron Backing Counter-Extremism Strategy Marks a Fundamental Shift'. *The Guardian*, 29 June, sec. Politics. https://www.theguardian.com/politics/2015/jun/29/cameron-backing-theresa-may-counter-extremism-strategy-fundamental-shift.

Turner, B.S. 2001. 'Charisma and Charismatic'. In *International Encyclopedia of the Social & Behavioral Sciences*, 1651–3. Elsevier. https://doi.org/10.1016/B0-08-043076-7/04023-7.

Utaberta, Nangkula, Fariba Samia Omi, Siti Balkish Roslan, and Noor Fazamimah Mohd Ariffin. 2018. 'An Analysis of Women's Access and Participation in the Mosques in the Contemporary World'. *IOP Conference Series: Materials Science and Engineering* 401 (October): 012032. https://doi.org/10.1088/1757-899X/401/1/012032.

Van Velsen, Jaap. 1967. 'The Extended Case Method and Situational Analysis'. In *The Craft of Urban Anthropology*, edited by Arnold Leonard Epstein, 1st ed., 29–53. London: Tavistock.

Verter, Bradford. 2003. 'Spiritual Capital: Theorizing Religion with Bourdieu against Bourdieu'. *Sociological Theory* 21 (2): 150–74. https://doi.org/10.1111/1467-9558.00182.

Victorian Society. 2017. 'West Midlands Group 2017 Conservation Award Winner Announced'. *Victorian Society*. 12 January. https://victoriansociety.org.uk/news/west-midlands-group-2017-conservation-award-winner-announced?fbclid=IwAR20EFnyJ0SichBxrzg7vwJvppguXAMgPnu6i8VxPmS6TXbo7qjyZhcykcw.

Vinding, Niels Valdemar. 2018. 'Churchification of Islam in Europe'. *Exploring the Multitude of Muslims in Europe*, March, 50–66. https://doi.org/10.1163/9789004362529_005.

Wadud, Amina. 1999. *Qurʾan and woman: rereading the sacred text from a woman's perspective*. New York: Oxford University Press. http://hdl.handle.net/2027/heb.04755.

Wadud, Amina. 2018. *Inside the Gender Jihad: Women's Reform in Islam*. Reprinted. A Oneworld Paperback Original. Oxford: Oneworld.

Walzer, Michael. 1998. 'The Idea of Civil Society: A Path to Social Reconstruction'. In *Community Works: The Revival of Civil Society in America*, edited by E. J Dionne, 293–304. Washington, DC: Brookings Institution Press.

Wang, Yuting. 2017. 'Muslim Women's Evolving Leadership Roles: A Case Study of Women Leaders in an Immigrant Muslim Community in Post-9/11 America'. *Social Compass* 64 (3): 424–41. https://doi.org/10.1177/00377686 17713660.

Waqar, Ahmad. 2012. 'Creating a Society of Sheep? British Muslim Elite on Mosques and Imams'. In *Muslims in Britain*, edited by Ziauddin Sardar and Waqar Ahmad, 1st ed., 171–91. London: Routledge.

Wardak, Ali. 2002. 'The Mosque and Social Control in Edinburgh's Muslim Community'. *Culture and Religion* 3 (2): 201–19. https://doi.org/10.1080 /01438300208567192.

Ware, Rudolph T. 2014. *The Walking Qur'an: Islamic Education, Embodied Knowledge, and History in West Africa*. Islamic Civilization and Muslim Networks. Chapel Hill, NC: The University of North Carolina Press.

Webb, Sam. 2017. 'Manchester Didsbury Mosque Panic after "white Powder" Letter Delivered'. *The Sun*. 5 November. https://www.thesun.co.uk/news/4843056/ manchester-didsbury-mosque-suspicious-white-powder-letter/.

Weeks, Douglas. 2019. 'Barking Mosque and Quintessential Insight: Overcoming the Problematic Government/Community Counterterrorism Partnership in the UK'. *Studies in Conflict & Terrorism* 42 (8): 735–54. https://doi.org/10.1080/1057610X .2018.1425087.

Wells, Anthony. 2006. *NOP Poll of British Muslims*. http://www.webcitation.org/query ?url=http://ukpollingreport.co.uk/blog/archives/291&date=2013-03-21.

Werbner, Pnina. 1990. *The Migration Process*. Oxford; Rhode Island: Berg.

Werbner, Pnina. 1996. 'The Making of Muslim Dissent: Hybridized Discourses, Lay Preachers, and Radical Rhetoric among British Pakistanis'. *American Ethnologist* 23 (1): 102–29. https://doi.org/10.1525/ae.1996.23.1.02a00060.

Werbner, Pnina. 2002. *The Migration Process: Capital, Gifts and Offerings among British Pakistanis*. 1st ed. New York; Oxford: Routledge.

Werbner, Pnina. 2003. *Pilgrims of Love: The Anthropology of a Global Sufi Cult*. London: Hurst.

Werbner, Pnina. 2017. 'Seekers on the Path: Different Ways of Being a Sufi in Britain'. In *Sufism in the West*, edited by John R. Hinnells and Jamal Malik, 127–41. London; New York: Routledge.

West Midlands Police and Crown Prosecution Service. 2007. 'CPS Press Release: Joint Statement Regarding Channel 4 Dispatches Programme'. 8 August. https://web .archive.org/web/20080516004431/http://www.cps.gov.uk/news/pressreleases/ archive/2007/153_07.html.

Westbrook, Caroline. 2016. 'Amazon Prime's Christmas Advert Spreads a Touching Interfaith Message'. *Metro*, 18 November, sec. Entertainment. https://metro.co.uk/2016/11/18/amazon-primes-christmas-advert-spreads-a-touching-interfaith-message-6266536/.

Wiktorowicz, Quintan. 2006. 'Anatomy of the Salafi Movement'. *Studies in Conflict & Terrorism* 29 (3): 207–39. https://doi.org/10.1080/10576100500497004.

Williams, Melvin D. 1984. *Community in a Black Pentecostal Church: An Anthropological Study*. Prospect Heights, IL: Waveland Pr Inc.

Williams, R. R. 2010. 'Space for God: Lived Religion at Work, Home, and Play'. *Sociology of Religion* 71 (3): 257–79. https://doi.org/10.1093/socrel/srq048.

Winter, Timothy. 2003. *British Muslim Identity: Past, Problems, Prospects*. Cambridge: Muslim Academic Trust.

Wood, Richard L. 2002. *Faith in Action: Religion, Race, and Democratic Organizing in America*. Morality and Society Series. Chicago: University of Chicago Press.

Woodberry, Robert D. 1998. 'When Surveys Lie and People Tell the Truth: How Surveys Oversample Church Attenders'. *American Sociological Review* 63 (1): 119–22. https://doi.org/10.2307/2657483.

Woodhead, Linda. 2016. 'Why "No Religion" Is the New Religion by Professor Linda Woodhead, The British Academy Lecture'. *The British Academy*. https://www.thebritishacademy.ac.uk/video/why-no-religion-new-religion-professor-linda-woodhead-british-academy-lecture.

Woodhead, Linda and Rebecca Catto. 2012. *Religion and Change in Modern Britain*. London; New York: Routledge.

Woodlock, Rachel. 2010. 'The Masjid Is for Men: Competing Voices in the Debate about Australian Muslim Women's Access to Mosques'. *Islam and Christian–Muslim Relations* 21 (1): 51–60. https://doi.org/10.1080/09596410903481853.

Wright, Mike. 2018. 'Church of England Sees Regular Attendance Rise but Churchgoers Struggle to Make Traditional Sunday Services'. *The Telegraph*, 14 November. https://www.telegraph.co.uk/news/2018/11/14/church-england-sees-regular-attendance-rise-churchgoers-struggle/.

Wuthnow, Robert. 1997. *The Crisis in the Churches: Spiritual Malaise, Fiscal Woe*. New York: Oxford University Press.

Wyatt, Tim. 2021. 'New Board of Scholars Is Unifying Fragmented Muslim Communities'. *Religion Media Centre* (blog). 11 January. https://religionmediacentre.org.uk/news/new-board-of-scholars-is-unifying-fragmented-muslim-communities/.

Yilmaz, Huseyin. 2018. *Caliphate Redefined*. Princeton: Princeton University Press. http://www.myilibrary.com?id=1054900.

Zschomler, Danny. 2018. '"A Road to Prosperity?": The Values and Value Struggles of Members of the Prosperity Movement on the Old Kent Road in the UK'. Ph.D., Goldsmiths, University of London. https://doi.org/10.25602/GOLD.00025976.

Zulfikar, Teuku. 2014. 'Researching My Own Backyard: Inquiries into an Ethnographic Study'. *Ethnography and Education* 9 (3): 373–86. https://doi.org/10.1080/17457823.2014.919869.

Glossary

adab	Arabic. Now a loanword in many Muslim contexts, generally means 'etiquette', 'good manners' or 'respectful behaviour'.
adhan	Arabic. 'Call to Prayer', announced from mosques at times of the five daily prayers.
ʿalim / pl. ʿulamaʾ	Arabic. Muslim scholars, usually an individual trained in Islamic law though not exclusively. In the singular form, it will usually refer to men. In the plural, it can include men and women.
ʿalima	Arabic. Literally female scholar. See entry for *ʿālim / pl. ʿulamaʾ*.
ʿaqīda	Arabic. 'Creed', the theological beliefs and precepts of Islam.
ʿaqiqa	Arabic. A celebration, usually in the form of a feast, to celebrate a child's birth.
ʿashuraʾ	Arabic. Usually refers to the tenth day of Muharram. Shia Muslims mourn the killing of Husayn bin Ali on this day.
ʿasr	Arabic. The third of the five daily prayers for Muslims, held in the late afternoon.
baraka	Arabic. 'Blessings', the transcendental quality evoked in Muslim sacred spaces.
Barelvi	South Asian reform movement that seeks to maintain traditions of Sufism from South Asia but combined with a scholarly legal background.
barkat	Urdu. See *barakah*.
bukhoor	Incense.
Darul Uloom	Literally 'House of Knowledge', and it refers to an educational institution. In the British context, it more often refers to a full-time Islamic seminary.
Deobandi	South Asian reform movement, founded in Deoband, with an emphasis on erudition and fidelity to the (Hanafi) tradition.
duʿaʾ	Arabic. Supplication to God. Usually less formal and regulated than other forms of prayer, such as the *salah*.
duha	Arabic. An optional (supererogatory) prayer Muslims observe in the mid-morning (after sunrise, before noon).
fajr	Arabic. The first of the five daily prayers for Muslims, held at dawn before sunrise.

fard	Arabic. 'Obligatory', a religiously mandated action for every individual.
fard kifaya	Arabic. 'Communal obligation', a religiously mandated action that the community must fulfil rather than the individual.
fatwa. / pl. fatwas	An Islamic legal opinion offered by a Muslim scholar or Islamic authority. They are usually non-binding unless issued as part of formal judiciary or state in a Muslim-majority country.
fiqh	Arabic. Islamic jurisprudence or the study of Islamic law.
Fultoli	South Asian reform movement associated mainly with Muslims from Sylhet, Bangladesh.
fuqaha (pl)	Arabic. Muslim legal scholars, especially those who specializes in Islamic jurisprudence.
hadith / pl. aḥadith	Arabic. A historical oral tradition or written text that describes something the Prophet Muhammad did or said.
halaqa / pl. halaqas	Arabic. A gathering of Muslims with a teacher, usually educational (though sometimes for ritual purposes).
'ibadat	Arabic. Literally 'acts of worship', refers to actions of ritual obedience to God and thus are theocentric. Contrast with *mu'amalat*.
Ibadi Islam	Small but historic denomination of Islam that can be traced to the first century after the death of the Prophet Muhammad.
iftar	Arabic. The opening meal to break the fast.
al-Ikhwan al-Muslimun	Arabic. 'The Muslim Brotherhood'. Middle-Eastern reform movement that emphasizes political as well as social religious reforms.
'isha'	Arabic. The last of the five daily prayers for Muslims, held after the twilight after sunrise ceases.
Isma'ili	A denomination of Shi'i Islam.
Ithna Asharis	The Twelvers. Largest denomination of Shi'ism.
Jama'at-i Islami	South Asian reform movement that emphasizes political as well as religious social reforms.
Jamia Masjid	In Muslim-majority countries, this generally refers to the largest mosque in area that holds the Friday congregational prayer and the Eid prayer. In Britain, this distinction no longer applies.
janaza	Arabic. The funeral prayer.
jumu'a	Arabic. The Friday prayer. The weekly congregational prayer all Muslim men are expected to attend, and women are encouraged to attend.

Kaʿba	Arabic. The cube-shaped mosque at the centre of Masjid al-Haram, the direction of prayer for Muslims globally.
khatib	Arabic. The individual appointed to deliver a sermon (usually, but not exclusively, the sermon of the Friday prayer).
khurooj	Arabic in origin, though the specific meaning in this context emerges from a South Asian context. A practice maintained by the Tablighi Jamaat movement of visiting mosques for a set period of time, for example 3 days or 40 days.
khutba	Arabic. A sermon, usually but not exclusively the sermon part of the Friday prayer.
laylat al-Qadr	Arabic. Literally 'the Night of Power'. Referring to an indeterminate auspicious night in Ramadan.
madhhab	Arabic. 'School of thought', referring to jurisprudential methodologies. In Urdu, 'religion'.
madrassa	Refers to a school. In certain Muslim-majority contexts, it can refer to a full-time seminary (similar to a *dār al-ʿulūm*) but in the United Kingdom it refers most often to after-school supplementary education.
maghrib	Arabic. The fourth of the five daily prayers for Muslims, held just after sunset.
maktab	Arabic. It can refer to a library, or office, but in a British-mosque context most commonly refers to the supplemental after-school Islamic education offered in mosques.
markaz	Arabic. Meaning 'centre', often used to describe a large mosque.
masjid	Arabic. Mosque. Literally 'place of prostration'.
mawlid al-nabi	Arabic. The birthday of the Prophet Muhammad. It's observation through worship or specific acts of devotion is a highly contested fault line between various Muslim denominations.
mihrab	Arabic. The prayer niche or decorated aspect of a mosque at which the Imam prays and communicates the direction of prayer to Muslims.
muezzin	The individual appointed to make the call to prayer.
muʿamalat	Arabic. The *muʿamalat* refers to the interactions between creations of God, namely between humans; so they are anthropocentric. Contrast with *ʿibadat*.
mufti	Arabic. A religious scholar qualified to offer formal religious opinions.
muhaddithun	Arabic. A religious scholar who specializes in *hadith*.
muqaddas	Arabic. Something sacred, holy or blessed.

musalla	Arabic. Literally 'a place of prayer'. It can refer to a small place allocated for worship (akin to a small room) or a spacious location for a large gathering of Muslims.
mustahabb	Arabic. An action that is 'recommended' but not compulsory in the Islamic moral schema.
nikah	Arabic. An Islamic marriage, specifically referring to the contract.
qudus	Arabic. Meaning sacred or holy.
Quran	The sacred text of Muslims.
ruh al-qudus	Arabic. Quranic term. Can be translated as 'The Holy Spirit', though it is most commonly understood to refer in Quranic cosmology to the Angel Gabriel.
sadaqa	Arabic. Charity, usually but not exclusively financial. Distinct from zakah.
Salafi, salafiyya, Salafism	Arabic origin. Referring to a distinct reformist movement in Islam with contested definitions and internal heterogeneity. In general, Salafi approaches attempt to recreate and prioritize early Muslim practice.
salah	Arabic. Literally 'to pray' but usually refers to the five daily prayers, mandated upon all capable Muslims, and one of the five pillars of Islam.
salam	Arabic. Literally 'peace'. A shortened form of the Islamic greeting *as-salāmu ʿalaykum,* meaning peace be upon you.
shariʿa	Arabic. Islamic law.
shaykh	Arabic though used more widely, a title of honour, usually to refer to an Islamic scholar.
Shiʿi / Shia / Shiʿism	Arabic. A large denomination of Islam in which religious authority after the death of the Prophet Muhammad is located in the family of the Prophet Muhammad. Contrasted with Sunnism.
sunna	Arabic. Literally meaning 'tradition', 'example' or 'habit'. It refers to speech, actions and approvals of the Prophet Muhammad. It can also refer to a recommended action in the Islamic moral schema.
Sunni	A large denomination of Islam in which religious authority after the death of the Prophet Muhammad was granted to Abu Bakr, his companion, and then other senior companions of the Prophet Muhammad. Contrasted with Shiʿism.
surau	Malaysian. A small prayer room.
Tablighi Jamaat	South Asian reform movement, associated closely with Deobandis but with a more missionary focus.

tarbiyya	Arabic word. Referring to education, instruction, moral upbringing or socialization.
tariqa / tariqas	Arabic. A Sufi brotherhood.
usra	Arabic. Literally 'family', though it can be used by members of the Muslim Brotherhood to describe a specific social organization of support for religious instruction.
wa ʿalaykum as-salam	Arabic. 'And upon you be peace'. The traditional response to the Arabic Islamic greeting *as-salāmu ʿalaykum*.
wali	Arabic. Referring to a 'close friend' of God. While not entirely synonymous with the Catholic conception of a Saint, it is often used to refer to especially pious individuals.
waʿz	Persian. Loanword in many South Asian languages, referring to religious sermon or lecture, sometimes devotional singing.
waqf	Arabic. A charitable endowment, similar to a contemporary legal trust.
zakat	Arabic. One of the five pillars of Islam, referring to giving 2.5 per cent of one's wealth over a certain amount to charity.
zawiya	Arabic. A Sufi lodge. Usually distinct from a mosque in that it is home to a specific *tariqa* and its activities.
Zaydism	Branch of Shiʿism.
zuhr	Arabic. The second of the daily prayers for Muslims, held just after noon.

Index

ablution   33, 79, 82; *see also* wudu
activism   11–13, 77, 103–4, 139
adhan   83, 88, 91; *see also* call to prayer
agency   18, 114, 116, 140, 158, 161, 176, 177
anglophone   6, 21, 38, 69, 73, 176–7
'aqīda   50
architecture   3, 33, 37, 82, 105, 148–50, 153
authority (religious and mosque)   6–7, 18, 27, 37, 43–4, 49–57, 63, 98–9, 104, 106–7, 110–11, 121, 148, 157, 159, 165, 170, 173, 177

Bangladesh   16, 31, 45, 48, 61, 102–3, 163
baraka   18, 27, 62, 72–6, 78–80, 84–92
Bengali   1, 18, 34, 45, 48
Birmingham   2, 3, 17, 29, 38, 40, 48–9, 51, 72, 76–7, 82, 93, 102–3, 105, 126, 127, 134, 149, 150, 153–4
bonding capital   112–13, 117
Bradford   1, 18, 29, 44–6, 51–2, 88, 149, 171–2, 182
bridging capital   112–13, 117, 120
bureaucracy   129, 141, 142, 167

calligraphy   31, 82–3, 148
call to prayer   83, 85–6, 89, 157; *see also adhan*
Cardiff   9, 12–15, 21, 30–2, 35, 51, 89, 96, 126, 127, 136, 143, 153, 162
carpet   21, 31, 71, 82
charity   26, 47, 54, 118–19, 127, 140, 168, 171
Christian and Christianity   5–6, 10, 13, 21, 33–4, 36, 43, 55, 57–9, 63–4, 67–8, 75, 94, 109, 112, 120–3, 128–30, 139, 141, 147
church   2, 21, 32–3, 46, 50, 57–9, 63–6, 68, 75, 80, 93–4, 112, 117, 120–2, 124, 126, 146–7, 164, 171

civil society   6–8, 67, 109–14, 117, 119–20, 124, 126–31, 133, 176
class (distinctions)   16, 38, 77, 118
communal   6, 17, 23, 25–7, 29, 35, 39–41, 43–4, 53, 56–8, 60–3, 68, 81, 102, 115, 121, 125
community centre   2, 24, 28, 87, 107, 128, 140
conflict   2, 4, 6, 8, 16, 77, 97, 106, 123, 133, 136, 143, 146–51, 176
congregational   7, 43–5, 47, 49–55, 57–69, 82, 86, 101, 107, 110, 112–13, 118, 121, 131, 158, 160, 162–3
convert property into a mosque   10, 19, 21–2, 31–3, 45, 77, 100, 103, 106, 140, 161, 164
convert to Islam   9, 10, 12–13, 105, 121, 133, 136, 170
council   46, 77, 123, 129–30, 140, 143–4, 150; *see also* local authority
council (of mosques)   3, 44–5, 51–3, 86
Covid-19   126–7, 145
creed   14, 77, 95
cultural   16–17, 39, 55, 57, 105–6, 114, 118, 125–6, 134–5, 148, 167, 172

Darul Uloom   27, 32, 100–1, 166
denomination   7, 15, 21–2, 29–30, 32, 35, 37–9, 41, 46, 48, 52, 57–8, 60, 62–3, 67, 85, 93–6, 98, 101–2, 105–8, 158, 163, 175
denominational   7, 15, 21, 29–30, 32, 35, 37–9, 41, 46, 48, 52, 60, 62, 85, 93, 102, 106–8, 158
digital   60, 86, 88, 124, 153, 176
discrimination   100
diversity   1–2, 6–8, 15, 21, 30, 35, 38, 41, 63, 67, 75, 93, 95, 98, 105–8, 112, 119, 141, 157, 159, 168–9, 175–6

dome   11, 21, 44, 82, 83, 147–9

ecumenical   7, 38, 93–8, 106, 117, 176
education   1, 23, 26–7, 31–7, 40, 45–6, 48–50, 56, 78, 80–1, 84, 86, 92, 104, 114, 121–2, 140, 162, 164, 166, 172–3, 175–6
Egypt   104, 108, 115, 137
Eid   34, 40, 62, 97
England   11, 36, 51, 65, 79, 93, 97, 102, 115, 119, 122, 125, 139, 171
equality   141, 153, 167–9
ethnic and ethnicity   7, 22, 46, 67, 96, 117–18, 127, 147
etiquette   72, 118

fard kifaya mosques   6, 23–4, 26–30, 33, 35, 38–41, 45, 46
fard mosques   6, 23, 24, 26, 29–30, 35, 38–9, 41, 46
feminism   169
festival   14, 45, 89, 118, 123
finance   6, 47, 53, 66, 113, 148
fiqh   33, 50, 82, 107, 169
Friday prayer   25, 27–8, 32–3, 40, 47, 50–1, 55, 61–2, 81–2, 85–6, 88–9, 116, 134, 140, 145–6, 157, 162, 170–1, 173
fundraising   3, 34, 37, 47–9, 119, 126, 173
funeral   1, 6, 23, 34, 48, 84, 118, 164; *see also* janaza

gathering   1, 26, 29, 57, 61, 64, 80, 150, 171
global   8, 15, 18, 35, 51, 60, 69, 91, 99, 101, 108, 135, 158–9, 177–8
grassroots   168

hadith   25, 73, 76, 83, 94, 105, 117, 156–7, 166
al-Hakimi, Abdullah Ali   12–15
house (use as mosques)   10, 21–2, 30–3, 40, 45–6, 124, 162

identity   5, 7, 18, 21, 26, 28, 30, 38, 59–60, 67, 76, 93–6, 98, 101, 103, 107, 115, 130, 133, 136, 141, 144, 148, 158, 182

imam   3, 14, 18, 24–5, 27, 30, 32–4, 44, 48, 51–4, 57, 61, 82–5, 100, 107, 115, 120–1, 123–4, 137–9, 155, 170, 172, 175, 177
independence   50–3, 119
India   11–12, 14, 16, 101, 163
interfaith   34, 120–4, 130, 160
interpretation   75, 115, 137, 140, 147, 156–7, 167, 172
interspatial   6, 19, 21–5, 27, 29–31, 33, 35, 37, 38, 41, 48, 92, 96, 110, 121, 163–4, 175
intra-religious   15, 38, 67
Iran   107, 136
Ireland   38
Islamophobia   134, 135, 151, 154–5, 169, 182

janaza   23, 27, 40, 84

language   4, 11, 24, 62, 73, 82, 84, 90, 97, 99, 105, 115, 141–52, 154, 176–7
lascar   10
leadership   3, 6, 7, 15, 17–19, 22–4, 33, 35, 38, 46, 63, 93, 95, 100, 106, 121, 159, 168–9, 171–3, 175
legal   16, 21, 23, 25–6, 37, 47, 51, 57, 102, 125, 137, 142, 156, 159, 164–7, 169–70, 173
local authority   46, 117, 125, 128–9, 182; *see also* council
lockdown   51
London   2, 9, 10, 12, 15, 17, 29, 36–8, 51, 63, 88, 99–101, 103, 107, 109, 115, 121, 122, 124, 128–30, 133, 136–8, 140–1, 143–5, 149, 162, 170–1

Madinah   28, 44, 73
Manchester   4, 17, 31, 40, 51, 88, 126, 136–7, 146, 182
Mecca   11, 55, 73, 159
migrants   16–17, 19, 31, 66, 77, 86, 97, 148, 150, 163–4
migration   8, 16–17, 29, 57, 102, 107, 114, 176
minaret   21, 44, 82, 86, 139–40, 149–50
modernity   5, 68, 166, 177

Muhammad, Prophet   23, 25, 27–9, 44, 49, 55–6, 76, 83, 88, 103, 107, 121, 156–7
Muharram   107
multicultural   12
Muslim Council of Britain (MCB)   2, 3, 17, 36, 44, 52–3, 66, 93, 104, 124–5, 155, 164, 168
Muslim Womens Council   155, 171

nation state   36, 53, 60, 104, 127
9/11   122
non-governmental organization (NGO)   131
Northern Ireland   38

open day (of mosques)   21, 124
Ottoman   10, 78

Pakistan   16–17, 29, 39, 45, 76, 99, 100, 107
philanthropy   48, 177
power (of mosques and Muslims)   8, 34, 43, 53–4, 104, 116, 129–31, 133, 139, 140, 147–9, 169
Power, Night of   119
protest   44, 129, 133–4, 145, 151, 170
purpose-built mosques   9, 11, 13, 15, 19, 21–2, 31, 37, 40, 45, 77, 81, 100, 143, 161–2, 164

qibla   31, 44, 76, 83, 88
Quilliam, Abdullah   9–15, 106, 121
Quran   27, 31, 33, 48, 62, 72–5, 78, 79, 81, 83–4, 87, 89, 94, 98–9, 102–3, 117, 119, 133, 137, 165–6, 169–70

radio transmitters   86, 88
Ramadan   14, 31, 46–8, 50, 62, 89, 119, 136
recitation   27, 33, 62, 78–9, 83
rhythm   4, 65, 67, 81, 83–4, 88–92, 118, 158, 162–3
rhythmanalysis   81, 91
rites   18, 23, 27, 34, 40, 112–13, 164, 175

ritual   18, 25, 27, 33, 60–1, 63, 71, 75–6, 78–81, 84, 88, 91–2, 121, 127, 175
rural   24, 50, 62, 76, 94, 96–7, 115, 117, 149–50

sacralization   7, 79
sacred power   91
sacred space   26, 73–81, 84, 90, 92, 147
sacred time   79–81, 84, 91
Salafi   37–8, 49, 71, 94, 98, 104–7
salah   24, 25, 45, 80, 85, 94, 157
Scotland   38, 51, 65, 97, 102, 168–9
sectarian   7, 46, 93, 94, 98
seminary   37
Shia   86, 98, 105, 107
shoes   71–2, 82, 109
shrine   76, 95, 163, 169
side entrance (to mosques)   160
social capital   7, 18, 48, 62, 112–13, 117–18
social media   86–8, 115, 141, 161
socio-economic   119, 164
Stornoway   87, 96–7
structure (of mosques)   9, 31, 33, 41, 43, 50, 53, 63, 81, 89, 93, 99–100, 107, 110, 135, 147, 171, 175
student   11, 27, 33, 56, 78, 87, 94, 153
Sufi   37, 39, 56, 72, 76–9, 83–4, 98, 102, 104, 159, 163; *see also* Sufism
Sufism   17, 37, 39, 56, 63, 76–7, 101–2; *see also* Sufi
sunna (practice of the Prophet)   71, 98, 105, 121, 165–6
sunna mosques   6, 23–4, 28–30, 35, 38, 40–1, 48, 145
Sunni   38–9, 46, 52, 63, 85, 94, 98–100, 103, 105, 107, 119, 158, 166, 172

technology   86–7
tension   3, 7, 14, 18, 80, 93, 101, 105, 147, 154
terrorism   122, 135–9, 170
timetables (of prayer)   86–8
translation   11, 99, 166
transnational   37, 53, 56, 111

ulama   37–8, 49, 52, 102, 166

volunteers   21, 49, 50, 78–9, 113, 119,
    125–7, 168

Wales   12–15, 21, 36, 38, 51, 96, 102, 115,
    137, 139, 150, 165
walking congregation   46, 49
weddings   27, 29, 34, 118, 164
women   2, 8, 13, 15, 17, 33, 47, 60, 65–6,
    105, 112, 116–17, 128, 139,
    153–73, 176–7

worship   7, 23, 25–6, 33, 35, 39, 44–6, 52,
    56, 58, 78–81, 87–90, 101, 107,
    119, 127, 137, 147, 150, 156,
    163, 165, 173, 175
worshippers   1, 7, 11, 15, 24, 31, 59–60,
    65, 71, 77–8, 86–7, 89, 134, 138,
    140–1
wudu   71, 78, 82; *see also* ablution

Yemen   12, 14–15, 107

www.ingramcontent.com/pod-product-compliance
Lightning Source LLC
Chambersburg PA
CBHW071835300426
44116CB00009B/1546